Networked Affect

Networked Affect

edited by Ken Hillis, Susanna Paasonen, and Michael Petit

The MIT Press
Cambridge, Massachusetts
London, England

MIT Press books may be purchased at special quantity discounts for business or sales promotional use. For information, please email special_sales@mitpress.mit.edu

This book was set in Stone by the MIT Press. Printed and bound in the United States of America.

Library of Congress Cataloging-in-Publication Data

Networked affect / edited by Ken Hillis, Susanna Paasonen, and Michael Petit.
   pages   cm
Includes bibliographical references and index.
ISBN 978-0-262-02864-6 (hardcover : alk. paper)
1. Affect (Psychology)—Social aspects. 2. Emotions. 3. Social networks. 4. Internet—Social aspects. I. Hillis, Ken. II. Paasonen, Susanna, 1975– III. Petit, Michael.
BF531.N48 2015
302.23'1—dc23
                                                                                    2014025224

10 9 8 7 6 5 4 3 2 1

Contents

Acknowledgments

Networked Affect results from a series of panels held at the 2011 Association of Internet Researchers (AoIR) conference in Seattle. While many of the original panelists have contributed to this volume, we would also like to extend our sincere thanks to Feona Attwood, Mary Bryson, Radhika Gajjala, Jillana Enteen, Daj Kojima, Ben Light, Sharif Mowlabocus, Theresa Senft, and Michele White for sharing their stimulating papers with us and for fueling debates at the crossroads of affect theory and Internet research. We would also like to thank the International Institute for Popular Culture (IIPC) for its support.

1   Introduction: Networks of Transmission: Intensity, Sensation, Value

Susanna Paasonen, Ken Hillis, and Michael Petit

Networked communications involve the circulation of data and information, but they equally entail a panoply of affective attachments: articulations of desire, seduction, trust, and memory; sharp jolts of anger and interest; political passions; investments of time, labor, and financial capital; and the frictions and pleasures of archival practices. As *Networked Affect* attests, the fluctuating and altering dynamics of affect give shape to online connections and disconnections, to the proximities and distances of love, desire, and wanting between and among different bodies, to the sense of standing out from the mass. In different but complementary ways, contributors examine how the cultural practices of production, distribution, and consumption increasingly rely on the internet and its convergence with other networked media forms (and media industries), as well as how these practices are underpinned by affective investments, sensory impulses, and forms of intensity that generate and circulate within networks comprising both human and nonhuman actors. As a whole, this volume works to demonstrate the value of affect theories for internet researchers.

The *Oxford English Dictionary* defines the verb *affect* as "to have an effect on something or someone." Most definitions of *affect* highlight the central role of intensity and agree on the presence of a quality of excess, a quality of "more than." While some theorists hold to a humanist inflection alone, others conflate affect with emotion or argue for the practical inseparability of the two, and yet others emphasize the meaning of being affected in a visceral manner as in, for example, theorizing an individual's precognitive "gut reaction" to someone or something as "more than" can fit into any fixed definition of emotion. As is the case with many contributors to this volume, authors have argued for affect's human and nonhuman sources, settings, and inclinations alike (e.g., Massumi 2002; Bennett 2010). These discussions of affect are often less focused on feeling and sensation as such than they are on how bodies or objects may produce or experience intensity as they pass from one state to another—whether this passage be one that produces horror at the physical reality of intense burns from radioactive fission, or whether the passage of a different kind of body, such as an online avatar, induces an affective jolt, or even an uncanny sense of awe, when signs once believed to be dead letters in books now stand up and point back to us in lively fashion from the networked settings they have also come to occupy on the internet (Hillis, this volume).

Our frequent if not near-constant prosthetic connections to information, communication, and media technologies underscore the importance of exploring the affective underpinnings of human-machine relations and the complex forms of agency that arise from these. A social networking site such as Facebook, for example, invites and facilitates the creation and maintenance of social connections with "friends," consisting of family, acquaintances, and strangers who are geographically dispersed. Facebook's circulations of links, images, invitations, videos, and pieces of text are driven by individuals' interest in and quest for affective encounters with others, and for waves of amusement and curiosity. More than an instrument or "tool" for social exchange, however, Facebook configures these interactions and encounters. An individual's wall is not based solely on her or his choice but is a continually self-updating news feed cogenerated by friends, corporate sponsors, site architecture and design, and the organization of data as modulated by the algorithms used. Intent, agency, and affect thereby become to some extent contingent outcomes of the network itself rather than of human agency alone.

In their enquiry into the ways that mediation constitutes the intermeshing of the human and the nonhuman, Sarah Kember and Joanna Zylinska point out, "It is not simply the case that 'we'—that is, autonomously existing humans—live in a complex technological environment that we can manage, control, and use. Rather, we are—physically and ontologically—part of the technological environment, and it makes no more sense to talk of us using it, than it does of it using us" (Kember and Zylinska 2012, 13). Humans do not simply manipulate or control machines, data, and networks any more than machines, data, and networks simply manipulate or control us. As the chapters that follow illustrate, complex networks of people and machines and assemblages of interaction and cohabitation are where data are automatically generated, where software and intelligent agents generate effects and potentialities, and where affective and immaterial forms of labor provide pleasure and gratification for individual users along with monetary value for the site involved.

At the moment when information machines are becoming so powerful and seemingly lively that we *know* we are no longer fully in control, theorizations of affect offer ways to understand and explain the implications of the particular technological conjuncture at which the "networked society" now finds itself. What are the theoretical and political implications, we would ask, when intelligent agents deployed by Amazon and Netflix offer recommendations on what to buy, watch, and read? When our Siri-enabled car tells jokes based on an algorithmic analysis of our "likes" to help pass the time on a long drive? When Google Calendar interrupts email or a FunnyorDie.com video to warn us that a scheduled meeting is but five minutes away? Or when metaphysically inflected "Getting Things Done" time and productivity management applications further technicize our day in the name of "efficiency" (Gregg, this volume)?

Our encounters with websites, avatars, videos, mobile apps, discussion forums, GIFs, webcams, intelligent agents, and "platforms"[1] of different kinds allow us to experience sensations of connectivity, interest, desire, and attachment. Even so, they equally allow us to experience detachment and boredom (Petit, this volume) and articulate issues of difference in heated and hierarchical terms, as in instances of hate speech and "flaming" that follow the dividing lines of ethnic difference or sexual orientation (Kuntsman 2009; Paasonen, this volume). Networked affect, however, also can be a mediating and mobilizing force that has the capacity to stir social action (Tzankova, this volume) and thus to constitute a potential channel for political agency. Such encounters, connections, and disconnections operate as human and nonhuman networks of influence and interrelation that affect the life of the individual (now too frequently reduced to the "user") on the micro level of quotidian operations and tasks, as well as in the rhythms of communication, thought, entertainment, and information management.

The affective encounters taken up in this volume involve positive jolts and attachments, as well as shocks and forms of psychic grabbing that allow for or induce negative registers of fear, disgust, and shame, along with complex and contradictory feelings and gut reactions that refuse any such dualistic distinctions. Extant social categorizations and identifications orient the actual and virtual forms that affective encounters take. The boundaries among different social groups are negotiated, built, bent, reinforced, reorganized, and eroded in such encounters. Consequently, to explore affective encounters is to "ask how encounters with different media engage senses and affects (emotions, feelings, passions) and, hence, have effects. ... Affects, in this sense, pose questions about the links between the subjective and the cultural, individual and social, self and other, inside and outside" (Koivunen 2001, 7–8).

Networked Affect considers how individual, collective, discursive, and networked bodies, both human and machine, affect and are modified by one another. A key objective of the volume is to outline the contemporary schematics and frameworks by which affect is theorized, and to explore the ensuing analytical possibilities and methodological reverberations for internet studies and internet researchers. The book asks what can be gained by turning to affect, what kinds of networked and affect-inducing moves are available, what are their implications, and what might be lost if affect remains unexamined in online settings. The considerations of affect addressed and conceptualized in this volume, though distinct intellectual projects, are united in their interest in the sensory, intensive, and material conditions of collective and individual action, practice, and existence.

Affect: Definitional and Theoretical Encounters

Gregory Seigworth and Melissa Gregg (2010, 19) note in their introduction to *The Affect Theory Reader* that the genealogical routes of the "turn to affect" in the humanities and social sciences are diverse to the degree that the issue is, in fact, not one of a single unitary turn but rather one of multiple entangled research traditions and agendas (also Koivunen 2010, 9–11; Blackman and Venn 2010, 8). Indeed, the rise in studies of affect overlaps and connects with a number of other "turns" diagnosed in cultural theory, such as the so-called somatic, corporeal, material, ontological, and nonhuman turns (e.g., Hemmings 2005; Sheets-Johnstone 2009; Bogost 2012; Dolphijn and van der Tuin 2012). Each of these turns extends theoretical investigations to the embodied, the sensory, and the lively in ways that question the anthropocentrisms of earlier intellectual inquiry.

Seigworth and Gregg (2010, 6–8) sketch out eight possible turns, or trajectories of thought, related to affect. These trajectories are broad; some are clearly interdependent, while others could be argued to be askance of if not hostile to one another. They include (1) the tradition of phenomenological and postphenomenological theories of embodiment; (2) explorations of human-machine relations in traditions such as cybernetics, artificial intelligence, neuroscience, and robotics; (3) non-Cartesian philosophical traditions drawing on the work of Baruch Spinoza, such as feminist research, Italian autonomism, political philosophy, and philosophically inflected cultural studies; (4) psychological and psychoanalytical inquiries; (5) feminist, queer, subaltern, and other politically engaged work concerned with materiality; (6) critiques of the linguistic turn and social constructivism in cultural theory; (7) studies of emotion and critiques of the ideal modern subject; and (8) science and science studies embracing pluralist approaches to materialism. Broadly contextualized in this vein, the affective turn is not particularly novel but rather an amalgamation, a revisiting, reconsideration, and reorientation of different theoretical traditions, some of which are more established than others.

The turn to affect has been motivated in part by a growing awareness of the limits to knowledge production inherent in research focused principally on representation, mediation, signification, and subjectivity, which has been dominant in cultural theory for some decades. Without necessarily rejecting the insights gleaned through the study of representation, affect theorists largely acknowledge the importance of researching phenomena located at the intersection of sensation, intensity, and materiality (cf. Massumi 2002; Clough and Halley 2007; Liljeström and Paasonen 2010; Dolphijn and van der Tuin 2012). According to this line of argumentation, the "textual turn" continues to constrain analytical attention to issues of ideology, meaning, and representation, even as it simultaneously downplays the material, the embodied, and the sensory in studies of culture and society. Tied to linguistics' structuralist legacy, the textual turn reproduces the logocentric dominance of language and the textual as *the* general framework for understanding the world. Human bodies, cityscapes, sounds, images, and videos—all of these, despite their specific materiality or modality, are routinely addressed as and therefore reduced to "texts" (Hillis 2009, 27). The centrality of the notions of subjectivity and identity in cultural theory has also been critiqued for steering attention away from more collective actions and assemblages, and for framing social exchanges through the negativity of "lack" as conceptualized in psychoanalytical theory (Braidotti 2002). In *The Affective Turn,* Patricia Ticineto Clough and Jean Halley (2007) alternatively present the notion of affect "as a promise to produce new research questions: from subject identity to information, from organic bodies to nonorganic life, from closed systems to complexity of open systems, from an economy of production and consumption to circulation of capacities" (Koivunen 2010, 18). In this framework, affect theory indicates and facilitates more life-affirming, progressive, and dynamic engagements with the world (also Maddison, this volume).

Anu Koivunen (2010, 23) notes, "As a rhetorical figure, the affective turn promises drama and change of direction." Turning toward affect, however, means turning away from something else, and this may, depending on the degree of the turn, lead to the rhetorical dismissal of existing forms of thought instead of the establishment of productive critical dialogue with them. While there is little doubt as to the limitations of reductive textual metaphors in studies of culture, economy, and society, there are also limitations to categorically turning away from studies of meaning, identity, and representation, given the fundamental entanglement of the material, the semiotic, and the political (cf. Hemmings 2005; Barad 2007; Ahmed 2008; Tyler 2008). When turning away from the representational and the subjective, new materialist theory in particular has been accused of turning away from issues of power, ideology, and politics in its embrace of the lively and the positive (Hemmings 2005; Tyler 2008). Imogen Tyler (2008, 88) argues that it "is important to refuse the absolute distinction between affects, feelings, and emotions not only because the purification of affect abjects an entire history of counterhegemonic scholarship but because affect is by definition unanalyzable and thus critically and politically useless." While Tyler's comment may seem rather bleak in terms of the potentialities afforded by affect theory, she nonetheless continues by pointing out that "affect is channeled within and across media with political consequences and we need to theorize these affects as not only unpredictable (which [they] can be) but also as strategic, and performed" (Tyler 2008, 89). The theoretical project to investigate the complex interconnections among affect, emotion, and politics has been taken up in recent titles such as *Political Affect* (Protevi 2009), *Political Emotions* (Staiger et al. 2010), and *Digital Cultures and the Politics of Emotion* (Karatzogianni and Kunstman 2012).

When turning to affect, it is problematic—not to mention lacking in rigor—to simply "add affect" onto one's existing research agenda without addressing the broad set of ontological, epistemological, methodological, and sociopolitical concerns and challenges that affect poses for one's conceptual and methodological practice. Given the tension between studies of representation and those of affect, for example, analyses incorporating the two must necessarily balance different traditions of thought when considering the intermeshing of the semiotic and the material in networked exchanges. It follows that bodies need to be considered in terms of their thick materiality alongside their manifestation as textual depictions, images, or surfaces encountered on the screen—while also conceptualizing the traffic in between (Hillis 2009; Kyrölä 2010; Coleman 2012).

Because of its use as a term across disciplinary and theoretical frameworks, affect remains open to mutually incompatible definitions. This malleability may explain some of affect's evident attraction as an object of intellectual focus. In new materialist investigations inspired by the philosophy of Gilles Deleuze and Félix Guattari, for example, affect translates as nonsubjective and impersonal potentiality, intensity, and force that cannot be attributed to any particular bodies or objects (Shaviro 2010; Kennedy 2000; Anderson 2010; Grusin 2010). In contrast, in the work of the psychologist Silvan Tomkins, which has animated a range of queer and feminist research (e.g., Sedgwick 2003; Sedgwick and Frank 1995), affect is defined as a biological system of input and output that is hardwired in the human body, much like the drives for breath, thirst, hunger, and sex. For Tomkins, affects are identifiable and specific as the physiological reactions of disgust, enjoyment/joy, interest/excitement, anger/rage, shame/humiliation, surprise/startle, fear/terror, distress/anguish, and "dissmell" (i.e., reaction to malodor). The embodied capacity for positive and negative affects of varying intensity is nevertheless "free" in the sense that any affect can be attached and related to any object or impulse. In other words, there is no causal connection between any particular object and any specific affect that may be evoked (Tomkins 1995, 54–55). As different as these two conceptualizations of affect are—one impersonal and autonomous, the other biological and highly definable—they have been brought together in research that attends to how humans are impressed in encounters with the world, how bodies meet and move, and what their capacities allow (e.g., Ahmed 2004; Probyn 2005).

Tomkins's conceptualizations of affect, based on his clinical practice, have been a means of rendering discussions on affect more concrete, as opposed to the explorations of affect inspired by the philosophy of Spinoza and developed further within new materialist philosophy. Spinoza (1992) reflects an anti-Cartesian interest in how bodies are constantly shaped, modified, and affected by encounters with other bodies, encounters that may increase or diminish, affirm or undermine their life forces. For Spinoza, *affectus* refers to the modifications of bodies (through their encounter with others) that "result in increases or decreases of the potential to act" (Brown and Stenner 2001, 90). Bodies are distinguished from one another with respect to motion and rest, quickness and slowness—that is, in terms of movement and tempo—as well as their capacity to affect and be affected (see Deleuze 1998, 125; Parikka, this volume). It follows that the bodies affected and affecting one another can be human, animal, individual, collective, linguistic, and social, as well as bodies of thought (Deleuze 1998, 127; Gatens 2000).

In studies of art, conceptualizations of affect have opened the realm of aesthetic analysis to the corporeality of encountering images and texts, and to the mutual inseparability of sense and sensation, sensing and making sense (Armstrong 2000; Sobchack 2004). Here, a turn to affect can be seen as entailing analyses of intensities and modes of expression particular to twenty-first-century art and culture, as well as both continuing and extending studies of aesthetics understood as the investigation and theorization of sensation and experience (e.g., Grusin 2010; Shaviro 2010; Sundén, this volume). These studies range from considerations of the force and impact of images and sounds in relation to experiences of the sublime (Richardson 2010) to conceptualizations of embodied and reparative reading (Gallop 1988; Pearce 1997; Sedgwick 2003). In these works, affect is evoked as an active, contingent dynamic or relation that orients interpretation and moves readers, viewers, and listeners in very physical ways. Similar conceptualizations have been expanded to account for the intimate, tactile, and disturbing qualities that online practices often entail (Paasonen 2011).

A consideration of affect is further present in work that engages the concepts of immaterial and affective labor. The concept of immaterial labor describes forms of work that are about the production of value that is "dependent on a socialised labour power organised in assemblages of humans and machines exceeding the spaces and times designated as 'work'" (Terranova 2006, 28). Italian autonomist Maurizio Lazzarato (1996, n.p.) introduced the concept to describe work that produces "the informational and cultural content of the commodity." Instead of tangible objects, such work generates services, information, text, sounds, images, and code. For their part, Michael Hardt and Antonio Negri (2001, 293) identify two complementary forms of immaterial labor. First, immaterial labor produces "ideas, symbols, codes, texts, linguistic figures, images and other such products." Second, as affective labor, it both produces and manipulates affects, social networks, and forms of community. The term affective labor, then, simultaneously grasps "the corporeal and intellectual aspects of the new forms of production, recognizing that such labor engages at once with rational intelligence and with the passions or feeling" (Hardt 2007, xi). The intensities and affective investments present in online settings—the repetitive, frustrating, and potentially rewarding series of searches for a plane ticket on Orbitz or Expedia; the work of searching on Google; eBay's countless online postings on the part of experienced sellers freely giving away their expertise to newbies (Robinson 2006)—have been theorized in terms of immaterial and affective labor, particularly so within the framework of autonomist theory. In the business models of sites such as Amazon, Google, and Facebook that rely on advertising income, and which work to naturalize the attention and experience economy, the various layered exchanges of users add up to virtual value. This value depends both on the immaterial labor of usage—acts that are hardly experienced as labor even as they are frequently engaged in at the expense of routine work tasks—and on the overall value of data-mined information about individuals' consumer and lifestyle preferences, travels and visits, and values and beliefs (Terranova 2003; Jarrett 2006; Lillie 2006).

It must be noted that, as investments of human time and energy, such forms of labor are much more uncertain, unpredictable, and malleable in their outcomes and effects than predicted or theorized by binary or idealist models of pure exploitation or empowerment. Both forms of immaterial labor are found, for example, in the ways that users of social media, both unknowingly and voluntarily, generate data from which ideas can be derived in exchange for the online services used, and in how these same individuals are affectively attached to other users *and* the sites in question (Coté and Pybus 2007; Jarrett, this volume; Karppi, this volume; Pybus, this volume). As Dean argues (this volume), social media "produce and circulate affect as a binding technique." While the immense databases of consumer preference generated by sites such as Facebook and Tumblr remain to be fully capitalized, the virtual value created on the most popular sites is considerable, albeit volatile, as Facebook's sharp plunge in market valuation following its 2012 IPO launch demonstrates. The widespread abandonment of the once dominant MySpace for Facebook and the resulting collapse in the value of MySpace—the most visited website in the United States in 2006 sold for 35 million dollars in 2010, less than one tenth of its 2005 selling price—points to the increasingly explicit correlations between affective and market values.

Internet Studies and Affect

Discussion of online networks too often has been conducted through a presumption of their immateriality as well as a positioning of them as neutral tools and conduits through which information smoothly passes between so-called senders and receivers who are always, at least implicitly, enlightened and rational bourgeois subjects. This Shannonesque conceptualization of networked media as instrumental channels of information exchange, together with an assumption of the supposedly rational user, who operates the technology to send and receive, manage and retrieve information, has been central to information society discourses and, consequently, to certain strands of internet research since its early days. In the 1990s, however, a parallel yet incompatible discourse of cyberspace emerged, where internet usage was framed as immersion in a virtual online space "behind the screen" (Paasonen 2009). By counterposing the online and the off, the virtual and the actual, the dystopian and the utopian, much of cyberculture studies in the 1990s did generate nonproductive binaries. This theoretical cul-de-sac, however, needs to be understood in terms of its intimate connection to the technological world as it existed in the 1990s: desktop computers; dial-up telephone modem connections; text-based Usenet newsgroups, MUDs, and MOOs; newly introduced graphic web interfaces; and experimental immersive virtual reality applications. It should be noted that cyberculture theory, largely American in derivation, gained prominence at the same time as actor-network theory (ANT, discussed below) and new materialist theory achieved recognition and were debated and applied in the social sciences and the humanities. Cyberculture theory nevertheless largely failed to draw from their insights, though early considerations of affect, nonhuman agency, and even ANT, are present in 1990s research (e.g., Dery 1993; Manovich 1995; Stone 1996; Hillis 1999).

Within the framework of new materialist theory, rather than understanding the virtual as separate from the actual, as was the case in much early utopian cyberculture theory, the virtual is understood as that which orients the actual as it unfolds. The virtual, therefore, can be understood as the potentialities, investments, and imaginations concerning the present and the possible shape of things to come. Following Deleuze (2002, 148), every actual object is surrounded by a cloud of virtual images that are "composed of a series of more or less extensive coexisting circuits, along which the virtual images are distributed, and around which they run." The virtual is then "a pre-individual or even trans-individual register of *life* which produces the affective tone of experience" (Blackman and Venn 2010, 20). In their discussion and embrace of multiple virtual lives on the screen, cyberculture theorists Sherry Turkle (1995) and Sandy Stone (1996) implicitly support the idea that "cyberspace" (as the internet and virtual reality applications were then often called) produces the affective tone of experience—in effect, a "trans-individual register of life." Their online ethnographic research began to articulate the entangled relationship between the virtual and the actual at the level of the interface, but did so within an understanding of cyberspace as somehow ontologically separate from the offline world. The inadvertent effect was to wall off the virtual and to encourage individuals to imagine that its actualization could take place only in entirely virtual settings. Other strains of 1990s cyberculture theory focused on virtual reality's immersive goggles, data gloves, the internet as prosthetic extension, and the figure of the cyborg (Grey 1995). The utopian acceptance of the deterministic notion that technology itself leads to social change arguably can be seen to promote, even proselytize for, forms of nonhuman agency.

The technological advances of the 2000s, such as the continual refinement of smartphone technology, along with the networks that support its applications and practices, which have increasingly made obsolete the distinctions between what is wired, what is wireless, and what is ubiquitous, have largely put to rest the idea that the virtual operates independently from the offline. And, as pointed out above, ubiquitous networked collectivity through multiple platforms, applications, and interfaces for purposes of work and play, consumption and production alike, has equally undermined the figure of the rational user in control of technology. In sum, recent intellectual activity at the crossroads of affect theory and internet research is fueled by the acceptance of network technologies and applications as constitutive elements of everyday life, as well as by the rearticulation of the rational and the passionate (or the affective) as interconnected, parts of the continuum of human perception and activity (Hardt 2007, x).

Once the technological is understood as not merely instrumental but as generative of sensation and potentiality—as agential, to use ANT terminology—it becomes crucial to investigate what emerges in our networked exchanges and encounters. ANT draws on Bruno Latour's argument for the need to focus on connections and relations in studies of action and agency. Latour suggests that "a subject only becomes interesting, deep, profound, worthwhile when it resonates with others, is effected, moved, put into motion by new entities whose differences are registered in new and unexpected ways" (Latour 2004, 210; also Seigworth and Gregg 2010, 11–12). For Latour, subjects are defined by the connections through which they are impressed and formed. Actors, such as human individuals, are best understood through the networks of people, technologies, objects, and practices of which they are a part—through their connections and reverberations within these networks (Latour 2011, 806). ANT, defined by John Law as the consideration of "entities and materialities as enacted and relational effects" (Law 2004, 157), focuses on such connections and points of contact that give rise to contingent networks—or, in Deleuzian terms, assemblages. While ANT is not always included in the genealogies of the affective turn, these trajectories of thought are deeply entangled, and nowhere more so than in the framework of networked communications.

ANT theorizes agency as distributed, networked, and emergent in its forms and effects, rather than as an issue of solely individual intention or activity. Actors are in a state of constant interaction, learning, and becoming, and are always connected to other actors and factors. An individual looking at a display screen, for example, is connected to a computer, itself an assemblage of hardware, protocols, standards, software, and data. Once connected to an information network by means of modems, cables, routers, hubs, and switches, the computer affords access to other computers, online settings, people, groups, and files. All this entails a rethinking of both human and nonhuman actors and how affect is generated and circulated. Nonhuman actors include, in this instance, the processes, agents, and networks involved in information and communication technology research and development, design, manufacture, promotion, and consumption; the infrastructure, policies, and labor of energy production; the global distribution of profit and harm; and the functions and affordances of code. Human actors engage with and through this technological assemblage. ANT's framework conceptualizes the connection of singular technological objects and human-technology encounters to the broader—indeed global—networked flows of money, labor, commodities, and natural resources. Considerations of individual intention, agency, technology use, and identity construction are, therefore, both complemented and complicated by the need to acknowledge their entanglement in technological networks of transmission and communication, as well as in the (social) networks of privilege and inequality.

Writing Affect

In his consideration of the methodological reverberations of actor-network theory within the social sciences, Law insists on the necessity of resisting the imperatives of coherence and neatness when addressing phenomena that are complex, diffuse, and messy, and on incorporating some of this messiness into scholarly practice, since "much of the world is vague, diffuse or unspecific, slippery, emotional, ephemeral, elusive or indistinct, changes like a kaleidoscope, or doesn't really have much of a pattern at all" (Law 2004, 2). Research therefore needs to make room for ambivalence and ambiguity while not reducing complexity into singular and coherent narratives, and to acknowledge the limits of language when tackling sensation, emotion, and affect (Law 2004, 90–93, 147). Coherence, Law argues, is imperative for scholarly writing, yet comes at the significant risk of flattening out complexities and ambivalences. Broadening the debate from the framework of ANT and the social sciences to both internet research and affect theory, the argument for accommodating and accounting for messiness and complexity in a rigorous way remains vital—theoretically as well as semantically.

When affect theorists tackle the complex, the extralinguistic, the precognitive, and the intense—elements that depend on and flow through human embodiment—the forms of writing that result sometimes border on the metaphoric and the elusive, seemingly at the expense of the evidentiary. That is, the acknowledgment of ambiguity, incoherence, and the limitations of scholarly prose may result in opaqueness of expression. Definitions of intensity, for example, risk a kind of tautology, circling recursively on themselves to suggest that intensity refers to that which is intense, or an intense experience, without a further unpacking of the term. Similar risks of tautology may be involved in the lax use of the concepts of potentiality and capacity, so that they become detached from the very theoretical framework within which the terms first were introduced. Floating and circulating free from theoretical frameworks, terminology becomes ephemeral.

Considered as a precognitive intensity or force, affect, as Tyler (2008) observes, is highly elusive. When identified or named, it is already gone and impossible to precisely recapture or pin down. As that which escapes the structures of language and attempts at meaning-making, affect has evoked experimental, and even lyrical, modes of scholarly writing, as authors try to grasp and convey some of its elusive yet visceral intensity (e.g., Stewart 2007; Seigworth and Gregg 2010). While it may seem ironic for there to be a certain seduction by, and preoccupation with, language when writing about the extralinguistic, such attention and care evince a need to rethink established research concepts and to imagine and develop alternatives to them (Cho, this volume; Petit, this volume).

It is further worth noting that authors can only ever have a *firsthand* knowledge of affect on the basis of their own experiences. This reality informs Bertrand Russell's distinction between "knowledge of" (firsthand/experience) and "knowledge about" (representation/theory). Scholars can speculate about other people's sensations, but they cannot directly know them. As Elaine Scarry (1985, 5–6) notes about pain, the experiences of others always remain out of grasp while pain itself remains inaccessible to words—and remarkably resistant to language and description. Or, as Niklaus Largier (2007, 14) puts it, "words *go around*" physical sensations and practices, the importance of which lies largely beyond the confines of signification. Writing is therefore an act of mediation where bodily impressions, modulations, arousals, and motions are translated in order to be brought into the representational space of the text. While much is unavoidably transformed and lost in such translation, this mediation between the sensory and the textual is nevertheless a key aim in affective forms of writing (Paasonen 2011, 200–205).

If not grounded in the assessment of specific bodies, however, academic reflections about the sensory may "lose their specificity and become generalized to the point where particularities or collective difference between bodies fade from view" (Kyrölä 2010, 8). To counter this, and to anchor their argumentation in lived experience, some scholars of affect have drawn on their own mundane observations (Stewart 2007) and evoked "a strategic I" for mounting an argument through autobiographical rhetoric and anecdotes (Kyrölä 2010, 24). The necessity of working with and through one's own experiences may, however, evoke accusations of nominalism very resonant with the widespread, hyperindividuated culture of "me": if we can only account for that which we have ourselves sensed, and if the affective encounters under review are unpredictable and contingent (and hence impossible to generalize), then what can meaningfully be said about the more collective workings of affect, or of affect on a more abstract level? One answer may be found in the forms of personal writing evoked in studies of affect that link to the tradition of feminist autobiographical writing (of which Virginia Woolf's 1929 novel, *A Room of One's Own,* is a classic example). The so-called autobiographical turn (Miller 1991; Gallop 1988; Pearce 1997) is a means of connecting personal experience to the broader flows of culture, economy, politics, and society while also conceptualizing one's implicatedness and situatedness within these. When exploring the bodily, and particularly the sexual, personal writing necessitates breaching the conventions of scholarly detachment and the predominance of the disembodied, often passive, textual voice in academic narration. The difficulties of incorporating the visceral and the corporeal into academic writing, therefore, speak to the tenuous—and necessarily risky—process of mediation between the embodied and the semantic, as well as to the difficulties involved in articulating the intimate, the personal, and the private. Experimental and personal forms of writing open up possibilities for bridging the gaps between the sensory and the semiotic, the personal and the collective, and for mediating the physical within the textual.

For many new materialist scholars, however, phenomenological accounts of affect—including those reliant on personal writing—fall short precisely because they do not address those qualities of force and sensation that are not human by definition, such as the force of color, or that of rhythm (Deleuze 2003). A focus on the personally sensible, therefore, is seen to limit the investigation of life forces to the realm of the autobiographical and anecdotal, and to flatten the conceptualization of force to the level of emotions as "intensity owned and recognized" (Massumi 2002, 25–30; Shouse 2005). In order to avoid this, new materialist scholars detach affect from the specific materiality of human bodies and address it on a more abstract level of intensity, sensation, and liveliness that animates and moves all kinds of bodies, not just human ones (Ash, this volume; Parikka, this volume). This line of intellectual inquiry decenters the human subject—especially the individual—as the main focus of scholarly exploration, with the aim of conceptualizing and making more apparent the energies of life that animate our world (Clough and Halley 2007; Grosz 2008).

Nevertheless, writing that focuses on affective force understood as a general vitality and potentiality in relation to cultural products such as visual art, film, and literature, regularly congeals around instances of resonance, as sensed and made sense of by the author in question (e.g., Deleuze 2003; Shaviro 2010). Resonance and potentiality, as identified in these analyses, are generalized into a broader, general, affective dynamic—or a property of particular images, seen in Deleuze's (2003) work on Francis Bacon's paintings as encapsulations of intensity and sensation. As noted above, one motivation underpinning the turn to affect has been a departure from linguistic structuralism. Paradoxically, abstracted analyses of potentiality, liveliness, and intensity may evoke an uncanny resemblance to structuralism when certain artistic creations (such as Bacon's paintings) are seen as encapsulating or generating affect, independent of the particularities of the sensing human viewer. In *Post-Cinematic Affect*, Steven Shaviro (2010), for example, discusses films as "machines for generating affect." For Shaviro, affect refers to a surplus that escapes confinement in individual emotion even as it forms it, transpersonally and transversally. His analysis works to chart the structure of feeling particular to contemporary culture by drawing on films as "affective maps" (Shaviro 2010, 3–4). These maps, however, are then generalized as an underlying cultural dynamic (or structure) that is simultaneously about everybody and no particular body at all.

Once the subjective is detached or even removed from the analysis, it becomes possible to connect forces, potentialities, and intensities with certain objects and phenomena, and to account for life forces that are not human by definition. Opening up to the world, its flora, fauna, and object life, scholars operating within the turn to the nonhuman can now consider nonhuman sensoria and "alien phenomenology" (Bogost 2012). Yet at the same time, these investigations are conducted from within the confines of specifically human sensoria, cognition, phenomenological experience, as well as language, the boundaries of which are imaginatively and conceptually breached through acts of writing. While there are no simple solutions to such epistemological dilemmas, the balancing act between the highly particular and the general—and between things sensed and made sense of—cuts through most work on affect, including this volume's chapters.

Intensity, Sensation, and Value

The forms of writing presented in the chapters that follow vary from the personal to the more detached, and the authors' foci move, for example, from sexual dynamics to the liveliness of computer code to the disaffection present in the "smart" classroom. Rather than anchoring itself in any one paradigm of affect theory, *Networked Affect* incorporates and interconnects several paradigms and frameworks in order to produce a multifaceted understanding of how affect matters for internet researchers. Chapters reflect the various tensions, theoretical tendencies, divergences, and convergences that have been a principal subject in our discussion above. As editors, our intention has been to gather a range of work focused on the lively intersection of networks and affects *and* to do so in a way that acknowledges the array of practices, theorizations, and methods found across contemporary affect theory. The power of affect to generate different and newly emergent forms of sensation, along with the sociopolitical implications of these forms, organizes our contributors' approaches to networked affect as they home in on the intensities and resonances of specific platforms, applications, exchanges, techniques, practices, and investments; the properties of file formats; and the creation of affective and possibly political value.

While all chapters tie issues of circulation and connectivity to theorizations of networked affect, they do so in three broad ways. The first set of chapters—organized under the thematic heading of *intensity*—considers the oscillations, reverberations, and resonances of affective intensity and the connections and disconnections that such intensity brings forth in online exchanges. The second set of chapters—organized under the theme of *sensation*—interrogates the materiality of technologies at the core of networked affect along with the interrelations among human and nonhuman bodies as they "inhabit" networked digital media. In the book's third section—*value*—contributors assess networked communications as sites of immaterial and affective labor, analyzing the creation and accumulation of value and the complex ways by which affective value ties in with political economy, human agency, and the networked technologies with which many of us now daily engage.

Intensity

In "A Midsummer's Bonfire: Affective Intensities of Online Debate," Susanna Paasonen investigates a Facebook wall debate about Helsinki club culture and heteronormativity. This chapter considers the particular dynamics and public reverberations of the thread in terms of affective stickiness that both congeals and sharpens when online participants interpret the messages of others, often by skimming through them and extrapolating meanings. The format of Facebook's discussion thread encourages interaction with the most recent posts on a thread, which, Paasonen argues, helps produce stickiness in the form of constant discontinuity and rupture. With trolls abounding, the Helsinki club culture exchange gave rise to multiple divisions among and categorizations of the participants. One of the most central to emerge is being a "feminist killjoy." In recursive fashion, practices of trolling and flaming evoke sharp reactions in other participants and help drive the exchanges further. Paasonen argues that the ability of online affective sharpness to both appeal and disturb, attract and repulse, results in forms of intensity that attach individuals to specific exchanges, groups, threads, and platforms such as Facebook.

Drawing from his extensive participant observation in Tumblr LGBTQ communities, in "Queer Reverb: Tumblr, Affect, Time" Alexander Cho provides a meditative yet analytic set of reflections about the affective dynamics at play in the practices of queer Tumblr users. These include the circulation of vintage erotica and ephemera, a call to action amid the wrenching aftereffects of gay youth who have committed suicide, as well as events logged over the lifespan of Cho's own posted and lyrical photos. Cho asserts that attention to cyclicality and repetition is crucial to understanding the flow of affect in these situations, and he underscores how these dynamics are useful in understanding the intensity of Tumblr's traffic in affect. He also traces in these practices the contours of a possible resistant queer politics through a stubborn persistence of the past. The chapter closes by offering the metaphor of "reverb" to explain the interplay of temporal cycles of felt experience that structure the flow of affect in online settings.

Paasonen and Cho focus on sites generating specific forms of intensity that circulate through online threads and resonate with groupings composed largely of Finnish- and English-speaking participants. In "Affective Politics or Political Affection: Online Sexuality in Turkey," Veronika Tzankova theorizes the political potential of networked affect through her exploration of Turkish sexual *itiraf* sites—online platforms where individuals share their sexual experiences, fantasies, and reflections in the form of short textual narratives. Tzankova demonstrates how networked affect has facilitated the emergence of a sexual counterpublic, along with alternative forms of ideological resistance, within the highly repressive political environment of Turkey's ongoing Islamization. Through the narratives they post, members of these sites circulate a gamut of intensities that necessarily engender a multiplicity of meanings—explicitly somatic and sexual, but implicitly political—which convey a sharp anti-Islamist positioning. The chapter's timely discussion of the role of affect in Turkish-language online settings concludes that, given the ubiquity of internet and web technologies, networked affect has the potential to influence and even help constitute the sociopolitical.

If intensities circulate through exchanges of text-based messages and photographs, they can also be produced when we experience visceral or gut reactions to moving images. In "The Avatar and Online Affect" Ken Hillis focuses on the digital avatar, such as one might deploy or encounter on sites such as Second Life, in order to assess how reactions to moving images are rendered and made possible in online settings. He outlines four networked phenomena that, when conjoined, constitute a multilayered mechanism capable of producing networked affect. These phenomena are metaphors of virtual space, the allegorical nature of networked telepresence, the use of lively indexical signs that take the form of digital avatars, and the contemporary reification of virtual mobility. Hillis argues that while many individuals may feel that they are "stuck" and insufficiently mobile for the dictates of today's just-in-time, do-it-yourself, disintermediated world, their avatars can depict the mobility they may feel they lack. In such a way do avatars accrue intense affect as they perform an imagistic body politics, seemingly independent of their embodied human operators, which can serve to redress these individuals' relative lack of desirable forms of mobility. The chapter demonstrates how, at a moment of great support for the idea of mobility as a major resource of contemporary life, the online moving image pulls us along in its tow, catching us in an emergent, oscillating tension between material fixity and digital flow.

In "Affect and Drive" Jodi Dean examines how feedback loops connecting computers and people give rise to affective networks—to fields of intensity, action, and enjoyment. Like Paasonen, Dean argues that social media produce and circulate affects that manifest a binding technique, as individuals attach themselves to sites and applications. The reverse is also the case when these applications press themselves on individuals and drive their activities. Dean argues that, within the framework of a communicative capitalism whereby communication has become inextricable from capitalist processes of expropriation and exploitation, affective intensity has become inseparable from incessant technological renewal and automated techniques of surveillance. Affect, or *jouissance* in Lacanian terms, is, she observes, what accrues from reflexive communication, from communication for its own sake through social media, from the endless circular movement of commenting on Facebook, adding notes and links, bringing in new friends and followers, and layering and interconnecting myriad communication platforms and devices.

Sensation

"Ethologies of Software Art and Affect: What Can a Digital Body of Code Do?" asks two questions: Can we use affect to understand human-nonhuman relations? And, if we can, how does affect's circulation inflect the various layers of abstractions that brand networked culture? To answer these questions, author Jussi Parikka extends theories of nonorganic affect in order to focus on the ways that software itself now circulates as a form of art. He exemplifies his discussion though software art projects such as Google Will Eat Itself and Biennale.py, and in so doing uncovers some of the heterogeneous relations by which software functions as a crucial though underacknowledged component of our contemporary culture of perception and the global digital economy. Projects such as Google Will Eat Itself expose the affective materiality of software. They do so through their transposition of spheres of sensation (the visual interface, machine processes) and of the intensities and the information that individuates and informs agency. In such circumstances, Parikka argues for the crucial importance of better understanding the meaning and nature of the relationship between a body of software and a body of humans. Any answer, he observes, must account for the potentialities that bodies are capable of in interaction with other bodies—and only in such interactions. The chapter concludes that software is not only a stable body of code, but an affect in itself, an affordance, and a potentiality for entering into human and human-nonhuman relations.

"Sensation, Networks, and the GIF: Toward an Allotropic Account of Affect" continues in the vein of new materialist theory in its examination of animated GIFs (Graphic Interchange Format), those winking, blinking, moving images of prairie dogs, dancing babies, and snippets of popular culture that have gained wide cultural prominence in recent years. Although GIFs have been examined as internet memes, author James Ash provokes a more robust consideration by examining them from a technical and material perspective. Drawing on Deleuze's work on Bacon, Ash develops the concept of allotropy to theorize how affect travels around and through networks and how it is translated by and travels between human and nonhuman entities. In his examination of a number of popular GIFs, he explains how their technical structure as a file type shapes their capacity to produce affect. Rather than being totally open in their potential, however, GIFs modulate forces into either sensations or affects that shape the possibilities of emergence when these animations are viewed. In making this argument, the chapter contributes to debates around affective transmission and suggests that affect must always be understood in relation to the specificity of the technical media that enable it.

In the midst of the affective networks of contemporary digital cultures, something seemingly of the opposite order is taking shape: steampunk, an aesthetic-technological movement incorporating science fiction, art, engineering, and a vibrant twenty-first-century do-it-yourself counterculture characterized by a retro-futuristic reimagination of the steam-powered technologies of the Victorian era organized around the question, "What if we continued as an analog society instead of a digital one?" In "Technologies of Feeling: Affect between the Analog and the Digital," Jenny Sundén turns to steampunk culture as a compelling example of a contemporary affective investment in the analog that is coupled with intense digital connectivity. Sundén formulates a critique of Massumi's notion of the superiority of the analog and suggests that steampunk, rather than being understood as analog nostalgia, is more aptly understood in terms of what she terms the transdigital. The term transdigital accounts for analog passions that are shaped through the digital in ways that concretely activate, but also move across or beyond the borders of the digital. Steampunk, Sundén argues, rather than indicating a return to a bygone era, is a reconsideration of the (digital) present.

In "'Make Love Not Porn': Entrepreneurial Voyeurism, Agency, and Affect," Stephen Maddison argues that online pornography is a critical arena in which to consider the relationship among bodily sensation, networked communication, and the relentless commoditization of reality enacted under the aegis of the "enterprise society." This chapter synthesizes theories of affect and recent work on immaterial labor and the entrepreneurial subject in order to assess the differing ways that two exemplary alt-porn websites entice paying viewers and encourage entrepreneurial individuals to post "authentic" self-made porn that others will pay to watch. FuckforForest is a nonprofit site that subverts the commercial model of online porn to raise money for ecoactivism, whereas "Make Love Not Porn" is a pay porn venture launched in 2012 by Cindy Gallop, former brand adviser to Coca-Cola and Levi's jeans. Maddison likens the rise of such sites—with their free previews and sensational "peeks" into the intimate, carnal realms inhabited by porn performers—to the parallel rise of the enterprise society, with its constant exhortations to work harder and longer and therefore, by implication, to have less time and affective energy for fulfilling sexual experience.

"Digital Disaffect: Teaching through Screens" is a meditative piece based on a first-year undergraduate humanities course in inquiry and reasoning. Michael Petit draws on information and data he collected on the topic "emotions and the internet" from more than one hundred students through qualitative interviews and quantitative surveys of peers. He provides an affective portrait of contemporary undergraduates who have grown up immersed in digital sensations and an environment of screens and media technologies. This generation surfs the web seeking and finding its affective potentialities in what many of them see as a vast and stimulating place. Yet as students move routinely, even robotically, through Facebook, Twitter, and Tumblr, they simultaneously use the internet to study, to download and read class materials, and to relieve the boredom of writing class papers. What Petit terms digital disaffect coexists with and within the affective responses students find on the internet. Petit's discussion is conveyed as much through affective resonance and writing as through linear structure, and the second part of the chapter takes the form of a series of printed "hyperlinks" that draw from his observations, comingled with interviews, class assignments, and students' observations. This chapter points to the normalization of digital disaffect within contemporary culture and considers what this might mean for the North American university classroom.

Value

The relationships among affective value, political economy, agency, and networked digital technologies are complex, as this set of chapters on value demonstrates. Melissa Gregg investigates the prehistory of contemporary time management and productivity services that are a feature of networked culture in "Getting Things Done: Productivity, Self-Management, and the Order of Things." Here she focuses on the synergies that exist between the practices of professional self-management encouraged by the self-help literature of the past three decades and those being reprised in today's online Getting Things Done (GTD) movement. Gregg offers a critique and a caution, given that the dominant logic of GTD is to espouse asociality as superiority. GTD produces a corporatized idea of human efficiency that is only imaginable through the mutually constitutive discourses of computation and management. It elevates an elite class of worker beyond the concerns of ordinary colleagues as well as many of the most conventional social bonds. Gregg observes that productivity's current mandate is to obliterate what remains of voluntary sociability in the otherwise coercive networking context of the modern workplace. This is a mode of thinking that takes seriously the possibility of transcending the social, of focusing attention and assessment of value purely on the consequential, at least for predetermined periods of time. Such an aspiration relies on a hierarchical workplace in which trivial tasks can be delegated to less powerful employees. By celebrating this structure as freedom, GTD draws together troubling philosophical legacies of exceptionalism under the affective guise of successful entrepreneurialism.

"'Let's Express Our Friendship by Sending Each Other Funny Links instead of Actually Talking': Gifts, Commodities, and Social Reproduction in Facebook" explores the tensions between processes of commodification and the affectivity of interactions through the social networking site Facebook. Like Gregg, author Kylie Jarrett argues that as advertising and capitalist economic imperatives saturate our digital networks, there has been a corresponding reduction in the viability, quality, and actuality of meaningful sociality. In Marxist terms, she argues that the use values of gifts based in richly complex reciprocal relations have been ceded to the abstractions of readily exploitable exchange value. This chapter challenges the simple binary relation between gifts and commodities—between use value and exchange value—by identifying their coexistence in Facebook's affective networks. Jarrett argues for the existence of reciprocal obligations between users and Facebook's technological platform, obligations that demand not only the contribution of abstract data for conversion to economic value but also the affective intensities that validate, legitimate, and perpetuate social networking sites and the commodity logic upon which they rely. The inalienable affective pleasures—the gifted use values—of our digitally mediated networks, she concludes, are implicated in capitalism through their ability to reproduce subjective orientations that support the existing social and economic order.

In "Happy Accidents: Facebook and the Value of Affect" Tero Karppi analyzes Timeline, Facebook's personalized user interface, as well as the site's related protocol called Open Graph. Karppi argues that Timeline entails a new, affective turn in Facebook's history that cannot be reduced to a mere updating of the site's graphical user interface (GUI). Instead, with the introduction of ideas of "serendipity" and "frictionless sharing" that are part of Timeline's launch, Facebook is moving toward building and controlling intensities—affects. Following Massumi's notion of the autonomy of affect,

Karppi explores how Facebook transforms its members into affective points of contact. By focusing on the nonsubjective side of affect theory, he challenges the idea of conscious and active user participation and argues that, through protocols and other platform-specific functions, Facebook renders individuals automatic and autonomous participants in the production of affects. Actions such as listening to music are made Facebook-compatible and then turned into affective streams—"happy accidents" that potentially attract the attention of other users as well as advertisers. Karppi emphasizes that Facebook's value, therefore, is less related to market value per se than to its capacity to affect its users, given that the former is based on the latter.

It has been argued that social media are creating a new culture of disclosure, particularly for younger users, one predicated on a distinct set of beliefs, norms, and affective practices that legitimate the constant uploading of personal materials. In the book's final chapter, "Accumulating Affect: Social Networks and Their Archives of Feelings," Jennifer Pybus examines the important position that digital archives now occupy within the information economy as sites for the accumulation of value, both social and economic. Reworking Ann Cvetkovich's notion of an "archive of feeling" as a paradigm for understanding the influence of social media on the everyday lived experiences of users, Pybus posits a digital archive of feeling, one within which we can examine the choices that determine which information is selected to represent us, enacting affect with others and, subsequently, ourselves. The deep and complex sociality and forms of immaterial labor embedded in such choices constitute the reasons, this chapter argues, that so many corporations are invested in rendering social networking databases profitable.

Networked Affect is international in scope, with authors from Australia, Bulgaria, Canada, Finland, Ireland, Sweden, the United Kingdom, and the United States. Though their work in some cases is rooted within specific national circumstances and particular places—a Toronto classroom, Helsinki club culture—the volume as a whole moves through and across increasingly interpenetrating forms of identification, whether they be sectarian or secular, place-based or global, machinic or humanist, corporate or resistant, sexual or social—and any combinations thereof. As authors and editors, we hope to encourage further conversations within internet studies and new media studies, and more broadly about how understanding affective networks, constituted in the sensory, the intensive, and the material, can illuminate our collective and fragmented actions and practices across networks.

Note

1. See Tarlton Gillespie (2010) for a productive discussion of the political implications of "platforms."

References

Ahmed, Sara. 2004. *The Cultural Politics of Emotion*. Edinburgh: Edinburgh University Press.

Ahmed, Sara. 2008. Imaginary Prohibitions: Some Preliminary Remarks on the Founding Gesture of "New Materialism." *European Journal of Women's Studies* 15 (1):23–39.

Anderson, Ben. 2010. Modulating the Excess of Affect: Morale in a State of "Total War." In *The Affect Theory Reader*, ed. Melissa Gregg and Gregory J. Seigworth, 161–185. Durham: Duke University Press.

Armstrong, Isobel. 2000. *The Radical Aesthetic*. Oxford: Blackwell.

Barad, Karen. 2007. *Meeting the Universe Halfway: Quantum Physics and the Entanglement of Matter and Meaning*. Durham: Duke University Press.

Bennett, Jane. 2010. *Vibrant Matter: A Political Ecology of Things*. Durham: Duke University Press.

Blackman, Lisa, and Couze Venn. 2010. Affect. *Body and Society* 16 (1):7–28.

Bogost, Ian. 2012. *Alien Phenomenology*. Minneapolis: Minnesota University Press.

Braidotti, Rosi. 2002. *Metamorphoses: Towards a Materialist Theory of Becoming*. Cambridge: Polity.

Brown, Steven D., and Paul Stenner. 2001. Being Affected: Spinoza and the Psychology of Emotion. *International Journal of Group Tensions* 30 (1):81–105.

Clough, Patricia Ticineto, and Jean Halley, eds. 2007. *The Affective Turn: Theorizing the Social*. Durham: Duke University Press.

Coleman, Rebecca. 2012. *Transforming Images: Screens, Affect, Futures*. London: Routledge.

Coté, Mark, and Jennifer Pybus. 2007. Learning to Immaterial Labour 2.0: MySpace and Social Networks. *Ephemera: Theory and Politics in Organization* 7 (1):88–106.

Deleuze, Gilles. 1998. *Spinoza: Practical Philosophy*. Trans. Richard Hurley. San Francisco: City Lights Books.

Deleuze, Gilles. 2002. The Actual and the Virtual. In *Dialogues II*, ed. Claire Parnet, trans. Eliot Ross Albert, 148–152. New York: Columbia University Press.

Deleuze, Gilles. 2003. *Francis Bacon: The Logic of Sensation*. Trans. Daniel W. Smith. London: Basic Books.

Dery, Mark. 1993. Flame Wars. In *Flame Wars: The Discourse of Cyberculture*, ed. Mark Dery, 1–10. Durham: Duke University Press.

Dolphjin, Rick, and Iris van der Tuin, eds. 2012. *New Materialism: Interviews and Cartographies*. Ann Arbor: Open Humanities Press.

Gallop, Jane. 1988. *Thinking through the Body*. New York: Columbia University Press.

Gatens, Moira. 2000. Feminism as "Password": Re-thinking the "Possible" with Spinoza and Deleuze. *Hypatia* 15 (12):59–75.

Gillespie, Tarlton. 2010. The Politics of "Platforms." *New Media and Society* 12 (3):346–367.

Grey, Chris Hables, ed. 1995. *The Cyborg Handbook*. New York: Routledge.

Grosz, Elizabeth. 2008. *Chaos, Territory, Art: Deleuze and the Framing of the Earth*. New York: Columbia University Press.

Grusin, Richard. 2010. *Premediation: Affect and Materiality after 9/11*. New York: Palgrave.

Hardt, Michael. 2007. Foreword: What Affects Are Good For. In *The Affective Turn: Theorizing the Social*, ed. Patricia Ticineto Clough and Jean Halley, ix–xiii. Durham: Duke University Press.

Hardt, Michael, and Antonio Negri. 2001. *Empire*. Cambridge, MA: Harvard University Press.

Hemmings, Clare. 2005. Invoking Affect: Cultural Theory and the Ontological Turn. *Cultural Studies* 19 (5):548–567.

Hillis, Ken. 1999. *Digital Sensations: Space, Identity, and Embodiment in Virtual Reality*. Minneapolis: Minnesota University Press.

Hillis, Ken. 2009. *Online a Lot of the Time: Ritual, Fetish, Sign*. Durham: Duke University Press.

Jarrett, Kylie. 2006. The Perfect Community: Disciplining the eBay User. In *Everyday eBay: Culture, Collecting and Desire*, ed. Ken Hillis and Michael Petit, 107–122. New York: Routledge.

Karatzogianni, Athina, and Adi Kuntsman, eds. 2012. *Digital Cultures and the Politics of Emotion: Feelings, Affect and Technological Exchange*. London: Palgrave.

Kember, Sarah, and Joanna Zylinska. 2012. *Life after Media: Mediation as a Vital Process*. Cambridge, MA: MIT Press.

Kennedy, Barbara M. 2000. *Deleuze and Cinema: The Aesthetics of Sensation*. Edinburgh: Edinburgh University Press.

Koivunen, Anu. 2001. Preface: The Affective Turn? In *Conference Proceedings for Affective Encounters: Rethinking Embodiment in Feminist Media Studies*, ed. Anu Koivunen and Susanna Paasonen, 7–9. Turku, Finland: University of Turku.

Koivunen, Anu. 2010. The Affective Turn? Reimagining the Subject of Feminist Theory. In *Working with Affect in Feminist Readings: Disturbing Differences*, ed. Marianne Liljeström and Susanna Paasonen, 8–29. London: Routledge.

Kuntsman, Adi. 2009. *Figurations of Violence and Belonging: Queerness, Migranthood and Nationalism in Cyberspace and Beyond*. Bern: Lang.

Kyrölä, Katariina. 2010. *The Weight of Images: Affective Engagements with Fat Corporeality in the Media*. Turku, Finland: University of Turku.

Largier, Niklaus. 2007. *In Praise of the Whip: A Cultural History of Arousal*. Trans. Graham Harman. New York: Zone Books.

Latour, Bruno. 2004. How to Talk about the Body? The Normative Dimension of Science Studies. *Body and Society* 10 (2–3):205–229.

Latour, Bruno. 2011. Reflections of an Actor-Network Theorist. *International Journal of Communication* 5:796–810.

Law, John. 2004. *After Method: Mess in Social Science Research*. London: Routledge.

Lazzarato, Maurizio. 1996. Immaterial Labor. Available at http://www.generation-online.org/c/fcimmateriallabour3.htm.

Liljeström, Marianne, and Susanna Paasonen, eds. 2010. *Working with Affect in Feminist Readings: Disturbing Differences*. London: Routledge.

Lillie, John. 2006. Immaterial Labor in the eBay Community: The Work of Consumption in the "Network Society." In *Everyday eBay: Culture, Collecting and Desire*, ed. Ken Hillis and Michael Petit, 91–106. New York: Routledge.

Manovich, Lev. 1995. Potemkische Dörfer, Kino und Telepräsenz/Potemkin's Villages, Cinema and Telepresence. In *Mythos Information: Welcome to the Wired World*, ed. Karl Gebel and Peter Weibel, 343–353. Linz, Austria: Ars Electronica.

Massumi, Brian. 2002. *Parables for the Virtual: Movement, Affect, Sensation*. Durham: Duke University Press.

Miller, Nancy K. 1991. *Getting Personal: Feminist Occasions and Other Autobiographical Acts*. New York: Routledge.

Paasonen, Susanna. 2009. What Cyberspace? Traveling Concepts in Internet Research. In *Internationalizing Internet Studies: Beyond Anglophone Paradigms*, ed. Gerard Goggin and Mark McLelland, 18–31. New York: Routledge.

Paasonen, Susanna. 2011. *Carnal Resonance: Affect and Online Pornography*. Cambridge, MA: MIT Press.

Pearce, Lynne. 1997. *Feminism and the Politics of Reading*. London: Arnold.

Probyn, Elspeth. 2005. *Blush: Faces of Shame*. Minneapolis: University of Minnesota Press.

Protevi, John. 2009. *Political Affect: Connecting the Social and the Somatic*. Minneapolis: University of Minnesota Press.

Richardson, John. 2010. *An Eye for Music: Popular Music and the Audiovisual Sublime*. Oxford: Oxford University Press.

Robinson, Laura. 2006. "Black Friday" and Feedback Bombing: An Examination of Trust and Online Community in eBay's Early History. In *Everyday eBay: Culture, Collecting and Desire*, ed. Ken Hillis and Michael Petit, 123–136. New York: Routledge.

Scarry, Elaine. 1985. *The Body in Pain: The Making and Unmaking of the World*. New York: Oxford University Press.

Sedgwick, Eve Kosofsky. 2003. *Touching Feeling: Affect, Pedagogy, Performativity*. Durham: Duke University Press.

Sedgwick, Eve Kosofsky, and Adam Frank, eds. 1995. *Shame and Its Sisters: A Silvan Tomkins Reader*. Durham: Duke University Press.

Seigworth, Gregory J., and Melissa Gregg. 2010. An Inventory of Shimmers. In *The Affect Theory Reader*, ed. Melissa Gregg and Gregory J. Seigworth, 1–28. Durham: Duke University Press.

Shaviro, Steven. 2010. *Post-Cinematic Affect*. Winchester: Zero Books.

Sheets-Johnstone, Maxine. 2009. *The Corporeal Turn: An Interdisciplinary Reader*. Exeter: Imprint Academic.

Shouse, Eric. 2005. Feeling, Emotion, Affect. *M/C Journal* 8 (6). Available at http://journal.media -culture.org.au/0512/03-shouse.php.

Sobchack, Vivian. 2004. *Carnal Thoughts: Embodiment and Moving Image Culture*. Berkeley: University of California Press.

Spinoza, Baruch. 1992. *The Ethics, Treatise on the Emendation of the Intellect and Selected Letters*. Ed. Seymour Feldman. Trans. Samuel Shirley. Indianapolis: Hackett.

Staiger, Janet, Anne Cvetkovich, and Ann Morris Reynolds, eds. 2010. *Political Emotions*. New York: Routledge.

Stewart, Kathleen. 2007. *Ordinary Affect*. Durham: Duke University Press.

Stone, Allucquère Rosanne. 1996. *The War of Desire and Technology at the Close of the Mechanical Age*. Cambridge, MA: MIT Press.

Terranova, Tiziana. 2003. Free Labor: Producing Culture for the Digital Economy. *Social Text* 18 (2):33–58.

Terranova, Tiziana. 2006. Of Sense and Sensibility: Immaterial Labour in Open Systems. In *Curating Immateriality: The Work of the Curator in the Age of Network Systems*, ed. Joasia Krysa, 27–36. Brooklyn: Autonomedia.

Tomkins, Silvan. 1995. The Quest for Primary Motives: Biography and Autobiography of an Idea. In *Exploring Affect: The Selected Writings of Silvan S. Tomkins*, ed. E. Virginia Demos, 27–63. Cambridge: Cambridge University Press.

Turkle, Sherry. 1995. *Life on the Screen: Identity in the Age of the Internet*. New York: Simon and Schuster.

Tyler, Imogen. 2008. Methodological Fatigue and the Politics of the Affective Turn. *Feminist Media Studies* 8 (1):85–90.

Intensity

2   A Midsummer's Bonfire: Affective Intensities of Online Debate

Susanna Paasonen

Building and setting large bonfires is a Finnish tradition to celebrate midsummer. Especially in rural areas, midsummer celebrations involve dance parties, bonfires, liberal consumption of alcohol, and (at least fantasies of) sexual encounters in the white night. A different kind of bonfire occurred in June 2012, as the Finnish media reported a curious incident involving an ongoing Facebook discussion about a midsummer's eve club night organized under the brand We Love Helsinki (WLH).[1] A female club participant—whom I will call "Maria Korhonen"[2]—had voiced her disapproval of DJ announcements in a post on WLH's openly accessible Facebook event wall, and this had inspired heated debate. Her post read as follows:

Hi! I would have wanted to know beforehand that this club was exclusively for heterosexuals so I would've known not to come. I've considered this We Love Helsinki concept fresh and therefore didn't expect hetero-exclusiveness. This became evident as a DJ on the traditional dance music side [*one side of the club in question*] announced, "Three female couples are dancing, get a grip, men, and ask them to dance!" As if women couldn't primarily want to dance with just women and as if women dancing with each other were just "dancing for fun." On the Factory side [*the other side of the club*] it was announced that "the women are particularly beautiful since they've decked themselves up—they've decked themselves up for you, boys." I thought the midsummer dance tradition had been updated a bit more for this event but guess it's too early for that :) (1/1, posted on Facebook on June 23, 2012, 209 "likes").[3]

The WLH club night recycled the Finnish midsummer dance tradition within its retro framing and choice of music genres. Issues of sexuality and potential intimacy central to popular midsummer iconography were firmly at the heart of the online exchange, and the flames that followed were both affective and networked. The WLH discussion thread was specific in its focus and platform.[4] Short-lived yet heated, it marked a linguistically, regionally, and temporally limited peak of intensity in the flow of Facebook updates and comments that trickled to blogs, online newspapers, and coffee table discussions. I nevertheless argue that the debate connected to, and even exemplified, dynamics central to online exchanges and their affective resonances more generally. By drawing on 728 posts and comments made by 173 users in the WLH midsummer dance thread between June 23 and June 28,[5] I explore the incident through notions of intensity and stickiness in order to conceptualize the affective dynamics of online debate, and those of trolling in particular.

Sticky Intensity

From flame wars to persistent acts of trolling, from intense textual romances to the circulation of viral videos, affect—understood as intensities, sensations, and impressions created in encounters between and among people, online platforms, images, texts, and computer technologies—has played a crucial yet understudied part in the uses and user experiences of the internet since its early days. My premise is that affective intensities both drive online exchanges and attach people to particular platforms, threads, and groups. Jodi Dean (this volume) argues that affect accrues "from communication for its own sake, from the endless circular movement of commenting, adding notes and links, bringing in new friends and followers, layering and interconnecting myriad communications platforms and devices." Such accrual renders sites sticky in the sense that it encourages users to stay and revisit (Coté and Pybus 2007; Pybus, this volume).

According to Sara Ahmed (2004, 90), stickiness is *"an effect of the histories of contact between bodies, objects, and signs* [her italics]," an effect of both relationality and circulation. For Ahmed (2004, 45), "the movement between objects and signs converts into affect" since "the more signs circulate, the more affective they become." In other words, circulation increases the affective value of objects as it accumulates and oscillates in and through acts of communication. The WLH discussion thread quickly grew sticky, with its hundreds of dismayed and amused comments, thousands of likes, and large groups of readers and browsers. As the thread began to swell, columns and opinion pieces appeared in print and online platforms and the incident became national news. On June 26, the evening newspaper *Iltalehti* published an online article titled, "Managing director answers: No gays were discriminated against at youth midsummer dance!" YLE, the national broadcasting company, headlined its online news item enigmatically: "Heated online gay debate about midsummer dances." Considered in terms of traditional journalistic criteria, the news value of the incident—DJ remarks at a Helsinki hipster club that led to a Facebook debate—was low. The main content of the news items was that such a debate was taking place and that bloggers had picked up on it. In terms of the dynamic of the discussion thread, the articles generated new interest, attracted novel participants with little connection to the incident debated, and further added to its stickiness.

Looking more closely at the WLH debate, the number of likes on a Facebook thread is one way to account for the stickiness of individual posts and comments—how attention clusters around certain comments while perhaps sliding over others. Korhonen was by far the most active participant throughout the thread with 55 messages. Her opening post attracted 209 likes, the most of any in the thread (although some of the likes may have referred to the thread as a whole). The second-most-liked comment was "Trolli-Finlandia approves this" (265/52, 189 likes; Trolli-Finlandia is a Facebook group modeled after the national literary prize, Finlandia, and it shortlists and awards the best annual Finnish trolls).[6] Two comments by the DJ who had encouraged men to ask women to dance followed in popularity with 171 and 155 likes, respectively (4/4, 312/4). In these lengthy replies, the DJ detailed his experience and knowledge of club culture and dance etiquette in order to contextualize his comment, while apologizing for any hurt or dismay that he may have caused. Replying to the first of these, Korhonen insisted that she had not been hurt but was debating a matter of principle, thanked the DJ for his response, and wished him a good club night with a smiley (7/1).

Yet this—obviously—was not the end of the thread, which soon grew both antagonistic and fragmented. Long and thoughtful responses were followed by personal attacks, incredulous exclamations, and reflexive comments on the evolution of the thread itself. Before it became national news, the thread focused (more or less) on heteronormativity, discrimination against sexual and ethnic minorities, club and dance cultures, social relations of power, and the fairness of the critique targeted against WLH. As news items and blog posts circulated and accumulated, new people joined in to express surprise, amusement, and aggression, to add absurd comments and links, and to attack and support one another. Articulations of positive and negative affect layered, oscillated, and intensified, and the debate grew increasingly fragmented.

In *Premediation,* Richard Grusin (2010) conceptualizes contemporary media culture as one of securitization and anticipation, one where potentially traumatic events, such as the collapse of the World Trade Center towers, can no longer come as a surprise. According to Grusin (2010, 127), the culture of premediation aims to protect us from negative surprise. By reading psychologist Silvan Tomkins by way of Eve Sedgwick and Adam Frank, he argues that broadcasting and social media aim at minimizing negative affect—such as fear, shame, or disgust—while optimizing the positive. His symptomatic cultural analysis assists in comprehending phenomena such as the "like" button on Facebook, through which one can only express positive affect (there being no button for "dislike"), or the cute and odd cat videos and pictures extensively shared online, which provide positive jolts of surprise and merriment (Grusin 2010, 4). Yet a closer look at how "like" buttons are used—or explorations into the unsettling qualities that cat pictures often involve—soon makes evident the equally pronounced ubiquity of negative and mixed affect. I argue, therefore, that in uses of networked media, positive and negative affective intensities intermesh and cluster in complex ways to the degree that their qualities are difficult to tell apart and their intersections hard to precisely determine (also Paasonen 2011, 231–240). Such oscillation of intensity involves more than securitization in the positive register.

I further argue that social media uses are largely driven by a search for intensity—a desire for some kind of affective jolt, for something to capture one's attention (also Dean, this volume). This desire for intensity provokes the interest and curiosity of users; it grabs their attention, and drives their movements across networks, sites, files, and discussion threads. Yet the promise of intensity often is not delivered, and the search for thrills, shocks, and jolts continues despite, or perhaps because of, the boredom involved in browsing from one page to another (Petit, this volume). The stickiness, or "the grab" (Senft 2008, 46) of a discussion thread, then, depends on the intensities it affords.

Heated Feelings

In the 1990s, even before the pervasive use of the web, scholars and journalists were both fascinated and puzzled by the particularities of online communication on list-servs, Usenet newsgroups, Internet Relay Chat (IRC), and bulletin boards. Much of their bewilderment had to do with the intentionally aggressive and provocative mode of interaction: why were people composing vitriolic messages, intentionally provoking and attacking each other? Answers to these troubling questions were found in the purportedly weak social ties facilitated by anonymity. Assuming that their posts could not be traced—apart from IP numbers and cookies deployed—and that they need not encounter other discussants face to face, users were said to feel free to play in a nastier fashion than in face-to-face communication (e.g., Wallace 1999). In his 1994 introduction to the anthology *Flame Wars*, Mark Dery (1994, 1) poetically wrote of how "the wraithlike nature of electronic communication—the flesh become word, the sender reincarnated as letters floating on a terminal screen—accelerates the escalation of hostilities when tempers flare; disembodied, sometimes pseudonymous combatants tend to feel that they can hurl insults with impunity (or at least without fear of bodily harm)." Dery (1994, 2–3) further noted that despite the use of smileys, online textual exchanges seemed to encourage misinterpretation due to the lack of physical cues and embodied characteristics such as pitch, intensity, stress, tempo, and volume—resulting, he suggested, in communication with flattened affect.

Emoticons such as the smiley have been a means of textually mediating affect that would otherwise be conveyed through facial expressions, gestures, or tone of voice (Walther and D'Addario 2001). Smileys have been deployed in online communication since the late 1970s in order to ensure that humorous intentions, puns, or irony do not go unnoticed or get misinterpreted as imbued with negative intent (Hafner and Lyon 1996, 217–218). Smileys were much in use throughout the WLH thread, including the very first post. Rather than simply mediating a positive tone, however, their use was also interpreted as antagonistic, and even aggressive. One participant complained, "Maria's choice of words was intentionally provocative and sarcastic and occasionally plain bitching. … Throwing in a couple of smileys with comments really doesn't help but just provokes people more :) :)" (165/32, 29 likes). Here, smileys were attached to complex affective constellations where no clear distinction could be made between a friendly smile, a sarcastic smirk, and an intentional insult. Mercurial in their uses and interpretations, smileys both softened and sharpened the arguments made, and served to create both proximity and distance within the thread.

Returning to the theorizations of the early 1990s, analyses of the relative anonymity and distance facilitated by networked communication fail to fully account for passionate online exchanges, such as trolling and flaming, of the nonanonymous kind (cf. Wallace 1999; Herring et al. 2002). The WLH thread took place on the nonanonymous platform of Facebook as a debate among networked friends, acquaintances, and strangers. As people commented on the thread and shared links related to it, the heat of the flames reached news feeds and wall discussions and reverberated in the broader social network beyond the WLH Facebook event wall. Furthermore, in response to Dery's discussion on the flattening of affect, I suggest that online exchanges tend to involve the circulation and intensification, rather than the waning, of affect.

The fact that the affective dynamics of online communication differ from those of the face-to-face kind (with the exception of webcam exchanges) does not mean that they are any less rich or intense. For if they were, this would imply that textual communication itself involves flattened affect to start with and—by implication—that diaries, poems, novels, and letters equally convey and evoke flimsy or thin affective intensities. Yet this is hardly the case, considering that fears concerning the arousing and potentially harmful effects of the novel are as old as the modern literary genre itself (Schindler 1996; Hillis 2009, 153). Following literary scholar Isobel Armstrong (2000, 124–125), text can be seen as "generating new, unique affect patterns" and thought structures that are recognized "as dynamic shifters of meaning." For Armstrong (2000, 93), texts and readers produce reciprocal feedback loops, where energies build up and are released through acts of interpretation. In online communication, such feedback loops broaden into affective networks that encompass writers/readers/users; platforms and their information architecture; textual, visual, and audiovisual messages; and sensory experiences of connectivity and disconnection (to list only some of the actors involved). Attention shifts and clusters within the network while intensities grow and fade.

Individual posts in a discussion thread are often skimmed through quickly, by skipping over sentences, messages, and even entire sections. Such skipping is directly supported, or even encouraged, by the information architecture of discussion platforms that regulates the format and order in which posts are rendered accessible to users. In a Facebook discussion thread, users see the very first post, and the newest comments made on it above a box asking them to write a response of their own. In order to go back in the thread, some clicking is required. Each click renders more comments visible, and if the thread is long, getting to the beginning can be cumbersome. Since the WLH Facebook thread soon consisted of hundreds of comments, participants entering it later often stated their unfamiliarity with much of it beyond the first post. This was the result of both the laboriousness of reading through the mass of existing comments and of the site architecture, which encourages interaction with the most recent ones. As one new participant after another was provoked by the first message, or tried to provoke its author, the flames of the debate kept going. In other words, the platform itself helped the sparks fly.

On the one hand, the disjointedness and sharpness of the thread—users speaking, or shouting, past one another, and repeating similar comments—was intimately tied to the affordances and limitations of Facebook as the site of interaction. On the other hand, the fragmentation and polarization of the views expressed was also connected to the affordances and limitations of textual communication itself. As Dery noted, participants in an online discussion are left with room to interpret the tone, style, and content of the posts, and to imagine what the people writing them may be like. All this facilitates the creation of straw men—projections concerning what the other participants may value, feel, or intend to communicate. Even half a word can be read as indicative of a broader (albeit possibly hidden) agenda, argument, or stance. Reactions and replies may quickly grow stark.

In her analysis of online discussions on "chavs"—working-class youth in the UK—Imogen Tyler (2006; 2008) points out that as people respond to each other's messages, they try to outdo one another, and thereby the affective intensities of the exchange grow. Following Ahmed's work on how "language works as a form of power in which emotions align some bodies with others, as well as stick different figures together, by the way they move us" (Ahmed 2004, 195), Tyler argues that heated debates are both driven and animated by affect that circulates and sticks to certain comments and people. In Tyler's (2006) analysis, affective intensities adhere to young chav bodies as representing objects of middle-class disgust, and as presumably lacking a sense of style and proper demeanor. In the WLH thread, the circulation and stickiness of affect took complex routes that helped to mark the boundaries between groups of people as well as to constantly fragment them. Boundaries were drawn, among other things, between queer and nonqueer club participants; between heteronormative and nonheteronormative ones; between queer people sensing injustice in the incident discussed and those failing to do so; among queer people, white people, and people of color as objects of discrimination; between people with green and leftist political sympathies and those supporting the right-wing populist Finns Party (or standing accused thereof); between people living in the capital city of Helsinki and rest of the country; between feminists and nonfeminists; between people into dance cultures and those clubbing for casual fun and sex; and between those just wanting to enjoy themselves and those purportedly incapable of so doing.

Some discussed the equal rights of sexual minorities and the persistence of discrimination, while for others the matter was one of offhand DJ comments and, ultimately, therefore, much ado about nothing. Some zoomed out from the incident to address social power relations, while others zoomed in to address the events of the club night. These zooms were fast and out of synch with one another. For some the thread exemplified the unwillingness of straight people to acknowledge their own participation in social discrimination. For others it was a case of people being hurt when no hurt was intended, of overreacting or even desiring to be hurt. Some discussed matters of principle, even as others could not see the point. From these incompatible points of departure, the debate evolved into considerations of more accessible—ideal, nonheteronormative, nonracist, non-ableist—clubbing practices, as well as into trolling that aimed to provoke other participants. While it is possible to interpret the thread as an open forum for debating the politics of naming, it resulted in an increased polarization of views, rather than democratic negotiation or resolution, as is often the case with online political debates (cf. Robinson 2005). As Zizi Papacharissi (2002) notes, the Habermasian ideal of the public sphere as one of critical rational exchange can be mapped onto emotionally wired online discussions only with some difficulty. In fact the WLH thread points to how online exchanges, once heated up, are animated by a search for affective intensity rather than rational argumentation, and by provocation rather than a desire for negotiation.

Enter the Trolls

As argued above, affective intensity drives online discussion forward. Exclamations of aggression and support, waves of amusement, distanced sarcasm, descriptions of hurt and harm circulate, stick, and pull discussants and readers back for more. Trolling was one of the tactics that the WLH debate participants deployed in amping up the affective intensity of the thread. While flaming translates as hostility, aggression, and insult toward other participants, trolling, as intentional provocation of other users, involves more nuanced practices, such as posting opinions and views that one does not actually hold, coupled with a pretense of simplicity or literalness, or making comments abruptly off topic. Adi Kuntsman (2007) points out that flaming and trolling have been understood as negative and disturbing, yet also as facilitating community mobilization. Whereas some scholars see trolling as a gamelike practice producing a sense of belonging, for Kuntsman the issue is one of multiple and contradictory effects, where feelings of hurt and amusement intermesh with practices of violence and play (Kuntsman 2007, 101–102; cf. Herring et al. 2002). Trolls may mobilize and shape, as well as fragment, communities.

Trolls aim to provoke, disturb, and disrupt, and to amuse themselves and others while doing so (see Phillips 2013). This is social activity performed in front of others: a troll uses her forum as a stage where the reverberations of her actions can be followed and enjoyed by many. The pleasures of trolling, much like those of flaming, lie in the intensification of affect, this being a principal aim and goal of the activity. Users not identifying as trolls of any kind, or even disapproving of the practice, can take pleasure in the affective intensities that trolls engender on discussion forums, in social networks and online communities. This is not an issue of optimizing positive affect but of different affective qualities and intensities enhancing one another, moving the users and driving their exchanges further. As people feel hurt or amused and respond, the overall affective intensity—and temporary stickiness—of the exchange grows.

Trolls entered the WLH thread in the third contribution, a comment written by one of the club DJs, who quoted from a popular 1980s Finnish song, *Lähtisitkö* ("Would you go"), by Pave Maijanen, about a man proposing rowing on a lake, diving for white pearls, and gentle kissing (3/3, 7 likes). As a reply to the first two posts, which had a markedly serious tone, the comment was markedly absurd. A troll is only successful if it evokes a response. Since no reply was made, the DJ soon tried more abruptly with, "I am going to encourage the ones in floral dresses and those in corduroy pants to fuck each other!" (6/3, 28 likes). Again, no one replied until his response to the following comment:

This discussion has at least shown that everybody is not truly welcome in we love helsinki (go to gay clubs, hush, comments from DJs mocking transpeople in the thread). ... of course the most important thing is that if someone addresses problematic practices of power (such as DJ comments) they wouldn't need to fear this kind of sexist and homophobic counterattack and ridicule. Oppressive practices that maintain norms aren't necessarily always intentional (purposefully created) but this doesn't make them any less harmful. (214/29, 22 likes)

After reading these tirades a cock has grown out from my forehead, and I'm going to fuck men in the ass with it so that my whole upper body turns brown. (215/3, 12 likes)

This response was defined as homophobic (234/1) and truly degrading (280/7), and the DJ leveled additional accusations of homophobia in return (409/3). Any community, online, offline, or anywhere in between, relies on some kind of exclusion, for there can only be insiders insofar as there are outsiders (Joseph 2002). Trolls render such boundary work visible. By acting against shared assumptions and breaking down apparent consensus, they may also facilitate the articulation of the community's conventions and norms.[7] One of the central dynamics of the thread had to do with defining the stance of WLH on heteronormativity and the accessibility of public space to queer people. Korhonen insisted on hearing from the main WLH event organizer, whose initial replies—"We Love Helsinki clubs are always open to all!" (39/16), and "there's a bit more to do in event organizing than hanging out on Facebook" (188/16, a message sent while the Midsummer event was still under way)—left her annoyed by their vagueness and seeming lack of engagement. Her sharp replies to comments made by others helped to rekindle the flames of the debate as they burned from one day to another. By the time that the main organizer added a comment (569/16) stating that the values of WLH did not condone homophobia, racism, or any other form of discrimination, and emphasized that all participants should encounter difference with an open mind, the thread had gained a life of its own, with a sharpness resistant to attempts at community building. At this point, alignments with other participants were random and fleeting, and openness and good behavior were by no means a given.

Early on in the thread's brief lifespan, a participant suggested that everybody should move forward together in order to create events enjoyable to all (37/14). Korhonen replied sarcastically with, "I probably should've made penitence first and then sent a formal apology to the organizers that I participated in the event. I guess I just provoked bad blood with such selfish remarks when we should just all 'move forward together' with a 'positive attitude'" (87/1). As the discussion constantly fragmented in this vein, references to community creation were understandably ambivalent. WLH was critiqued for acting against its principles of communality, even as it was also thanked for creating it (148/37; 190/1; 280/7), and the thread was even seen as evolving into a community (of trolls) in its own right (372/28). Aggressive comments constantly blocked attempts at consensus, and the rhetorical tactics of trolls and nontrolls grew inseparable. As one participant noted, "I can't tell trolls apart from people who're 'serious' in this discussion. the whole thread is that absurd. ugh." (417/104)

Along with other participants, Korhonen was suspected of being a troll and congratulated for successful trolling despite her possible intentions: "The one who started the discussion should actually receive a prize. There possibly hasn't been such a successful troll in the history of the entire internet" (377/28, 5 likes); "Pretty nice opening for a discussion. It's inspired more than 400 comments already and the flames are climbing over the walls. :) Best entertainment since Top Gun where Maverick didn't ask Iceman to dance although he wanted to" (395/99, 4 likes). References to trolling were made throughout the thread, and it was named as a favorite candidate for the Trolli-Finlandia prize (111/3; 265/52). Four days into the discussion, active participants were already referred to as trolls: "Wow, even trolls are already growing tired. Makes me yawn. Try boys, once more" (415/60, 0 likes). Rather than being accidental, such gendering was indicative of the more general dynamics of the thread, where the sharpest opposition to critiques of heteronormativity, as voiced by Korhonen and those supporting her views, was identified as straight and male.

Killjoys

It is noteworthy that trolls were not the primary nodes of affective intensity in the thread. Although random provocations persisted, and increased toward the thread's end, not many participants picked up on them. Most comments referred back to those made by Korhonen: *she* became the sticky node of the discussion, and it was to her that most affective intensities stuck. Korhonen was accused of both unwillingness to have fun *and* willingness to intentionally spoil the fun of others—for turning fun sour:

Relax and have fun, that's what the whole event is about! (10/7, 46 likes)

Is the purpose of your suggestion to relax perhaps to belittle the whole thing and try to shut down the discussion? Not everybody can have fun in the same way if they're excluded through comments. Your fun, however, doesn't seem to be hindered by the exclusion of others since you want discussion on the topic bypassed. If you want to "have fun" then perhaps you shouldn't read these comments if they're not part of your fun :). Just let others discuss at least. (11/1, 14 likes)

Always those "boohoo heteronormativity boohoo" types that need to spoil the majority's fun. Let them dance at LGBT places if their sensitive minds can't take that. (12/8, 9 likes)

This exchange exemplifies Ahmed's (2012, n.p.) discussion about "feminist killjoys": "those who refuse to laugh at the right points; those who are unwilling to be seated at the table of happiness." Since they refuse to "go along with it," killjoys are seen as "trouble, as causing discomfort to others" and as ruining the atmosphere (Ahmed 2010, 69). If feelings "get stuck to certain bodies in the very way we describe spaces, situations, dramas" (Ahmed 2010, 69), then the body of Korhonen, together with the collective bodies of LGBT people, feminists, and supporters of the environmental party, were stuck with the label of killjoy both in the WLH thread and in the columns and comment pieces covering the incident. Facebook interface design relies on thumbs-up likes, pink heart graphics, and peppy yellow smileys that work to frame exchanges primarily in terms of positive affect. Such upbeat modality dovetails poorly with critique, which may seem inappropriate if it is perceived as geared toward killing the general aspiration toward joy in Facebook exchanges.

Historically, the term unhappy has referred to "causing misfortune or trouble": unhappy ones are those banished from happiness, "troublemakers, dissents, killers of joy" (Ahmed 2010, 17). Since happiness involves "reciprocal forms of aspiration," "one person's happiness is made conditional not only on another person's happiness but on that person's willingness to be made happy by the same things" (Ahmed 2010, 91). It could be argued that Korhonen adopted the strategic position of a killjoy by refusing to be made happy or to adopt the positive attitude suggested in some of the comments. Her replies (to both dialogical and rude comments) were often curt: "I'd like to know if you belong to the moron club or are you otherwise stupid" (33/1, 20 likes); "Hope you grow a spine as you grow up a little" (90/1, 5 likes); "That comment of yours really insults all intelligent life on earth" (109/1, 8 likes). Personal attacks were made against Korhonen who, in turn, made attacks of her own, for instance by labeling others as sympathizers of the nationalist-populist party, Perussuomalaiset (the Finns Party, 205/1). The following exchange exemplifies some of this dynamic:

Small things are large things. Those that you claim to be small things are not small things but they are big things. Supporting and maintaining existing unequal power positions is a very significant thing. Blindness to discriminatory practices and ignoring them are also big things. The ones who imagine themselves as being beyond such structures are the least free. (250/1, 8 likes)

Calling the opponents homophobic racist persus ["persu" refers to the supporters of the Finns Party: the term is very close to "perse," meaning arse] really helps the discussion a lot. (251/26, 45 likes)

No, Maria. Small things become large things when they move into the wrong context. None of us here is ignoring "discriminatory practices" and I at least don't imagine being above anybody. You're not intentionally ignoring my point are you? Since I can't say more clearly what I mean without sounding insulting. (252/46, 20 likes)

I believe that you haven't gotten the whole point and I really don't feel like explaining it any further. (253/1, 0 likes)

The affective dynamics of the thread circulated and intensified around—as well as through—Korhonen. As the thread evolved, comments made to and about her grew increasingly sharp and personal. She was accused of patronizing and belittling others, and characterized in a vitriolic vein as a "passive-aggressive sand-cunt" (383/45), "man-hating feminist" (391/96), and "attention-seeking narcissist" with "fascist ideas" (661/150). Other participants saw such comments as sheer bullying that evoked and necessitated sharp responses from Korhonen (675/15). For others still, this was an issue of her getting back what she deserved (696/165).

In Tyler's (2006) analysis of the figure of the "chav," the affective intensities of online debate reinforce social distinctions through articulations of disgust toward the working class. More specifically, a hierarchical division between "us" and "them" is drawn between the middle class and chavs as those lacking in cultural capital and social mobility. In the WLH thread, divisions were drawn in terms of political alliances, gender, education, and displays of cultural capital in ways that invert the class hierarchy of Tyler's analysis. It was those who used complex and academic terminology (such as "heteronormativity") that were likely to be mocked for imagining themselves to be superior to the rest, and some participants crafted pastiches of such apparently pretentious language: "unless you haven't noticed, the aim of my comment was to highlight through hyperbole the absurdity of his analogy as an argumentative move" (281/60). All in all, accusations were not made against "stupid assholes," as in Tyler's material, but against those who were seen to mark others as stupid assholes through "faux-academic brilliance" (383/45):

If something pisses me off then it's arrogance towards "the stupid." This thread is rife with academic jargon and everybody is assumed to be educated thinkers. If the stream of consciousness doesn't get through or people don't understand how the world will be saved through the use of right words, then they're "persus," aka arrogantly a little more stupid than you. … By insisting that people use certain words and by interfering with language we set ourselves above others. (718/86, 3 likes)

During the debate, Korhonen became a virtual embodiment of an academic-feminist killjoy. People shared their search results on Korhonen, identified her political interests and activism, and inquired after her sexual preferences in the thread. Bloggers and columnists published (often highly sarcastic) texts using her real name, and users uploaded pictures of her on discussion forums. She was even identified as something of a meme: "Must appreciate with a brownie point. Maria became a meme and not everybody achieves that" (299/75, 13 likes). The term meme—defined by some as a cultural gene—connotes viral online content that replicates through contagion (Knobel and Lankshear 2007; Shifman 2013). Whether taking the form of a misspelled word, an animated GIF (see Ash, this volume), a video, or a picture, a meme is generated through circulation, and as users comment on it, and create tributes to, variations, and parodies of it. Accessible and open to intervention, up for grabs, memes move within and across social connections, accumulate, and vary (Shifman 2012, 188–189). Since easy-to-use platforms such as Quick Meme and Meme Generator have increased in popularity, the volume of meme creation, circulation, and appropriation has exploded.

Memes are often used as shorthand: for example, a link to the viral YouTube video "Trololo"—an old Soviet TV song clip—indicates the presence of trolls (and perhaps tilts the discussion toward the absurd). The meme was shared early on in the WLH thread (38/15, with the message "Trolololo. Trolled.") to express a belief that Korhonen's first message had been a successful troll. Similarly, references to the meme-phrase "First World Problems" imply that the frustrations, complaints, and challenges voiced by others are particular to the privileged people of the affluent West and insignificant on a global scale. "First World Problems" was used in the thread as shorthand for the repeatedly expressed view that the debate was about overreaction by the overly sensitive, and lacking in appropriate scale and context (442/108, 535/128, 541/127). Soon enough, the incident inspired new variations of the meme (figure 2.1).

Memes were used in the thread as a means of distancing and metacommentary: "Trololo" helped to identify the entire debate as a troll thread while "First World Problems" helped to frame critiques of heteronormativity voiced within it as trivial whining, lacking a sense of proportion. In addition to the possible amusement they provided, both memes helped to efface the complexities of the debate by defining it through exaggerated traits and features. Positioned as a queer-feminist killjoy meme by some, Korhonen herself was identified with easy and excessive annoyance, as the one to be easily annoyed. Framed as a meme, she thus became shorthand for the overtly sensitive and the disproportionally critical:

A thank you and a bow for cheering up the work day. Staggering professional annoyance from the one who started the thread. respect! =) (533/127, 2 likes)

uh huh. people sure know how to be annoyed about no matter what these days. problem here seems to be homophobiaphobia rather than homophobia. :) (684/158, 1 like)

The whole event now needs some self-examination, does WLH have room next year for Korhonen and her friends, the professionally annoyed? How will safety be improved so that such professional complainers don't get to spoil the midsummer for others? I was considering coming but if they let in spoilers such as Korhonen, I'm not interested. What if such a professional complainer gets violent, you never know, it may even also be a persu. (separate post on WLH wall, June 27, 14 likes)

Figure 2.1
"I went to a midsummer dance. They even encouraged men to dance." http://www.quickmeme.
com/meme/3pvjv1.

Sticky Flames

All in all, the sudden height and bright heat of the midsummer flames seem dispro-
portionate. How did one comment made on an open Facebook event wall create such
a blaze? The question can be answered by examining the themes and discussion styles
particular to the debate: the various frustrations and political affinities expressed, and
the roles adopted during its course. As I have suggested above, explanations can also

be found in the dynamics of online debates more generally—their fast intensification and circulation, the sharpening of affect, and the possible flattening of people into types—as they tie into the particular affordances and limitations of online platforms.

The stickiness of online platforms involves appeal, investment, and circulation that result in the generation of affective, monetary, social, and/or political value. Such attachments are, nevertheless, of the fleeting kind. Formerly viral videos are soon forgotten, sites lose their stickiness as users migrate elsewhere, and flame wars come to a halt. Online, flames grow high within minutes and soon fizzle unless their heat is maintained. The WLH thread did not have a chance to die down into a smoldering heap as Korhonen removed it on June 28, five days after her first post.[8] The incident was discussed for a few days more, but as comments ceased to circulate its stickiness washed away—although lingering resonances remained.

Affect both congeals and sharpens in online debates, as readers and participants fill in the gaps of, extrapolate meanings from, and project values and assumptions onto the messages of others, read some words carefully and skip over the rest. The sharpness of affect grabs, appeals and disturbs, attracts and repulses, pulls users close and pushes them away again. The oscillation between different, often starkly posed and juxtaposed arguments is an important aspect of the overall rhythm of online exchange and social media use, of constant clicks and shifts from one page, site, video, and image to another, of refreshes and perpetual searches for new documents, images, and affective intensities. These movements are fast inasmuch as they are persistent, driven by a desire for something that will grab and stick, rather than just slide by—no matter how contingent and temporal such attachments may be.

Notes

1. WLH has organized club nights and urban culture events in Helsinki since 2008. Timo Santala is the founder and main organizer of WLH. His name is used with permission.

2. The alias was chosen since Maria is historically the most popular first name, and Korhonen currently the most common last name, in Finland.

3. All translations are by the author.

4. By way of context, Finland is a relatively wired country. According to the 2012 national statistics report, 90 percent of the population uses the internet regularly, the percentage being 100 percent for those under the age of thirty-four. More than 40 percent of the population has a social networking service account.

5. With the possible exclusion of some individual comments toward the very end, and those removed during the debate, the material studied covers the whole thread. I have also interviewed Timo Santala, the main organizer of WLH events, and "Maria Korhonen," the woman who opened the debate. The posts have been rendered anonymous by allocating each of them two

numbers: the first represents the chronological order of the comment in the thread and the second that of each new discussant. Thus (1/1) refers to the first comment—posted by Korhonen—and (728/130) refers to the final one: the last new participant entered the thread in the message (726/173). I would like to extend my thanks to Aino Harvola and Julia Koivulanaho for their valuable help with the research material.

6. The WLH thread was indeed shortlisted for the 2012 prize but failed to win.

7. In the amply referenced example of a "virtual rape" in LambdaMoo in the early 1990s, trolling led to community rules of conduct being articulated for the very first time. This is one of the first examples of community formation in relation to trolling. See Dibbell 1993.

8. In my interview with her, Korhonen explained that at this point the thread had somewhat spiraled out of control. She further explained that during the debate she did not read through the posts made about her on other public forums, and still remains unwilling to Google her name for fear of what she might uncover. In fact, she was unaware of much of the commentary made on platforms other than the WLH Facebook event wall during the debate.

References

Ahmed, Sara. 2004. *The Cultural Politics of Emotion*. Edinburgh: Edinburgh University Press.

Ahmed, Sara. 2010. *The Promise of Happiness*. Durham: Duke University Press.

Ahmed, Sara. 2012. A Willfulness Archive. Keynote presentation at the Crossroads in Cultural Studies Conference, Unesco, Paris, July 2, 2012.

Armstrong, Isobel. 2000. *The Radical Aesthetic*. Oxford: Blackwell.

Coté, Mark, and Jennifer Pybus. 2007. Learning to Immaterial Labour 2.0: MySpace and Social Networks. *Ephemera* 7 (1):88–106.

Dery, Mark. 1994. Flame Wars. In *Flame Wars: The Discourse of Cyberculture*, ed. Mark Dery, 1–10. Durham: Duke University Press.

Dibbell, Julian. 1993. A Rape in Cyberspace: How an Evil Clown, a Haitian Trickster Spirit, Two Wizards, and a Cast of Dozens Turned Database into a Society. *Village Voice* 38 (51):36–42.

Grusin, Richard. 2010. *Premediation: Affect and Materiality after 9/11*. New York: Palgrave.

Hafner, Katie, and Matthew Lyon. 1996. *Where the Wizards Stay Up Late: The Origins of the Internet*. New York: Simon and Schuster.

Herring, Susan, et al. 2002. Searching for Safety Online: Managing "Trolling" in a Feminist Forum. *Information Society* 18 (5):371–384.

Hillis, Ken. 2009. *Online a Lot of the Time: Ritual, Fetish, Sign*. Durham: Duke University Press.

Joseph, Miranda. 2002. *Against the Romance of Community*. Minnesota: University of Minnesota Press.

Knobel, Michele, and Colin Lankshear. 2007. Online Memes, Affinities, and Cultural Production. In *A New Literacies Sampler*, ed. Michele Knobel and Colin Lankshear, 199–227. New York: Peter Lang.

Kuntsman, Adi. 2007. Belonging through Violence: Flaming, Erasure, and Performativity in Queer Migrant Community. In *Queer Online: Media, Technology and Sexuality*, ed. Kate O'Riordan and David J. Phillips, 101–120. New York: Peter Lang.

Paasonen, Susanna. 2011. *Carnal Resonance: Affect and Online Pornography*. Cambridge, MA: MIT Press.

Papacharissi, Zizi. 2002. The Virtual Sphere: The Internet as Public Sphere. *New Media and Society* 4 (9):9–27.

Phillips, Wendy. 2013. The House that Fox Built: Anonymous, Spectacle, and Cycles of Amplification. *Television and New Media* 14 (6):494–509.

Robinson, Laura. 2005. Debating the Events of September 11th: Discursive and Interactional Dynamics in Three Online Fora. *Journal of Computer-Mediated Communication* 10 (4). Available at http://onlinelibrary.wiley.com/doi/10.1111/j.1083-6101.2005.tb00267.x/full.

Schindler, Stephan K. 1996. The Critic as Pornographer: Male Fantasies of Female Reading in Eighteenth-Century Germany. *Eighteenth Century Life* 20 (3):66–80.

Senft, Theresa M. 2008. *CamGirls: Celebrity and Community in the Age of Social Networks*. New York: Peter Lang.

Shifman, Limor. 2012. An Anatomy of a YouTube Meme. *New Media and Society* 14 (2):187–203.

Shifman, Limor. 2013. *Memes in Digital Culture*. Cambridge, MA: MIT Press.

Tyler, Imogen. 2006. Chav Scum: The Filthy Politics of Social Class in Contemporary Britain. *M/C Journal* 9 (5). Available at http://journal.media-culture.org.au/0610/09-tyler.php.

Tyler, Imogen. 2008. "Chav Mum Chav Scum": Class Disgust in Contemporary Britain. *Feminist Media Studies* 8 (1):17–34.

Wallace, Patricia. 1999. *The Psychology of the Internet*. Cambridge: Cambridge University Press.

Walther, Joseph B., and Kyle P. D'Addario. 2001. The Impacts of Emoticons on Message Interpretation in Computer-Mediated Communication. *Social Science Computer Review* 19 (3):324–347.

3   Queer Reverb: Tumblr, Affect, Time

Alexander Cho

Field Notes, March 13, 2011:

There is a picture of a young man, dark-haired, extreme close-up. A smooth young face that is on its way to premature age—you can see it around his eyes, in the smallest wrinkles. It is an old black-and-white photo, so old that the emulsion is deteriorating and his cheek fades into an indeterminate grayness. All I can really see are his sharp cheekbones, dark brow, and eyes, looking off to the side.

Queerlife[1] has been posting a lot of these vintage images recently. They go without comment, without clear historical referent. It is image upon image, times overlapping and redoubling. I can't help but feel that there is something erotic in voyeurism across time. Looking into the past of young men.

Like many people I know, I stumbled into Tumblr through porn. In early 2009, a friend of mine in Austin told me about a new "blog" some art-queer friends of his started that did nothing but post pictures, usually arty porn you'd never see anywhere else. I visited the site. I didn't realize I would step into a universe of porn portraiture, of images cascading upon images upon images, an endless saturation. But it wasn't just porn. Tumblr as a whole is a massive churning machine of evocative photos, image aggregation on steroids, 37.5 million posts *per day*.[2] It was disorienting, no one explained very much with words, there were no "profiles" like Facebook, there were no "friends," there were no clear ways to traverse or search the network—just post after post of explanationless images, traded from one anonymous Tumblr user to another. A gorgeous landscape photo of a tropical beach after a photo of a genderqueer boy wearing a three-piece suit after a galactic vision constellated with Lady Gaga in Alexander McQueen heels.

I realized very quickly that there is a huge queer ecosystem on Tumblr.[3] Queer Tumblr users circulate porn, flirt, provide support to deal with homophobia as well as advice on coming out, disseminate news pertinent to LGBT communities, organize real-life meet-ups, post pictures of themselves, "reblog" pictures of others, "like" pictures of sexy men and women, post seemingly unqueer pictures of art, design, architecture, landscape photography, and alter the HTML and CSS code of their Tumblrs in order to express their individuality. This was not surprising; historically, queer people have had a significant relationship with internet technologies, due to our precarious position as a sexual minority that must slip so-called private behavior in and out of public space. The internet, with its ability to link people across geography and under the cloak of anonymity, has historically afforded queer people the chance to express themselves in a way that may be awkward, uncomfortable, or unsafe in public (Alexander 2002a, 2002b; Egan, 2000; Campbell, 2004; Gross 2003, 2004; Hillis 2009).

However, Tumblr felt different from 1990s-era Web 1.0 blogs full of pages of long-form, cathartic HTML text. Instead of literal testimonial and narrative storytelling, it appeared that Tumblr users favored communication through image, mostly without attribution or caption; they relied less on text and more on the felt register of suggestive imagery, one of intimation, assemblage, intensity, and aesthetic. Tumblr seemed like a terrain of affinities speaking at a thousand miles a minute, one that regarded written language as a simple, runty cousin. My feeling of disorientation upon first entering the space was like being immersed in language that didn't quite make sense—all there was was the gist. I sensed that there was *something else* being circulated here, something that resisted definition and classic semiotic formulas. It seemed, from the first moments I was in the space, that Tumblr traded in affect.

I had the sense that to understand Tumblr, I needed to fully immerse myself in it. It is not a space that rewards piecemeal interloping. I decided to make my own Tumblr in the fall of 2009. I have made friends, flirted, posted a ton of pictures and videos, ranted, and gotten off. This chapter draws on three years of immersive participant observation in LGBTQ Tumblr communities to examine the affective dynamics of a subset of practices of queer users. These practices call attention to cyclicality, repetition, and refrain as crucial in understanding the flow of affect, and I suggest that the dynamics I outline here are useful in understanding the properties of the traffic of affect on Tumblr more generally and possibly across social media writ large. My discussion of these practices also traces the contours of a possible resistant queer politics rooted in the interplay of cyclical, erotic, and melancholic queer temporalities that linger in a stubborn persistence of the past. I also offer the metaphor of "reverb" as part of the effort to develop a vocabulary to describe how affect channels and circulates in social media environments.

The Shape of Affect

Affect is generally conceived as a force or intensity that exists somewhere in between an embodied, sensorial experience and the naming of an emotion. In other words, affect is a moment of suspense, a shift, an attunement between entities. As Gregg and Seigworth (2010, 1) explain, "Affect is found in those intensities that pass body to body … in those resonances that circulate about, between, and sometimes stick to bodies and worlds … visceral forces beneath, alongside, or generally other than conscious knowing, vital forces insisting beyond emotion." Contemporary affect theorists understand that beings are always in the process of becoming, entwined in a map of forces that ebb and flow, one with profound real, embodied consequences. In other words, an analysis vis-à-vis affect adopts a resistance to the neatness of the "subject" as the primary nodal point of reference in favor of an understanding of interlocking forces and fields of intensity. Massumi (1995, 2002) equates affect with intensity and emergence, a plane of the virtual, the generative potential of the event not yet determined. In contrast, "emotion" such as "anger" or "happiness" is the precipitate, the concretized fallout after a subtractive logic of cognition. Or as Thrift states, quoting Steven D. Brown and Paul Stenner, "Emotions we experience are merely the names given to differently assembled euphoric or dysphoric relationships, akin to chords" (Thrift 2004, 62).

A key concept for understanding this understanding of affect, inspired by Deleuze and Guattari (1987), is the idea of the assemblage, a way of thinking about interconnection as messy, overlapping, and inseparable. Where classical modernists saw discrete entities (such as a clean "subject"), and where structuralists envisioned a rigid schema of relations (such as in linguistics or kinship), the assemblage supposes constant multiplicities: "A multiplicity has neither subject nor object, only determinations, magnitudes, and dimensions that cannot increase in number without the multiplicity changing in nature" (Deleuze and Guattari 1987, 8). As queer theorist Jasbir Puar (2007, 212) explains, the idea of assemblage "is attuned to interwoven forces that merge and dissipate time, space, and body against linearity, coherency, and permanency." Nonlinear, incoherent, and impermanent are all very good ways to describe an initial encounter with Tumblr. You are the sum of your posts, which are a visualization of your connections to others—a porous, living assemblage.

An attention to affect recognizes the necessity but also the limits of a linguistic model of semiotic meaning. The two concepts should not be thought of as opposite, but rather as interrelated: affect is the condition of surplus and intensity; representational language is a system of codes and containment.[4] Rather than understand meaning strictly as a formula of signifier and signified, an attention to affect is a focus on excess, that which overfills or cannot be captured in language. As Jack Katz states, there is a whole register of "ways of expressing something going on that talk cannot grasp" (cited in Thrift 2004, 60). For this reason, unlike other social media, Tumblr offers a unique opportunity to trace the lines of intensity and affinity that connect people through affect. It is as if Tumblr's operational logic is the old saying, "A picture is worth a thousand words."[5]

In contrast to image-based networks such as Flickr or Instagram that emphasize amateur photography, the vast majority of images on any given Tumblr are reblogged from others in a stream, which were reblogged from others, and so on. Tumblr's structure and its users deemphasize the question of origin or authorship at the level of the image—often, the original poster of an image will have pirated that image from elsewhere on the net, posting it with no credit, leaving the question of origin unanswerable. In this way, the locus of authorship on Tumblr is less focused on the creation or capture of an original image and located instead around the personalized stream as a whole, a dynamic of constant movement and active selection. The authorial locus on Tumblr is not the act of creation; it is the act of *curation*. The experience of Tumblr is less like reading a LiveJournal blog and more like walking through a million different constantly shifting galleries—both may contain serious emotional heft and personal investment, but the latter relies much more on aesthetics, intimation, sensibility, and movement—in short, affect.

Field Notes: July 7, 2010:

Yesterday I had to wake up very early to take my friend Julie to the airport. I stood in front of my bathroom mirror with tousled bedhead, grey T-shirt, and squinty eyes. Sounds unsexy, but at that moment, at 5 a.m., it seemed cute. *I would want to wake up next to me,* I thought. I took a picture in the mirror. I posted it to Tumblr. It wasn't even GPOYW (gratuitous picture of yourself Wednesday). When I arrived back home I decided to go back to sleep. A few hours later, I woke up and checked Tumblr. Ursa had liked my photo. MathewMack reblogged it. Springeve liked it. And Claggwagg did too. It's bounced around the Tumblr sphere six times, as far as I can tell. I was surprised. I joined, for a brief blip, the Tumblr cute guy club. Technovalidation.

Queer Analytics

My use of "queer" as an analytic category is multivalent and slippery. I mean, on one level, that I train my attention toward the circulation of images and other posts among a highly visible group of Tumblr users that identify as LGBTQ, or any nonheteronormative permutation thereof. This is in step with a history of queer people using the internet from its earliest iterations to express identity and articulate connection in a way that spans real and virtual geographies as well as tempers the risk of expressing sexuality in a traditional public sphere.

In a broader sense, drawing inspiration from Cathy Cohen, I invoke "queer" as an agenda that is widely encompassing in the experience of alterity—a relational stance that trains its eye on a "shared marginal relationship to dominant power" (Cohen 2005, 43). I identify this stance less as a deliberately inclusive political movement and more as a palpable, subterranean rhythm of bad queer feeling[6] that runs through much of the Tumblr landscape I have observed, regardless of any one person's overt claim to static sexual orientation. It is the dark optimism of a hovering possibility for community, the release of self-expression in the midst of a system that you perceive to be tilted against you, and the potential for kinship and intimacy outside of heteronormative family and relationship structures. In a related vein, I am inspired by Sara Ahmed's "queer phenomenology" (2006) as a way of thinking about the sorts of objects that orient us toward a sensibility or disposition that traverses strict categories of identity. The Tumblr I have observed, in other words, is full of a lot of snark, vaguely antistatist politics, and frustrated sexual yearning.

The third use of "queer" in this essay draws on its older meaning—peculiar, unsettling, weird. Rather than apply it to a person or user, I invoke it to describe an overwhelming sensation of strangeness upon encountering and trying to "figure out" Tumblr. It is a feeling of eerie dislocation, it is elusive, a shock of dumbness, the sense that you may not be able to understand the (primarily visual) vocabulary being used around you, an alien architecture of affinity and attunement that at first glance evades literal understanding. In the following section, I explore this queer feeling as a function of image moving along the vector of time, a trajectory that is warped, coiled, broken, and multiple, or at the very least, *not straight*.

I want to be clear in that I am not attributing these specific affective dynamics as they manifest on Tumblr only to queer users. Instead, I am focusing on a very small subset of the practices of queer users because I believe they demonstrate well the underpinnings of affective dynamics that characterize user interaction on Tumblr generally. Because queer people have had a historically fraught relationship with expressing sexuality in public, they have long relied on underground economies of expression and relation that traffic in code, affinity, and intuition rather than the literal (Muñoz 1999; Warner 2005). In the words of Ann Cvetkovich (2003), queer people have long relied on an "archive of feelings"—ephemeral, unofficial, evasive—as opposed to literal institutionalized records in order to build community and share history. Queer users of Tumblr continue this tradition, and attention to their practices can highlight the felt dynamics of this social media platform, though they are in no way the only people who use Tumblr in this manner.

Ultimately, however, this argument is not simply about how queer people use Tumblr. Rather, it pays attention to a small subset of the practices of a group of queer people to demonstrate that there is a dynamic of connection and interaction on Tumblr based on a nonlinear, atemporal rhizomal exchange of affect and sensation, a "queer reverb" of repeat and repeat; and there may be a possibility for this sort of transmission to buoy an antinormative or resistant politics.

The following argument regarding the character of time and queer Tumblr users is in two parts. First, among the many practices of such users I focus on the circulation of images that invoke past times as a kind of affective archive, one that purposefully highlights silences and gaps in queer history with floating "recollection-images." Second, I consider the ways that *intensity* builds on Tumblr through user practices of repetition in various forms. I combine these to suggest the notion of "reverb" as a way of understanding how affect circulates in this social media environment.

Field Notes: October 12, 2010:

There was a very sexy picture of a young man in my Tumblr feed. I traced it back to the original poster, and to my surprise, it's a self-portrait. I sent him a message. We've been e-mailing pictures of ourselves back and forth, some NSFW. He, as far as I can tell, is about 25. Lives in Minneapolis. His room is painted dark green. Lit dimly with large table lamps with old yellow fabric lampshades, fringe and tassel. Short pile carpet. He traffics in prairie arcana. Old west curlicues. Here is a photo of him over his left shoulder, sitting on a large rock, at sunset. He is just inhaling a puff from a cigarette. Wavy hair, the suggestion of curls, suggestion of interiority. We trade compliments. He is flirty. Erotics reaching across space and time.

Archive and the Recollection-Image

Queer people have a troubled relationship with archives and "official" historical narrative. Queerness is systematically erased from the public record as a "private" thing and is difficult to pinpoint in artifacts that endure in institutional memory banks. A reading of queerness and history is a reading between the lines, whether in a coded dedication or an obvious erasure.[7] Often, queer history can only manifest in what we usually consider secret, ephemeral, or even intuited or felt (Cvetkovich 2003; Arondekar 2005; Dinshaw 2008). Recent efforts in queer studies have attempted to more clearly articulate queer people's relationship to time, or "queer temporality."[8] Queer temporality is a way of apprehending being-in-the-world that, in the words of Carolyn Dinshaw (Freeman et al. 2007, 178), insists on a "refusal of linear historicism." It is one that looks to moments of belatedness, stunted progress, omission from official records, histories of embodied feeling, asynchronicity and repetition as productive places of inquiry, recognizing that queer people, or rather queer*ness*, has been relegated as adjacent to or incompatible with Western heteronormative historical narratives.

According to Walter Benjamin (1940), one of the hallmarks of the modern era is a constant movement through "homogenous, empty time," as opposed to the hauntings and co-occurrences of premodern civilizations and religious time. Attention to queer temporality explodes the idea of such homogenous and empty time, indicting the public face of white, heterosexual Western normativity as its vanguard. Of particular significance to queer people is Freud's application of the famous assertion that ontogeny recapitulates phylogeny to the psychic self, so that the location of the "primitive," temporally, is equivalent to the infant, a location that, by assumed Western heteronormative extension, always places the adult straight white man at the endpoint of psychic maturity (Brickman 2003). In Freud's scheme the illogical and debilitating cyclical reliving of trauma or sadness is diagnosed as melancholy, usually a woman's affliction; proper mourning involves moving past and moving on. Likewise, non-Western "primitive" people are stuck in an infantile holding pattern of psychic development, and "inverts"—gay men and lesbians—have failed to progress to the logical endpoint of sexual development, are stuck in a sexual vector bending back on itself, an immature phase marked by same-sex attraction. According to this Western heteronormative temporal narrative, those who fail to line up in time's straight-and-narrow, those who are hopelessly primitive, melancholic and hysterical, queer, brown, or black, or some combination thereof, are unfortunately out of time.

How can we recuperate time that is not straight, according to this conception? Elizabeth Freeman suggests that we expand our heuristic to account for embodied experience: "something felt on, with, or as a body, something experienced as a mode of erotic difference or even as a means to express or enact ways of being and connecting that have not yet arrived or never will" (2007, 158); elsewhere she explains that "the stubborn lingering of pastness ... is a hallmark of *queer affect*: a 'revolution' in the old sense of the word, as a turning back" (2010, 8; emphasis added). Embodied experience of the stubborn past: dwelling, melancholia, nostalgia, and camp are a few queer examples, usually marked by deviance—precisely for this reason. So a "queer affect," in relationship to temporality, is one that lingers in a stubborn past, one that dwells in cycles and refuses the tidiness of progress, one that skirts through the archive in ephemeral or evasive ways.

One way the interplay of cyclical, erotic, stubborn, melancholic queer temporality manifests on Tumblr is in its massive traffic in vintage erotica, both male and female. One Tumblr I follow, Encyclopediaofcock, is an assemblage of retro gay porn, retro erotica that is less explicit, such as vintage photos of male sunbathers and pulp fiction covers, and present-day comic book geekery and self-portraits of the Tumblr owner. In one post, he states outright that he refuses to post any sort of contemporary porn. At fifteen to twenty posts a day, all sourced from other Tumblrs, Encyclopediaofcock is just one node in a large ecosystem of retro erotica available to queer affect.

About two weeks into my time on Tumblr, in 2009, I posted a close-up photo of two young men kissing taken by Wolfgang Tillmans, a famous gay male German photographer. There is something visceral about this photo—it looks like it was taken in a hot, sweaty gay club, at the height of the night's excitement. For these two young men it appears that nothing in the world is more important at that moment than their kiss. There is a whiff of something late 1980s, early 1990s about it, in the floppy hairstyles and the track suits that the young men wear—hearkening to a time just before our current tilt to neoliberal gay inclusion, which usually excises carnal display from mainstream depictions of homosexuality. These two young men are so unconcerned with the camera that I remember feeling slightly unsettled the first time I saw this photo, perhaps tapping into my own internalized fears regarding homophobic violence. Perhaps that is why I posted it. I captioned the photo with a link to Tillmans's official gallery homepage, providing no title and no other words.

Watching what happened to this post over the next few weeks was fascinating. It was the first time anything I had posted was reblogged. The long-format version of the post allows me to trace chronologically how this image shot around the Tumblr landscape. As of this writing, it has thirty-two "notes"—notes get added to a Tumblr post whenever anyone "likes" it by pressing the heart icon on the top of the post page or reblogs it on their own Tumblr—eighteen "likes" and fourteen "reblogs." To follow one thread: blueboy reblogged it from me, wolf90 reblogged it from blueboy, and conniealba reblogged it from wolf90. Two Tumblrs that have a large following, springeve and manphile, both of whom specialize in gay male sexy/erotic pictures, reblogged this photo, which further generated a number of reblogs from their followers.

We don't really know the stories behind these vintage posts. Without any sort of caption or credit viewers are simply left to fill in the blanks with their own assumptions of who these people are. On some level they are empty of narrative, while at the same time they hint at a subterranean queer history. In her work on intercultural cinema, Laura U. Marks (2000) also tackles the idea of history without specific referent. Writing about Marlon Fuentes's *Bontoc Eulogy* (1996), a film that tells a fictionalized story of a group of Filipino tribespeople who were exhibited at the St. Louis World's Fair of 1904, by using archival footage of the fair as well as ethnographic footage of anonymous women in the Philippines in moments of grief and despair, Marks employs Deleuze's idea of the "recollection-image" as a way to understand the relationship between image and gaps in history. As she puts it, "By using these archival images, Fuentes partially redeems them—not by filling in their stories, but by mourning the eternal loss of those stories. They are mediums of distant events that infect the present" (Marks 2000, 53). "Recollection-images," says Marks, are "those floating, dreamlike images that cannot be assigned a connection to history" (Marks 2000, 37). Following this logic, it is less important for us to know literally who/what/where these people are—*was the Tillmans photo taken in the 80s? 90s? 2000s? Berlin? New York? Were these guys gay? What happened to them? Are they yuppies now? Are they destitute? Are they even alive?*—than to think of them, much like Fuentes's Filipina elders, as floating images from some barely hinted-at space and time, *calling attention* to the fact that they are allowing us to fill in the blanks with affective charge by virtue of erasure. This is the generative meaning-space of queer temporality—it is a charged vacuum, a conduit for affect. It doesn't matter what these images are actual documents of—what matters more, in fact, is the "infinite deferral of historical truth" (Marks 2000, 37). It is the displacement and assemblage of these images through an affective archival pointillism that matters for the circulation of Freeman's "queer affect," not their actual place in linear historical narrative.

Queer Reverb

One queer Tumblr user explained to me that the best way to get followers and reblogs quickly was, in fact, not to post on queer-inclusive politics or blog sexy pictures, but to make simple repeating GIF animations (see Ash, this volume). These are short captures from movies or TV shows, only seconds long, with subtitled dialogue and no audio.

Significant moments from *Game of Thrones*, *Parks and Rec*, and the early John Waters film *Multiple Maniacs* (1970), for example, play on endless repeat. Often these GIF animations are comical, the punchline to a famous exchange, a silly moment, or simply an expression of feeling such as disgust or frustration—when Kristen Wiig's character from *Bridesmaids* demolishes an oversized wedding cookie, for example, or Jake the Dog from the cartoon *Adventure Time!*, rolling his eyes, declares, "I never really take anything seriously." One of my favorites is a two-panel GIF of grainy TV footage of Anita Bryant in 1977, looking proper and composed, with perfectly coiffed hair and demure hoop earrings in the left panel, mouth moving as a subtitle reads, "We were going to go on a crusade across the nation and do away with the homosexuals." In the next panel, a hand slams a cream pie into her face. The post has 5,500 notes.

I want to make a case for attention to this smallest and most innocuous of Tumblr practices, for I believe it encapsulates the queerness of time on Tumblr and hints at how users trade in affect across the site. The repeating GIF is a perfect moment of refrain, to invoke Deleuze and Guattari (1987). Their explication of the refrain: "It acts upon that which surrounds it, sound or light, extracting from it various vibrations, or decompositions, projections, or transformations. The refrain also has a catalytic function: not only to increase the speed of the exchanges and reactions in that which surrounds it, but also to assure indirect interactions between elements devoid of so-called natural affinity" (Deleuze and Guattari 1987, 348). Elsewhere Kathleen Stewart, in her essay "Worlding Refrains" (2010), explains the way we feel and move through the world on intuited and sensed registers; for Stewart, logics of discourse or semiotics are leaky and insufficient systems that do a poor job of capturing the flow of forces that create worlds. In her words, a refrain is "a scoring over a world's repetitions. A scratching on the surface of rhythms, sensory habits, gathering materialities, intervals, and durations. A gangly accrual of slow or sudden accretions" (Stewart 2010, 339).

Lorne Bertelsen and Andrew Murphie (2010) also explore the concept of the refrain in their analysis of the *Tampa* affair, in which more than four hundred refugees remained in stasis on a huge red tanker bound for Australia, halted in international waters as the Australian government deliberated over what to do with them. For Bertelsen and Murphie, the constant *presence* of the image of the looming red ship as it shot around Australian mass media itself was in itself world-making. Instead of thinking about the hulking red ship on the horizon as a part of a unidirectional semiotic formula, their assertion is that the incessant refraining of the ship was a locus of affective intensity that fed back upon itself: "The repetition of this image did not just *illustrate* a complex political event. It helped *bring it into being*" (Bertelsen and Murphie 2010, 138; emphasis in original). The ship's simple *immanence*, constantly refrained, created a *thing*.

Refrain is repetition, a scoring of affect fed back on itself, a way of apprehending that is not beholden to straightforward formulas of signification. To use Deleuze and Guattari's terminology, it is a territorializing, an intensity that encrusts and dissolves. It is in concert with but exceeds, or has the potential to slough off, discourses and systems of signs; thus it is not the same as a simple semiotics. In this way, an analysis through attention to refrain—that is, the dynamism and procreative sensibility of evocation, often clustered around feeling or affect—opens up the potential to fill in the blanks in leaky or insufficient systems of sign. This is the tie-in to the kinks of queer temporality. In other words, if queer temporality is the condition, then refrain is the mechanics.

Refrain, as it applies to Tumblr: user-created emotional/temporal prisms that span its multiplicity and simultaneously help define it as a set of urges, wants, and hurts, refracting affect through the rhizome in a nonlinear and hardly literal way. Anita Bryant getting pied over and over and over is a perverse queer temporality that has a catalytic function—bringing Tumblrs together by means of a shared affinity.

The most resonant image I have encountered during my time on Tumblr came to me in early October 2010. It was a photocollage of six adolescent boys' faces, most of them smiling broadly, on a purple background. The boys were already famous through most national news media, which had covered their suicides in a rare display of mainstream attention to the plight of bullied queer youth. This collage also carried text:

SPIRIT DAY. It's been decided. On October 20th, 2010, we will wear purple in honor of the 6 gay boys who committed suicide in recent weeks/months due to homophobic abuse in their homes or at their schools. Purple represents Spirit on the LGBTQ flag and that's exactly what we'd like all of you to have with you: spirit. Please know that times will get better and that you will meet people who will love you and respect you for who you are, no matter your sexuality. Please wear purple on October 20th. Tell your friends, family, co-workers, neighbors and schools.

Within several days the image garnered over thirty thousand notes. "Spirit Day" became a phenomenon in the United States, gaining national media attention in its own right when it occurred on October 20th, prompting major celebrities, such as talk show host Ryan Seacrest, to wear purple (Miller 2010).

This post, and the way it framed the suicides of these boys, did more than simply channel anger, grief, disgust, and frustration (though it certainly did do that). I want to move through platitudes of "tragedy" to think about the way the post operates as refrain, like Bertelsen and Murphie's red ship: it is a territorialization of a stubborn negative queer affective charge, constantly resurrected.

There are multiple refrains going on here. The text of the post demands that the occasion of these boys' suicides be refrained into productive public neoliberal logics of state-sponsored individual rights, gathered in a simple semiotics of purple on a single day, rather than attention to or intervention in systems of micropower that infiltrate every second of young queer peoples' lives. The image, however, works on a different refrain. The bizarre, almost perverse arrangement of smiling portraits of these young boys, probably uploaded to their Facebook pages at happier moments, is poignant on a whole other register for precisely what it masks—the duplicitous nature of systemic homophobic abuse, which demands that one keep a smiling public face because "it gets better," at the same time that it eats away at one's will to live. Heather Love states that we have not been able, under the recuperative impulse (e.g., Spirit Day at its most trite level), to allow for "sustained engagement with the stubborn negativity of the past: critics have ignored what they could not transform" (Love 2007, 147). This is the energy of the affective charge in circulation here, hidden behind the recuperative agenda of Spirit Day: a "stubborn negativity" (to put it mildly) that leads nowhere but the end of the road. I see this second refrain, in the words of Elizabeth Freeman, as a "queer hauntological exercise," a *longing*, in the sense that it "produces modes of both belonging and 'being long,' or persisting over time" (Freeman 2010, 13). These boys and their bad feelings persist on the refrain on Tumblr, skating on affective charge, weaving the network between users. One wonders if the creators of Spirit Day realize their double entendre: not simply honoring these boys' youthful spirit, but also regarding them as spirits, continually haunting us.

My final suggestion has to do with value, or force. If refrain is repetition and encrusting, a bringing-into-being and then dissolving, and if queer temporality describes the general character of the practices of queer Tumblr users described above, then how do we account for direction, force, and intensity? How do we describe the way in which some posts take off, while the vast majority linger with little circulation? Or the fact that some Tumblr users have inordinately large reach, whereas the vast number of Tumblrs I've observed and spoken with have small-to-medium reach at best? It is no coincidence that many people I've spoken to about Tumblr employ this same language, unprompted, when speaking about why they decide to follow someone or reblog an image. "Resonate," "immersion," and "strong reaction" are all frequent terms, though they seem like containers that can't quite carry what has already been felt. This phenomenon has been explored by Paasonen (2011, 16, 18) as "resonance," in terms of online pornography and its dynamics of "force and grab" with audiences who feel "sympathetic vibrations."

I offer "reverb" to further tweak this fruitful concept and posit it as a way to understand how intensity interacts with refrain over *time* and as a function of *repetition*. Though it is not a central focal point of her argument, Paasonen (2011, 185) hints at this ground in her use of terms such as "tempo." In my conception, reverb is refrain that has the additional quality of amplification or diminishment (intensity) through echo or refrain; in this sense, it can be modulated to serve a purpose. Reverb is a quality and a process, a way to understand the direction and intensity of the flows of affect. It has been startling to watch this pattern over the years: a post lingers until it hits a popular Tumblr, then takes off, dies down again, and takes off again, almost like a breathing thing. We can view any individual Tumblr, or any one of its posts, "as if an echo of irreducible excess, of gratuitous amplification, piggy-backed on the reconnection to progression, bringing a tinge of the unexpected, the lateral, the unmotivated, to lines of action and reaction"; in other words, affect is the irreducible excess, a "system of the inexplicable" (Massumi 1995, 87), always in emergence. Thrift (2004, 62) describes it similarly: "Affect [is] defined as the property of the active outcome of an encounter."

This is in keeping with Massumi's bottom line, and much of contemporary affect theory: that structural and poststructural analyses are all predicated on a static structural referent, and that, therefore, we need to understand relationality through a different vocabulary, one that accounts for movement and potential. I posit that we can think of reverb as a shorthand way to describe this potential as well as its observable traces: certain posts could be said to possess a high degree of reverb, and individual Tumblrs that have many followers enable or possess a high degree of reverb. Reverb describes a quality as well as a process, attention to movement rather than the fixed—this is another way of understanding Massumi's invocation of the suspense of the event, or as he would term it, the "virtual." It is "the pressing crowd of incipiencies and tendencies, [it] is a realm of *potential*" (Massumi 1995, 91). Like the movement of iron filings on magnetized paper, reverb is the directed territorialization of this affective charge. It is the encounter, prime. It is the multitude of notes that coalesce around a popular post, the saturation and flow of images in the dashboard feed, the pulsations and traces your own picture leaves behind as it traverses the Tumblr space, the wake of the affective charge.

Notes

1. All Tumblr names presented are pseudonyms.

2. Though detailed statistics are hard to come by, the site announced on March 8, 2010, that it was averaging two million posts and fifteen thousand new users every day (Karp 2010). In 2011 the site was due to pass ten billion posts, with an average of 37.5 million per day (Pingdom 2011).

3. There is a popular meme, "Rules of Tumblr," that reverberates in different permutations across the internet. In a YouTube video posted by JustKidding1026, called "What you need to know about Tumblr," a young woman gives snarky tips on the site's etiquette, saying, "If you're homophobic, you're prolly not going to last long on this website." The video goes further: "Seeing as most people on the site are either lesbian, gay, or they support homosexuality. Just saying. Just saying" (What You Need to Know 2010). Elsewhere, another version of Rules of Tumblr states: "[Rule] 8. Tumblr isn't for homophobes. Tumblr is mostly people who support gay people, or lesbian/gay people themselves. We don't discriminate on Tumblr" (Urban Dictionary 2010).

4. See Paasonen (2011, 8–12) for a discussion on the false binary between affect and representation.

5. Tumblr users create an account that is usually anonymous, identified only by a made-up Tumblr name, which is the basis of a unique URL and which can be changed at any time. Users can upload pictures, videos, text, or links, or, more likely, "reblog" these items from anyone else

on Tumblr. This means that with a minimum of two clicks, an image that you see on any Tumblr will appear on yours, and a corresponding "note" will be attached to the original post recording your action. Popular Tumblr posts can have hundreds of thousands of notes. All your posts, whether original or reblogged, gather on your own Tumblr, which is customizable with full malleability of HTML and CSS. Sometimes you don't even know the web page you're looking at is a Tumblr. When you have an account, you can "follow" other Tumblr users you like, and their most recent posts will accumulate in a dashboard or feed, reminiscent of Twitter. Following is nonreciprocal, also reminiscent of Twitter.

6. There are many strains of "bad queer feelings," and many authors in this list write against each other, but see collectively the debate on the "antisocial thesis" (Caserio et al. 2006); Edelman (2004); Love (2007); Halperin and Traub (2010); Ahmed (2010); Muñoz (2010); Halberstam (2011).

7. For example, a recent exhibition at Los Angeles's ONE Archives, entitled "To Whom It May Concern" (October 8, 2011–August 17, 2012), presented a collection of blown-up images of dedications from the inside covers of famous literary works by queer authors that are all veiled, insider, or tongue-in-cheek references to the author's sexual identity.

8. See the special issue of *GLQ: Lesbian and Gay Quarterly* on "Queer Temporalities" (Freeman et al. 2007) for an extended deliberation on this subject.

References

Ahmed, Sara. 2006. *Queer Phenomenology : Orientations, Objects, Others*. Durham: Duke University Press.

Ahmed, Sara. 2010. *The Promise of Happiness*. Durham: Duke University Press.

Alexander, Jonathan. 2002a. Queer Webs: Representations of LGBT People and Communities on the World Wide Web. *International Journal of Sexuality and Gender Studies* 7 (2/3):77–84.

Alexander, Jonathan. 2002b. Homo-Pages and Queer Sites: Studying the Construction and Representation of Queer Identities on the World Wide Web. *International Journal of Sexuality and Gender Studies* 7 (2/3):85–106.

Arondekar, Anjali. 2005. Without a Trace: Sexuality and the Colonial Archive. *Journal of the History of Sexuality* 14 (1/2):10–27.

Benjamin, Walter. On the Concept of History. 1940. Available at http://www.marxists.org/reference/archive/benjamin/1940/history.htm.

Bertelsen, Lorne, and Andrew Murphie. 2010. An Ethics of Everyday Infinities and Powers: Felix Guattari on Affect and the Refrain. In *The Affect Theory Reader*, ed. Melissa Gregg and Gregory J. Seigworth, 138–157. Durham: Duke University Press.

Brickman, Celia. 2003. *Aboriginal Populations in the Mind: Race and Primitivity in Psychoanalysis*. New York: Columbia University Press.

Campbell, John E. 2004. *Getting It On Online: Cyberspace, Gay Male Sexuality, and Embodied Identity.* New York: Harrington Park Press.

Caserio, Robert L., Tim Dean, Lee Edelman, Judith Halberstam, José Esteban Muñoz, Vitaly Chernetsky, Nancy Condee, Harsha Ram, and Gayatri Chakravorty Spivak. 2006. Forum: Conference Debates/The Antisocial Thesis in Queer Theory. *PMLA* 121 (3):819–836.

Cohen, Cathy J. 2005. Punks, Bulldaggers, and Welfare Queens: The Radical Potential of Queer Politics? In *Black Queer Studies: A Critical Anthology,* ed. Patrick Johnson and Mae Henderson, 21–51. Durham: Duke University Press.

Cvetkovich, Ann. 2003. *An Archive of Feelings: Trauma, Sexuality, and Lesbian Public Cultures.* Durham: Duke University Press.

Deleuze, Gilles, and Felix Guattari. 1987. *A Thousand Plateaus: Capitalism and Schizophrenia.* Trans. Brian Massumi. Minneapolis: University of Minnesota Press.

Dinshaw, Carolyn. 2008. Born Too Soon, Born Too Late: The Female Hunter of Long Eddy, circa 1855. In *Twenty-First-Century Gay Culture,* ed. David A. Powell, 1–12. Newcastle: Cambridge Scholars Publishing.

Edelman, Lee. 2004. *No Future: Queer Theory and the Death Drive.* Durham: Duke University Press.

Egan, Jennifer. 2000. Lonely Gay Teen Seeking Same. *New York Times Magazine,* December 10. Available at http://www.nytimes.com/2000/12/10/magazine/lonely-gay-teen-seeking-same.html.

Freeman, Elizabeth. 2007. Introduction. *GLQ: A Journal of Lesbian and Gay Studies* 13 (2):159–176.

Freeman, Elizabeth. 2010. *Time Binds: Queer Temporalities, Queer Histories.* Durham: Duke University Press.

Freeman, Elizabeth, Roderick A. Ferguson, Lee Edelman, Tan Hoang Nguyen, Carolyn Dinshaw, Carla Freccero, Annamarie Jagose, Christopher Nealon, and Judith Halberstam. 2007. Theorizing Queer Temporalities: A Roundtable Discussion. *GLQ: A Journal of Lesbian and Gay Studies* 13 (2):177–195.

Gregg, Melissa, and Gregory J. Seigworth, eds. 2010. *The Affect Theory Reader.* Durham: Duke University Press.

Gross, Larry. 2003. The Gay Global Village in Cyberspace. In *Contesting Media Power,* ed. Nick Couldry and James Curran, 387–404. London: Rowan and Littlefield.

Gross, Larry. 2004. Somewhere There's a Place for Us: Sexual Minorities and the Internet. In *Technological Visions: Utopian and Dystopian Perspectives,* ed. Marita Sturken, Douglas Thomas, and Sandra Ball-Rokeach, 255–269. Philadelphia: Temple University Press.

Halberstam, Judith. 2011. *The Queer Art of Failure.* Durham: Duke University Press.

Halperin, David, and Valerie Traub. 2010. *Gay Shame.* Chicago: University of Chicago Press.

Hillis, Ken. 2009. *Online a Lot of the Time: Ritual, Fetish, Sign.* Durham: Duke University Press.

Karp, David. 2010. Has It Been Three Years Already?! Tumblr staff blog. Available at http://staff.tumblr.com/post/434982975/a-billion-hits.

Love, Heather. 2007. *Feeling Backward: Loss and the Politics of Queer History*. Cambridge, MA: Harvard University Press.

Marks, Laura U. 2000. *The Skin of the Film: Intercultural Cinema, Embodiment, and the Senses*. Durham: Duke University Press.

Massumi, Brian. 1995. The Autonomy of Affect. *Cultural Critique*, no. 31 (October):83–109.

Massumi, Brian. 2002. *Parables for the Virtual: Movement, Affect, Sensation*. Durham: Duke University Press.

Miller, Carlin DeGuerin. 2010. Wear Purple 10/20. CBS News. Available at http://www.cbsnews.com/news/wear-purple-10-20-gay-rights-organization-glaad-asks-for-anti-bullying-support/.

Muñoz, José Esteban. 1999. *Disidentifications: Queers of Color and the Performance of Politics*. Minneapolis: University of Minnesota Press.

Muñoz, José Esteban. 2010. *Cruising Utopia: The Then and There of Queer Futurity*. New York: NYU Press.

Paasonen, Susanna. 2011. *Carnal Resonance: Affect and Online Pornography*. Cambridge, MA: MIT Press.

Pingdom. 2011. Huge Milestone: Tumblr Users Have Soon Cranked Out 10 BILLION Posts. *Pingdom*, September 9. Available at http://royal.pingdom.com/2011/09/02/huge-milestone-tumblr-users-have-soon-cranked-out-10-billion-posts.

Puar, Jasbir. 2007. *Terrorist Assemblages: Homonationalism in Queer Times*. Durham: Duke University Press.

Stewart, Kathleen. 2010. Worlding Refrains. In *The Affect Theory Reader*, ed. Melissa Gregg and Gregory J. Seigworth, 339–353. Durham: Duke University Press.

Thrift, Nigel. 2004. Intensities of Feeling: Towards a Spatial Politics of Affect. *Geografiska Annaler* 86 B (1):57–78.

Urban Dictionary. 2010. Rules of Tumblr. *Urban Dictionary*, December 19. Available at http://www.urbandictionary.com/define.php?term=rules%20of%20tumblr.

Warner, Michael. 2005. *Publics and Counterpublics*. New York: Zone Books.

What You Need. 2010. What You Need to Know about Tumblr. YouTube, user JustKidding1026. December 12. https://www.youtube.com/watch?v=0OnyleRw-3Q.

4 Affective Politics or Political Affection: Online Sexuality in Turkey

Veronika Tzankova

I am a woman of an average physical appearance. If seen from outside, I have the perfect marriage—me and my husband appear to be in love with each other. The love part is somewhat true, but we have lots of problems. If it weren't for our little dirty secrets, we would long be divorced. My husband is a macho and usually doesn't like sharing me, while I am a moderate [Muslim] believer and do my best to live a moderate life. It all began with my husband's innocent fantasy to share our amateur sex pictures and videos on the net. Next step: despite my superficial verbal disapproval—group sex with his best friend. I cried a lot afterward because it was morally wrong, but I must confess, I really enjoyed it. I guess the angel and the devil are fighting inside my body. The result is that despite my average physical appearance, I have a much-above-average sexual life.

I am married and have an incredible sex life with my husband. But despite this, I can't ignore the bisexual beast in me. The fantasy of being fucked by a woman with a strap-on is driving me crazy.

Reading all the stories about the pleasures of sandwich-experiences, I feel sorry to have missed all the sandwich offers during my years at the university.

—Narratives translated from Turkish sexual *itiraf* (confession) sites

Sexuality in Muslim societies has long functioned under the prescriptive norms of religious principles of conduct and social institutions informed by these principles (İlkkaracan 2008; Shannahan 2009). For more than a decade a significant political revitalization of Islam has been ongoing in several Middle Eastern countries, and most overtly in Turkey (Kadioğlu 1994). The politico-religious dynamics involved in the reintroduction of Islamic values have played a significant role in the normative cultivation of affect, sexuality, and body politics. In this chapter, I explore the political potential of networked affect in the context of contemporary Turkey through an analysis of Turkish online sexual *itiraf* (confession) sites—social network sites dedicated to the distribution and public sharing of sexual adventures, fantasies, and reflections.

Although the English word "confession" carries a Christian connotation, the corresponding Turkish term, *itiraf*, is not associated with any religious practice but, instead, commonly signifies the expression of something supposed to remain hidden, such as forbidden love. Turkish *itiraf* sites exemplify the political charge of online affective modalities. By situating the social dynamics mediated by these online platforms within the broader context of political Islam in Turkey, I argue that networked affect facilitates a collective gathering of a sexual counterpublic (Warner 2002) along with alternative forms of political resistance.

The political charge of networked affect is closely connected to the ability of public engagement to radically challenge the production, assemblage, and normality of social relations. The desire to question societal apparatuses based on sexual practices presents various potent political opportunities. Lauren Berlant and Michael Warner (1998) argue that established sexual normativity does not tolerate the confusion of categories; a strict boundary is maintained between good and evil, right and wrong. Nevertheless, a visible public operating outside or on the margins of sexual categories opens a path for the transformation of normative sexual conduct. Based on this understanding, I expand on Berlant and Warner's position by arguing that publicizing sex in Turkish *itiraf* networks produces affective states that challenge not only sexual norms but also the totality of the politico-religious system that underlies them.

Christine Ogan and Kursat Cagiltay (2006, 803) describe Turkish confession sites as online platforms that have "evolved into a community where users tell their stories, compete to get them published and even create new language based on their interactions." Sexual *itiraf* sites, then, are online platforms where community members share their sexual confessions—experiences, fantasies, reflections—as short textual narratives:

Reading the extended discussions on sex during menstrual periods, I remembered the old days when I was practicing unprotected sex with my ex boyfriend. He loved my periods. Why? Because he was tired of cumming outside.

There are numerous Turkish sexual confession sites, but I base my study on kirmiziitiraf.com (redconfession.com) (figure 4.1) and erotikitiraf.com (eroticconfession.com) (figure 4.2). Erotikitiraf.com, the oldest and most popular Turkish sexual confession site, has an extended network of partner sites such as sekspartner.com (sexpartner.com) and kamerarulet.com (cameraroulette.com). These networks provide a wide range of opportunities for social contact through chat, video chat, instant messaging, and email. The posts on sexual confession sites can be openly read by all users who state they are above the age of eighteen and who have internet access.

Apart from the option of organizing submissions by the contributor's gender, there are generally no confession channels for categorizing or filtering topics or for the sexual preferences addressed. All narratives appear in a chronological and linear manner according to the time of submission. The confessions read like letters to intimate acquaintances, yet they are accessible as a public virtual file to thousands of people the writer has never met and likely never will. What is unusual about the confession sites, particularly within a Turkish context, is the broadcasting of the most intimate and

Figure 4.1
Screenshot of kitmiziitiraf.com with ad for female escorts.

potentially stigmatizing details of the writers' sex lives. The sites form a bricolage of publicly available sexual stories predominantly concerned with explicit explorations of human bodies as a source of pleasure.

Bodily Pleasure and Political Affect

In this section I provide a theoretical framework to address the pursuit of bodily pleasure in terms of the political affect that it involves, generates, and configures. I start with the premise that affect has an allegorical essence that supports a fundamental mixing of conceptual categories. Affect functions as a form of ontological participation,[1] and I define it as a stream of intensities operating at individual and group levels, which enable the collective experiencing of one thing in terms of another. Within this definition, the role of the internet as a platform of affective mediation is important. It defines the disjuncture between affect as a chain of physio-psychological intensities, and affect as a collective meaning maker of subjective and intersubjective experiences. The bodies that experience affective states are separated from the entities that disseminate them. Such a separation is by itself a mixing of categories. On one hand, affect as bodily experience is associated with immediacy and nonrationality (Gould 2010). On the other hand, the production and dissemination of affect through online platforms and networks is codified in discursive and representational practices that necessitate a

Figure 4.2
Screenshot of erotikitiraf.com showing links to partner sites.

level of consciousness and intentionality (Wetherell 2012). Networked affect, therefore, is a complex set of intensities associated with rational and nonrational modalities. In this context affect possesses the force to produce meanings that are only implicitly articulated in online discourse and representations. This is where, I argue, the political charge of affect lies—in its potential to convert implicit meanings into political agency.

For the purposes of this chapter, I understand political affect as the potential of affect to organize a sexual counterpublic that transgresses and challenges politico-religious boundaries and thus becomes a force of social struggle. Networked political affect lacks a tactile or determinate form of presence (Ahmed 2004; Gould 2010; Paasonen 2011); in this light the work of John Protevi (2009) on political affect offers a useful framework for the systematization of such intensities. Protevi identifies three compositional layers of political affect: personal, group, and civic. These layers form an imbricated whole and are in a process of continuous interaction. The personal layer is constituted by the establishment of values in relation to the body and body politics at the individual level. For example, the cases of Turkish women who abandon their homes and families in order to escape arranged, consanguineous, or endogamous marriages illustrate this layer.[2] Such cases exemplify how a point of intensity for a single individual can implicate body politics and trigger a flow of transformative dynamics at group and national levels.

The group layer of political affect is an intersubjective dynamic that mediates between the individual and civic layers and constructs non- or semi-rational intensities and identifications for more than one individual. An example of this layer of political affect is the feminist group Femen, which organizes topless protests to focus attention on religious, institutional, and sexist issues of significance to women.[3] Femen exemplifies the circulation of affective intensities at a group level. These intensities have the potential to trigger political sentience and thus also to mediate between individual and national political agency.

The civic layer of political affect projects the formation of body politics at a national, governmental level. This layer occupies a position of control in relation to the human subject and focuses on the broader social context of affective cognition. Governmental interventions and regulatory involvement in social issues such as abortion and marriage rights, among many others, are examples of the civic layer of political affect. In the sections that follow, I use Protevi's tripartite scheme of affect as a conceptual frame to capture the political charge of social and body interactions mediated through online sexual confessions. I begin with the civic level of political affect for three reasons. First, it provides an explanation for the basic premise of my study—that sexuality in Turkey, as experienced outside online sexual networks, is highly regulated. Second, it contextualizes sexual normativity and provides details essential to its meaning. Third, it emphasizes the contrast between the expectations of a stigmatizing sociopolitical environment and the values disseminated through online networks. This contrast is significant, since it signals the presence of ambivalent codes regarding the interpretation and conveyance of sexual meanings, where the level of ambivalence defines the force of affective intensities.

The Civic Layer of Political Affect: Turkey's Neo-Ottomanist Organization of Sexuality

Contemporary Turkish politics involves an ideological conflict between secular forces and the rise of Islamism at a governmental level. This comes as a result of the autocratic power of the major political party—AKP[4]—which explicitly promotes Islamism (Hale and Özbudun 2010; Casier and Jongerden 2011). Although the Republic of Turkey is purportedly governed by constitutional secularism, AKP has merged many aspects of government under its own ideological, political, and organizational umbrella. The term neo-Ottomanism refers to a return to the spiritual, cultural, and political inheritance of the Ottoman Empire (Tanasković 2010). The return to Ottoman values closely coincides with the ongoing Islamization of the country at a governmental level:

> In the 1980s and 1990s, Islamists attacked secularist hegemony in Turkey and transformed everyday behaviour and uses of the body. The political party, municipalities, and radical groups led this attack, thoroughly shaping the activities of associations, foundations, communities, and networks. These activities included teaching people how to pray or the proper way of praying, arranging Islamic ways of clothing and Islamic facial hair, wedding ceremonies, and imposing alcohol bans or making people quit alcohol. (Yavuz 2003, 243–244)

The Islamist infiltration of the government (Narli 1993; Yavuz 2003; Hale and Özbudun 2010) with respect to issues and practices of individual or private concern began through well-camouflaged propaganda on popular TV channels. It appeared somewhat harmless at first; in the early 2000s, it took the form of conversations ranging from personal hygiene to the proper Islamic way for men to urinate—whether standing or sitting. In 2004, Prime Minister Tayyip Erdoğan—along with the ministers of foreign affairs, justice, state, and health—made an unsuccessful attempt to criminalize adultery in an effort to "protect human honour, family and the right of the deceived woman." In this case, adultery was equated with theft and drug-related crimes (Hale and Özbudun 2010, 70–71). In 2012, the AKP government focused on the criminalization of abortion. Erdoğan expressed an absolutist opinion that abortion is a crime that no one should be granted the right to perform, and that there is no difference between a fetus killed in utero and a child killed after birth (MSNBC 2012). In support of the prime minister, Minister of Health Recep Akdağ added that even in cases where pregnancy has occurred as a result of rape, the mother should give birth, and if necessary the state would take care of the child (BirGun Halkin Gazetesi 2012). Various other officials worked to buttress this stance by adding that Turkey needed to increase its population.

In the shadow of such strong official condemnation of abortion, discussions about limiting access to cesarean sections passed almost unnoticed. Yet the most significant, albeit hidden, implications of these legal and political debates lay in their reductionist reconstruction and resignification of the sexual body. The abortion debates served to firmly locate both male and female sexual agency in a public and national discursive framework characterized by political oppression.

This official approach to body politics and sexuality has been reproduced in various forms of mainstream media. The TV show *Yaprak Dökümü* (*Fall of the Leaves*), for example, depicts the process of social degradation which purportedly results from "modern" forms of sexual activities. One of the show's main storylines traces the ways in which the premarital and extramarital affairs of two sisters lead to mental disorders, severe crime, messy pregnancy situations, and death. Such mass media representations of the ruling party's body politics aim to reintroduce a non-secular neo-Ottomanist cultural agenda.

The Group Layer of Political Affect: Community, Discursive Sex, and Transgression

Protevi (2009) argues that the essence of political affect involves a constitution of intensities for a batch of individuals—the group composition of affect. This layer is an intermediary positioning of political intensities that transgress the individual yet remain below the range of the national. In a way, at this level affect is an intersubjective sentimental cognition, where private sensibilities are compiled externally in collective intensities that teach how and what to feel (Gould 2010). In my reading, the group composition of political affect within Turkish online sexual networks is defined by the following interlacing conditions: the existence of a supportive online community, experiences of linguo-sexual pleasure, and socio-sexual transgression.

Online Community

The basic condition for the formation of a group layer of networked affect is the existence of an online community within which the sharing of sexual narratives and alternative body politics is constituted as social and intersubjective activity. Jodi Dean (this volume) argues that such communities "enable mediated relationships that take a variety of changing, uncertain, and interconnected forms as they feed back each upon the other in ways we can never fully account for or predict." Because online communities emerge from the indefinite web of social and intersubjective interactions among network members, they contain the potential to influence social realities, as articulated in the following sexual narratives shared online:

I know we haven't met in real life, but we all feel somehow like brothers and sisters here.

—Male confessor

The fantasy of sharing my wife with several other men is filling me up with desire. Before discovering this network, I thought I was crazy. But now I know I am not alone;)

—Male confessor

Both postings identify and address the presence of an online community which exists through technologically mediated (but potent) social relations. Dean (this volume) argues that affective networks generate a feeling of community. If we reverse Dean's statement, we could argue that the feelings of community within online networks produce the condition for the existence of an affective network. As exemplified by the above narratives, Turkish sexual networks involve the potential of affective networks. If we want to affirm the presence of affect, however, we have to consider the ways in which these networks operate. Sexual narratives function as allegories, much like human interest stories in newspapers. Everyone can relate to the subject of a human interest story on the basis of a shared set of emotions.

The infamous sexual liaison between Bill Clinton and Monica Lewinsky,[5] for example, provoked a tornado of public opinion and the articulation of such affective states as disgust, disproval, sympathy, and envy, among others. The explosive dimensions of the public's reaction resulted partly from the ways in which people were able to relate to the story emotionally, and these emotional reactions and investments moved them toward or away from the story and its individual protagonists. Such forms of orientation enabled the creation of communal spirit on a different basis than one rooted in rational standards alone. Similarly, the stories told by Turkish confessors solicit discursive intimacy and form community based on motives beyond the purely rational. Sex and sexuality constellate a domain to which most people can relate—and say something about—on the basis of life experiences that cannot be solely confined to the conscious and the rational. A statement such as "I love oral sex" (female confessor), for example, is reflective only of one's appreciation of a sexual practice, but not of the motives which underlie such appreciation. The "liking" of a sexual practice is a result of life experience, exemplified by sensation and feeling, and not by objects of thought (Feenberg 1999). Such experience-fueled sensations and feelings support the circulation of shared affective intensities that again support the existence of sexual communities online.

Linguo-sexual Pleasure

While all of my family was sitting at home and watching TV, I fucked my girlfriend in the bathroom. But what is even more exciting—I am writing this here.

—Male confessor

Turkish online sexual networks mediate affective states by providing the conditions for transforming or expanding the physical sexual body (that of scientific physiology) into a verbal abstraction able to elevate itself above concrete hegemonic social and political norms. The physiological body is externalized from itself and embedded into linguistic practices of conceptual value. This presupposes a very different pattern of body significance. The body transcends its physical limits and is recontextualized into discursive modes of social production. Talk about sex articulates an alternative, social sexualization of the body and its acts. It brings to language a change appearing in the bodies, actions, and values of the network members. Sex becomes a hybrid entity entangled within physical acts and linguistic representations, where it acquires different boundaries and the organs play different roles, as do the partners and social institutions.

In Turkish *itiraf* sites bodily practices are conflated into a world of words with social implications, where the world of words "authorizes selected feelings and actions while downplaying and even invalidating others" (Gould 2010, 33). But the conversion of sexual experiences into sexual narratives is also motivated by the quest for immediate gratification. I call the immediate gratification of reading and writing about sex a "linguo-sexual pleasure": a type of pleasure that exists on the boundary between cognitive and bodily impulses and is triggered by the interlacing of linguistic and sexual stimuli. Sex jokes or bull sessions that focus on sexual adventures are examples of such pleasure. Linguo-sexual pleasure within Turkish online sexual networks bears significance because it is a constituent of affect's group layer. Some network members explicitly identify the reading, writing, and sharing of verbal confessions as a linguo-sexual pleasure:

Fuck, fuck, fuck, fuuuuuuuuuuuck; even the typing of this word is ecstatic ...

—Female confessor

In this confession, "fuck" becomes a discursive entity sufficient to compensate for the lack of an actual sexual act and to provide a parallel level of pleasure. An affective, ecstatic, rippling intensity is born into a language that has already been inscribed into an indeterminate range of sexual sensations. Online platforms that allow the verbal and the sexual to interconnect also allow language to induce sexual production. This assemblage of the sexual and the textual produces intensive linguo-sexual pleasure, which—when shared and disseminated within a group setting—gains affective resonance through its capacity to "exceed what is actualized through language or gesture" (Gould 2010, 27). What is of significance here is affect's allegorical capacity to facilitate the experience of one type of thing in terms of another (see Ash's discussion of the allotropic, and Hillis's discussion of the avatar, in this volume). It is precisely this interchangeability of experiences that unleashes the political potential of affect as the collective gathering of a sexual counterpublic.

Affect is not produced in fixed frames of conventional meanings but in contextually explicable allegories. Sexual discourse is a convenient milieu for the production of affect, because sex signifies a plethora of things—most of them abrupt and incomprehensible to those who cannot grasp the various associations accompanying divergent sexual practices. This viewpoint offers a productive framework for thinking about the political significance of online Turkish sexual confession. The sexual and the political are fundamentally intermeshed in such acts of confession. They involve the quest for linguo-sexual pleasure and fantasy, as well as a desire—explicit or implicit—to challenge the regulatory frameworks governing sexual encounters and representations within Turkey. The networked realm of sexual confession is further intensified through what Sara Ahmed refers to as "the 'rippling' effect of emotions ... [and] 'sticky' associations between signs, figures and objects" (2004, 44–45), which transform sex into a form of political action and an affective gathering of a political counterpublic.

Socio-sexual Transgression

The political potential for networked affect is exemplified by the intensified, transgressive nature of desire exhibited on Turkish sexual networks. Georges Bataille (1986) argues for the significance of transgression within the sexual. For Bataille, the idea of crossing a boundary or limit elevates human sexuality beyond the reproductive function and intensifies the dynamics of desire. There is a codependence between sexual prohibition and the sexual violation of social boundaries. Considered in this vein, Turkish online sexual networks effect a double movement: on the one hand, they violate Turkish sociopolitical and religious rules of sexual conduct. Such violation or transgression adds to the intensification of desire. On the other hand, the sexual networks aim to normalize sexual transgression. These apparently contradictory movements of transgression and normalization seem to function in symbiosis in the realm of networked communication. Their mutual dynamic can best be visualized as a circular relationship within which social control is transformed into sexual pleasure, which then gives shape to alternative forms of social control. This dynamic bears resemblance to Michel Foucault's (1990) discursive thematization of sexuality, where the emergence of a system of epistemic operations such as *scientia sexualis* pursues the "truth" of sexuality while simultaneously privileging sexual mores that contribute to social welfare and national power. Similarly, Turkish sexual network members engage in the discursive utilization of sex and sexuality in an attempt to uncover sexual truths obscured behind dominant, purportedly "given" sexual mores. This is not an easy task, since such unveiling contains within itself a critique of dominant or hegemonic political, cultural, and religious norms and conditions. Such a critique questions the broader Turkish social context of body politics and works to articulate (and possibly even promote) the need for cultural modernization. Discourse on sexuality in a Muslim context bears so much social significance that it should be treated as having political agency in itself. Thus, online sexual confessing is political precisely because it challenges Islam's predicament regarding cultural modernity (Tibi 2009).

The following narratives identify the transgressive nature of sex and sexual confessions in two different ways, as exemplification and reflection:

What has been classified as a taboo has always got me hyper-excited [sexually]. But the thought of talking about these with a same-minded woman is driving me crazy.

—Male confessor

In response to the above confession:

Two of the best features of this site are: (1) to explicitly know that there are other people with crazy sexual preferences, and (2) to be able to bravely communicate such crazy preferences here. Let's all break the taboos together.

—Female confessor

What I learned from this site is the repressive conditions under which Turks live and experience their sexuality. But even worse, apart from all sexual taboos, talking about repressed sexuality appears to be an ever greater taboo. Women that wander the streets without underwear and the first thing they do when they get home is "confessing" it here is an example of that. How are such confessions "confessions"? I am sick of it.

—Male confessor

Such talk should not be understood as purely sexual. While it critiques social norms concerning sexual demeanor, desire, and acts, it also provokes critique aimed at sex talk itself. Such circular critique is important, since it negotiates the essence of sexual discourse and directs it back to the transformations occurring in the bodies and actions of individual confessors. The members of Turkish sexual networks implicitly articulate and negotiate the transitions that are happening for them at both the collective and individual level.

The Personal Layer of Political Affect: Fifty Shades of Green

The personal composition of political affect is the terrain on which individuals engage in the production of their own body politics. I exemplify this layer by analyzing how members of Turkish sexual networks participate in the construction of a particular and publicly observable form of body politics that is in an oppositional relation to the normative political physiology of reemerging Islamic values. Here affect mediates what Deborah Gould describes as "the tension between dominant accounts of what is and what might be" (2010, 32). Turkish sexual network members make their points by telling stories of how sex reflects and influences their somatic experiences. The sexual networks they use create spaces for political agency where personal accounts of body politics are exposed and made publicly available. Accounts of affective states—desire, lust, and approval—evoked in sexual narratives posted to these sites generate affective responses and intensities in their readers. Such affective states can facilitate the reconsideration of deeply embedded patterns of thinking and feeling and thereby open a channel for new imaginings (Gould 2010, 32). Consider the following narrative:

I came back from my vacation yesterday. I couldn't resist all the vacation opportunities, so I gave it up at the end. I met two boys in a nightclub. Generally, even if I stay late at night, I don't drink much—I know when to stop. But the guys were buying the drinks, so I got over my limit. The night continued at the hotel. I realized that handling two guys at a time is not easy. Without much effort, they got me undressed. Now, in case you ask when I got conscious about what was happening—it was not in the next morning when I woke up! It was when I was sandwiched between them! I must confess it was great! I think I couldn't have continued living without this experience.

—Female confessor

The posting provides a sense of the conformity required by public normativity in regard to female sexuality: a woman should not get drunk in the presence of a man or men, because intoxication renders her as sexual prey, and sex for pleasure should never be part of a woman's expectation or repertoire. In conformity to this rule, the confessor projects an image of partial innocence by announcing her ability to control her drinking habits. But to the reader's eventual surprise, she not only ends up in the sexual company of two men simultaneously, but gets "sandwiched" and enjoys it. Her confession is organized according to the following moments that sharply oppose Turkish public principles regulating the sexual body:

1. Getting drunk
2. Having sex outside the boundaries of marriage
3. Having sex with more than one partner
4. Having sex with more than one partner *simultaneously*
5. Having anal sex
6. Enjoying all of the above

The narrative is twice intensified toward the end: first, by emphasizing that the experience was great; and second, by arguing that it would have been impossible to continue living without that experience. Such affective intensification of the sexual episode is important, since it raises the following question: is the woman who made the post trying to present an obscene image of herself, or is she, effectively, challenging the boundaries of established body politics?

Obscenity is likely not a personal value the woman sought to project, even though the affective intensification (of both sexual desire and narration) of her post contradicts socially and politically established norms. Instead, her post speaks of a struggle for the acceptance of sexual practices deemed deviant by dominant forces and the discourses they circulate. In these complex dynamics the female sexual body tries both to conform to and to resist the norms of political physiology, and by doing so, it expands itself into a critical oppositional space where it can be inscribed with new meanings, embedded in new social relations, and layered with the political potential of imagination. Thus, the simple textual exposition of affective states through the discursive mediation of ecstatic "sandwiching" inscribes Turkish networked public space with alternative forms of body politics.

The Significance of Affect in Turkish Online Sexual Networks

While Turkish governmental politics have extensively reinforced morally conservative sexual norms for the last decade, Turkish online sexual networks have expanded sexual practice, expression, and understanding. The pursuit of liberal sexuality and sexual values within these networks involves a counterpublic political investment. These dynamics are exemplified in the following post, which provides a firsthand overview of the tensions involved in the political regulation of sexuality in Turkey and makes its political message crystal clear:

I can't understand our governors. They try to blind us and limit our sexual freedom. Although people cannot be socially active anyway, they [the governors] try to block any possibility of even innocent sexual exposures. The suppressed sexual feelings then burst into instances of perversion, rape, and harassment. I can't understand why sexuality has been systematically converted into such a taboo. Good that we have this online space here.

—Female confessor

Tiziana Terranova (2004, 2) observes that there "is a tendency of informational flows to spill over from whatever network they are circulating in and hence to escape the narrowness of the channel and to open up to a large milieu." Terranova's insight focuses our attention to the multiplicity of indeterminate experiences that information networks may provide or into which they may mutate. Based on these possibilities for shift and mutation, I have argued that Turkish sexual networks are indeed affective networks with real political potential. The examples I provide illustrate how these networks have continuously organized themselves around two overlapping and mutually complementary fields of experience: those of sexual desire and of political counteraction. These fields produce affect while also being produced by it.

The intermeshing dynamics of sexual and political affect evoke two types of mediation. On the one hand, I identify a type of *explicit* mediation, where the language and content generated by sexual confessors captures the focus of networked community around sexuality and its somatic impulses. On the other hand, there is a level of *implicit* mediation, which triggers what Ahmed (2004, 45) identifies as a "rippling effect." This effect impels network members to reconsider the social processes involved in sexual normativity. I classify these dynamics as political, because they are at the center of shaping alternative body politics and thus serve as political counteractants within the larger Turkish social context. Considering the sensitivity of the Turkish government to criticism and oppositional political stances,[6] networked affect constitutes a viable channel for political agency, due to its capacity to stir social action outside tangible or distinctive structures. Given the ways in which the AKP government tries to control individuals at intimate levels and to limit sexual freedom, the role of networked affect as a collective gathering of a sexual counterpublic becomes obvious. The political success of Turkish online sexual communities lies in their ability to push back on the government's conservative Islamist agenda by publicly violating what is considered sacred in Islam—the practice of sex as an act of worship within the morality of marriage. The AKP government has realized the political charge of sexual confession sites and has abortively tried to shut them down on multiple occasions. Erotikitiraf.com has managed to find its way around such situations by consistently switching servers and domain names.

In the hope of opening up further discussion, I conclude with an argument made by Andrew Feenberg and Norm Friesen (2012, 3): "Although they appear marginal to politics in the usual sense, [online communities] are redefining the political in response to the omnipresence of technology." Feenberg and Friesen point out the centrality of the internet in the broadening of the public sphere to include new issues and problems. As I have argued above, networked affect can be a mediating and mobilizing force for producing new forms of social and political awareness through its ability to interlace somatic, social, and political intensities. The existence and circulation of affect within Turkish sexual networks is thus crucial for the transgressive resistance to a reactionary regime of body politics.

Notes

1. In her reading of Fanon's *Black Skin, White Mask*, Sara Ahmed (2004) analyzes how a black man becomes an object of fear as declared by a white child. Ahmed suggests that the fear experienced by the child is induced by memory traces of black men. This is an epitome of the ways in which affective intensities (in this case, fear) evoke confusion in taxonomies and conceptual categories: the body of a black man is dissolved within the memory of black men. Similarly, black bodies from memories do not simply resemble the body of a black man, but *are* the body of a black man. Within the given moment and context, bodies from memory and reality are merged into the same order of being.

2. For more information on arranged marriages and honor killings in Turkey, see Sev'Er and Yurdakul (2001).

3. Femen's website is http://femen.org/en/.

4. AKP is the acronym of Adalet ve Kalkınma Partisi, translated literally as "Justice and Development Party." Their website can be found at http://www.akparti.org.tr/english.

5. More on the story and people's reactions to it can be found at http://www.cbsnews.com/news/15-years-ago-bill-clintons-historic-denial/. The comments posted in the discussion section radiate a gamut of strong affective states.

6. Prime Minister Erdoğan's sensitivity toward political criticism is well documented. Erdoğan "has made no secret of his disdain for Turkish newspapers, which he accuses of bias and says he no longer reads," and he has filed "a $30,000 lawsuit against *Penguen*, a humorous magazine, for

depicting him as a series of animals, including a frog and a snake. The cartoonists did this to show solidarity with a fellow draughtsman who had been fined some $3,500 on charges of assailing the prime minister's honor by depicting him as a cat" (Economist 2005).

References

Ahmed, Sara. 2004. *The Cultural Politics of Emotion*. New York: Routledge.

Bataille, Georges. 1986. *Erotism: Death and Sensuality*. San Francisco: City Lights.

Berlant, Lauren, and Michael Warner. 1998. Sex in Public. *Critical Inquiry* 24 (2):547–566.

BirGun Halkin Gazetesi. 2012. Akdağ: Tecavüze Uğrayan Doğursun Gerekirse Devlet Bakar [Akdağ: a Rape Victim Should Give Birth; the State Will Take Care of the Child If Necessary]. *BirGun Halkin Gazetesi*, May 30. No longer available.

Casier, Marlies, and Joost Jongerden. 2011. *Nationalisms and Politics in Turkey: Political Islam, Kemalism, and the Kurdish Issue*. Abingdon, UK: Routledge.

Economist. 2005. Europe: Censored; the Turkish Press. *Economist*, April 2, 37.

Feenberg, Andrew. 1999. Experience and Culture: Nishida's Path "to the Things Themselves." *Philosophy East and West* 49 (1):28–44.

Feenberg, Andrew, and Norm Friesen. 2012. *(Re)inventing the Internet: Critical Case Studies*. Boston: Sense.

Foucault, Michel. 1990. *The History of Sexuality*. Vol. 1, *An Introduction*. New York: Random House.

Gould, Deborah. 2010. On Affect and Protest. In *Political Emotions*, ed. Janet Staiger, Ann Cvetkovich, and Ann Morris Reynolds, 18–44. New York: Routledge.

Hale, William M., and Ergun Özbudun. 2010. *Islamism, Democracy and Liberalism in Turkey: The Case of the AKP*. Abingdon, UK: Routledge.

İlkkaracan, Pınar. 2008. How Adultery Almost Derailed Turkey's Aspiration to Join the European Union. In *Deconstructing Sexuality in the Middle East: Challenges and Discourses*, ed. Pınar İlkkaracan, 41–64. Aldershot: Ashgate.

Kadioğlu, Ayşe. 1994. Women's Subordination in Turkey: Is Islam Really the Villain? *Middle East Journal* 48 (4):645–660.

MSNBC. 2012. Erdoğan: Kürtaj Cinayettir [Erdoğan: Abortion Is a Crime]. MSNBC. Available at http://www.ntvmsnbc.com/id/25352507.

Narli, Nilufer. 1993. The Rise of the Islamist Movement in Turkey. *Middle East Review of International Affairs* 3 (3):38–48.

Ogan, C. L., and Kursat Cagiltay. 2006. Confession, Revelation and Storytelling: Patterns of Use on a Popular Turkish Website. *New Media and Society* 8 (5):801–823.

Paasonen, Susanna. 2011. *Carnal Resonance: Affect and Online Pornography*. Cambridge, MA: MIT Press.

Protevi, John. 2009. *Political Affect: Connecting the Social and the Somatic*. Minneapolis: University of Minnesota Press.

Sev'Er, Aysan, and Gokcecicek Yurdakul. 2001. Culture of Honor, Culture of Change: A Feminist Analysis of Honor Killings in Rural Turkey. *Violence against Women* 7 (9):964–998.

Shannahan, Dervla Sara. 2009. Sexual Ethics, Marriage, and Sexual Autonomy: The Landscapes for Muslimat and Lesbian, Gay, Bisexual, and Transgendered Muslims. *Contemporary Islam* 3 (1):59–78.

Tanasković, Darko. 2010. *Neo-Osmanizam—Doktrina i Spoljnopolitička Praksa* [Neo-Ottomanism—Doctrine and Foreign-Policy Practice]. Belgrade: Službeni Glasnik.

Terranova, Tiziana. 2004. *Network Culture: Politics for the Information Age*. London: Pluto Press.

Tibi, Bassam. 2009. *Islam's Predicament with Modernity: Religious Reform and Cultural Change*. London: Routledge.

Warner, Michael. 2002. *Publics and Counterpublics*. Cambridge, MA: Zone Books.

Wetherell, Margaret. 2012. *Affect and Emotion: A New Social Science Understanding*. Los Angeles: Sage.

Yavuz, M. Hakan. 2003. *Islamic Political Identity in Turkey*. Oxford: Oxford University Press.

5   The Avatar and Online Affect

Ken Hillis

The introduction to this volume sets forth a number of definitions of affect and observes that most privilege the generation and experience of forms of intensity as central. Intensity is "more than." Its direct relationship to affect is analogous to the way that an individual's affective visceral or gut reaction to someone or something can be understood as more than an emotion but less than the overflowing excess that attends such experiences as sublimity and awe. Humans increasingly experience the affective qualities and capacities of this visceral reaction in networked digital settings. How is such a form of experience rendered and made possible? Answering this question through focusing on the mechanisms, assemblages, metaphysics, and economies by and through which affect generates and circulates across digital networks is the objective of this chapter.

I organize my discussion around the figure of the avatar in multiple-user virtual environment (MUVE) platforms such as Second Life and also make reference to a subset of MUVEs, massively multiplayer online role-playing games (MMORPG) such as World of Warcraft.[1] While avatars can be operated by forms of artificial intelligence, one of the acknowledged purposes for which humans fabricate avatars is so that they can serve as stand-ins for human individuals seeking to communicate affectively with one another both in and through virtual environments or space. Within digital public spheres such as Second Life that have become meaningful components of the public sphere for many networked individuals, online avatars have come not only to represent but also to supersede the individual operator (Hillis 2009). Avatars have a capacity to generate seemingly independent forms of networked affect unrelated to their human operators. An avatar in Second Life that turns to look back and wave at its human operator as it walks across a virtual space, for example, has the potential to induce for that operator and others the perception that it has about it intense qualities of liveliness that are seemingly independent of its operator. Avatars in MUVEs have been designed with the proprioception-influencing capacity to move their virtual bodies with a full six degrees of freedom within the two-dimensional frame of the screen interface, and their lively mobility across networked settings works to suggest that they possess independent qualities, affective affordances, and capacities equal to those of the humans who remain this side of the screen.

There is an ironic decentering of the human at play here that comes at the expense of a fuller acknowledgment of the human agency entailed in designing, implementing, and maintaining the technology that allows operators to experience avatars metaphorically and allegorically *as if* they really were human and therefore alive. Operators' and viewers' implicit acceptance of avatar agency, born in part from seeing avatars move independently and interact with other avatars, appearing to constitute something lively, runs parallel to the emphasis, within new materialist studies, on the affective agency of technological forms such as the algorithm (Ash, this volume; Parikka, this volume) and intelligent agents in the form of mobile apps. Identifying and assessing the fields of intensity produced and experienced through human engagement with avatars that do human bidding across digital networks and platforms is important for internet studies and research, given the distributed forms of agency such avatars exemplify, advertise, assemble, and support. In the following sections I examine four networked phenomena that, when conjoined, constitute a mechanism or assemblage capable of producing a range of fields of intensity also identifiable as forms of networked affect. These are (a) metaphors of virtual space, (b) the allegory of networked telepresence, (c) the use of indexical signs and sign/bodies that take the form of lively digital avatars, and (d) the contemporary reification of virtual mobility. I conclude by assessing some of the sociopolitical implications lodged within and flowing from the avatar in virtual space.

Virtual Space and Telepresence

Textual and visual metaphors of virtual space abound on the web. We get to the internet with Safari and Explorer. We "visit" "sites" on "platforms" and sometimes find "pages" that are "under construction" in retro but by-no-means abandoned "cyberspace." Such metaphors work to naturalize the idea of internet addresses as material places one might visit, even though we know intellectually that we don't really go "there." The reliance on using them to describe the internet has been present since its earliest days, including the use of textual metaphors of space in "chatrooms" on IRC (Internet Relay Chat) and in the descriptions of the imaginary spaces of MUDs (multiuser dungeons) and MOOs (MUDs, object-oriented)—e.g., "you enter a darkened room." With the development of the World Wide Web, spatial metaphors have taken a more visual turn. One example apposite to my argument is the often intricate, frequently sexualized, idealized, and increasingly photorealistic online simulations of virtual space through which avatars move (figure 5.1).

Metaphors of virtual space operate by positing a relationship between two-dimensional digital images on a screen and three-dimensional space this side of the interface.

Figure 5.1
Second Life avatars in virtual space.

A digital image of a tree, for example, has a metaphorical correspondence with a living tree. Understanding the digital as metaphoric is necessary, otherwise operators and viewers could not recognize the images they see. Visual spatial metaphors in MUVEs also operate allegorically. They invite an immersion with the interface that allows operators to imaginatively place themselves within the spatial metaphor depicted and allegorically enact components of their lives. This invitation and operators' acceptance of it draw in part on the long-established literary and visual trope of a hero-guide negotiating a journey through an allegorical landscape. This journey may take the form of a voyage of self-discovery, a quest to feel part of a community, or an attempt to seek one's fortune in trade, as do many who maintain an avatar in Second Life. The story of Christian's journey through the seven deadly sins in John Bunyan's *Pilgrim's Progress* (1606) is sometimes credited with establishing the literary genre in English, yet, as Jungian-inflected mythologist Joseph Campbell demonstrates, the trope occurs across cultures and throughout human history (Campbell 1968). Humans retell the story in myriad ways, textual and visual; MMORPGs such as World of Warcraft and Star Trek Online are predicated on it.

The trope of a hero negotiating a journey through an allegorical landscape has broad cultural affect, and its availability for individuals to enact its components through interactive and lively avatars has assisted its passage or translation into digital realms. That a spatial metaphor might be worth enacting as an allegory is connected to the second networked phenomena noted above, telepresence. Telepresence is key to any experience of virtual environments as lively in their affective nature and quality. Defined succinctly, it is the phenomenological experience of presence at a distance and is authorized and supported by the use of networked information and communications technologies. An example would be the practice of spouses, partners, and lovers separated by distance who leave audio-enabled webcams (such as Skype) open so that they can be with each other through the night and wake up together (Diep 2012; Neustaedter et al. 2012). Telepresence is, then, also allegorical to the degree that it allows for an experiential interchangeability between material and virtual presence. It authorizes the imaginative sense of a journey, or a passing between two places, as if I might materially be with you on Skype.

The possibilities for achieving greater affective intensities through telepresence have grown in parallel with increased bandwidth and more powerful software and hardware applications. Together they have moved the internet from a purely textual medium to the multisensory web that allows for more telepresent forms of intensely affective engagements with online moving images. There seems to be a broad, even transcendent desire to experience online virtual environments as ever more affective, a desire at perhaps its most extreme in Ray Kurzweil's "singularity" (2005), the time in the supposedly near future when human mind is conjoined with machine mind and individual immortality is achieved by uploading oneself to the network. Pierre Lévy (1998), Pierre Teilhard de Chardin (1964), and Kevin Kelly (1994) have offered complementary visions in the hyperbody, the noosphere, and the Hive Mind, respectively. An experience of online virtual environments as seeming to constitute actual space for lively forms of interaction has been possible for quite some time, and these engagements, in turn, increasingly bridge or possibly even bulldoze the divides between the virtual and the actual, the image and the text. The desire to view electronic networks as if they are equivalent to actual material places and spaces is a desire for an alternative or parallel ecosystem amenable to our physical occupation, though in exchange it requires our accepting its psychic colonization of us.

Indexical Signs

Indexical signs are a third mechanism and a component of the assemblage that works to produce networked affect. The idea of the indexical sign was first theorized by Charles Sanders Peirce (1839–1914) and is arguably his most important contribution to semiotics and sign theory. (Peirce's theory of the indexical sign is subsequently refined by Jacques Derrida (1976), with his provocative reading of "the trace.") Peirce recognized that the relationship between a sign and the object to which it refers lies not only in connotative mental associations between representation and referent but also in a direct, denotative, existential, or causal relation of the sign to its object. An indexical sign always points to an object or is a sample of that object. Smoke, for example, is an indexical sign of fire. Peirce writes that the index "signifies its object [or referent] solely by virtue of being really connected with it" (cited in Short 2004, 220) and that it is "independent of the mind using the sign" (Peirce 1992, 226). An index, Peirce writes,

is a sign which would, at once, lose the character which makes it a sign if its object were removed, but would not lose that character if there were no interpretant. Such, for example, is a piece of moulding with a bullet-hole in it as a sign of a shot; for without the shot there would have been no hole; but there is a hole there, whether anybody has the sense to attribute it to a shot or not. (quoted in Innis 1984, 9–10)

A crucial point here is that Peirce's identification of the index "compels us to recognize a relation of sign to object that is distinct from signification" (Peirce 1992, 223). This relation is "more than." It is the sign itself, independent of mind, *and* the direct, visceral connection between the indexical sign and the interpretant, the human being who interprets the relation between sign and object. As referents seemingly independent of human mind yet dependent for their meaning on human interpretation, indexical signs exceed modernity's binary understanding of representations as mere disenchanted stand-ins for their referents. Indexical signs convey liveliness.

The "more than" quality of indexical signs is powerfully affective. Peirce writes that the index "takes hold of our eyes, as it were, and forcibly directs them to a particular object, and there it stops [or arrests them]" (Peirce 1992, 226). "Like a pointing finger, [the index] exercises a real physiological force over the attention, like the power of a mesmerizer, and directs it to a particular object of sense" (Peirce 1992, 232). This mesmeric appeal to human perception is not unlike the potentially violent affect contained in the original meaning of conception: "to seize or tame" (Hillis 1999, 69). Daniel Defoe (1660–1731) captures the affective potential of indexical signs in *Robinson Crusoe* (1719) when the shipwrecked Crusoe discovers "the Print of a Man's naked Foot on the Shore" (Defoe 2007, 153) of the island where he has spent years stranded in solitude. The footprint directly and viscerally indicates to Crusoe, the sign's interpretant, the reality of the object (the presence of assumedly savage cannibals who wish to eat him). It seizes Crusoe's perceptive faculties. He is "Thunder-struck" and "like a Man perfectly confus'd and out of my self" (Defoe 2007, 154). Only in the safety of his fortification can he reflect on the footprint's meaning and describe himself as "terrify'd to the last Degree" (Defoe 2007, 154.). As index, the footprint is an uncanny trace made by a body that in its absence is rendered even more affectively there.

Online avatars operate in a parallel manner. They are indexical signs of their operators. As moving images that speak and circulate in and through online virtual environments composed of naturalized spatial metaphors that their operators allegorically enter, avatars direct attention to themselves less as representations and more as actual traces of human operators, rendered lively and available through telepresence. This indexical relation between sign (avatar) and object (operator) is tacitly understood by all who witness the avatar. Peirce's theory would identify the avatar's operator as the object to whom the avatar always points. Writing in a mid-Victorian context, he could not anticipate that the sign and the object would merge with the interpretant. In MUVEs such as Second Life, human operators, networked and telepresent, are interpolated as both sign and its interpretant. They are affected by and connected through the sign to themselves and others as interpretants who make affective meaning of the signs that point back to themselves as interpretants. In such a recursive fashion, avatars become flickering indexes hovering between conscious and nonconscious, human and machine, forms of agency.

Sign/Bodies

Carolyn Marvin and David Ingle point out that media "re-create the illusion of bodily presence, the most basic of all ritual gestures" (1999, 140). Images of gesturing and moving bodies on the web constitute part of that illusion and are crucial to forms of networked affect. Gilles Deleuze writes that "movement is … explained by the insertion of duration into matter … [where duration] is called life when it appears in this movement" (1988, 94). Human perception accords the quality of liveliness to movement, and the concept of the sign/body, a term coined after taking account of Deleuze's theory of the "movement-image," offers an explanatory framework for how avatars instinctively hail human perception. And they do so in ways that serve to generate a field of intensity around them, together with affective responses on the part of their operators and other viewers.

In proposing his concept of movement-image in *Cinema 1*, Deleuze (1986, 56–61) acknowledges his considerable debt to Peirce's concept of the indexical sign. Deleuze identifies the rise of the cinema as pivotal in revealing the phenomenological limitations that ensue from the naturalized binary that places images in the qualitative realm of consciousness and movement in the different realm of quantifiable space. Deleuze notes that such a binary—one erected between idealism and materialism, interior and exterior, and, by extension, sign and referent—serves to divorce consciousness from the thing itself. The movement-image allows a film's spectators or interpretants to bridge this gap between perception and ideology.

Cinema, a technology that renders image equal to movement and, therefore, sign equal to reality, erases the psychological distinctions between the image as a psychic or experiential reality and movement as a physical reality dependent on moving through space. Just as in online MUVEs, in cinema there are no actual moving bodies distinct from spectators' perception of movement. The image's ability to move confers on it an intense quality of immanence, which for Deleuze leads to a situation of "more than," one in which "the image exists in itself. ... The identity of the image and movement leads [spectators] to conclude immediately that the movement-image and matter are identical" (Deleuze 1986, 59). The experience Deleuze identifies relies on the image passing at the level of human experience from one state to another. Bodies and objects may produce and experience intensity as they so pass, and I link this to Deleuze's insight, which I extend via actor-network theory, to suggest that the avatar and the human being to whom it directly points are also instinctively experienced as co-constitutive parts of a networked whole. The sign/body occupying networked virtual space points to those online forms of signification mounted by web users and participants, whose practices and techniques reveal the broader project of using the web to collapse the binary that Deleuze identifies; that is, to render the web as the realm both of the image and consciousness and of space and movement, and thereby to reconnect consciousness to the thing.

Brain science research using immersive virtual reality (VR) technology confirms that individuals lose track of their body locations in virtual settings. H. Henrik Ehrsson reports that it is possible to determine the experience of embodiment through "visual perspective in conjunction with correlated multi-sensory information from the body" (Ehrsson 2007, 1048). To induce the sensation of out-of-body experience in subjects, Ehrsson had them wear immersive virtual reality head-mounted displays that transmitted images of the subjects filmed from behind. The display prevented these subjects from seeing any other spatial representation or image of themselves in the virtual space. Ehrsson then used the end of a rod to press on the subjects' chests while at the same time holding a different rod in front of the camera behind them, which made it seem as if the virtual individual viewed from behind was also being poked in the chest. Subjects reported perceiving their chests being probed, yet they also sensed that it was the virtual individual lodged within the display (in other words, their avatar) that was being touched by the rod. In a second experiment Bigna Lenggenhager et al. (2007) demonstrated that the sight of a humanlike figure, such as an avatar in virtual space, combined with the actual stroking of the subject's body, can induce an experience of relocating the subject's sense of self away from bodily location in material space and toward what the avatar "sees" from its point of view in virtual space. As Ehrsson (2007, 1048) comments, "We feel that our self is located where the eyes are."

Deleuze, Ehrsson, and Lenggenhager, et al. confirm in different ways that moving images hail perception autonomically, and the viewing of a moving image of an object, thing, or event has the potential to authorize the perceptual sense of experiential access to a trace of the referent. The dynamics of signification further suggest to human perception that the moving image/icon connects metaphorically and allegorically to the thing it stands for and points toward: the body of its human operator or referent. The autonomic reception of the moving image online, operating as if it were the trace of an actual human being located elsewhere, parallels the psychic desire to receive this image in the same way—that is, as if it were a transmogrification that could render actually present the distant individual it represents. In such a way does communicability become an end in itself, so as to lend credence to the idea and even the sensation that our avatars are ourselves.

The dynamic of passing from one state to another (or at least the sense of so doing) that informs Deleuze's theorization of the cinema is phenomenological and allegorical. The online moving avatar also operates in a phenomenological and allegorical fashion in relation to the human user with whom others perceive it has telepresent connection. Avatar, a Sanskrit term, translates as "he passes or crosses down." Avatars online reflect the widespread interest in adopting digital forms that can "pass or cross down" into the virtual world, to become inherently more mobile, and to move beyond bricks and mortar in order to reach networked individuals focused on the display. Allegory can be defined as "the aesthetic device of personification" (Nelson 2001, 202), and whether deployed in TV ads or as an avatar in a networked virtual world it remains a figural device serving to simulate the possible.

Allegory is a means by which what remains immaterial or potential—in this case actual humans in digital form—is given imaginative yet figural embodiment, so that this figure then may seem to exist or be probable. This is the discursive value of calling a moving image, such as one's online avatar, a virtual object—it pushes the image, in this case that of the avatar, toward seemingly greater materiality, yet at the same time conveys the value of exchangeability between the virtual and the material that lies at the intersection of the simulation. Conceptually, this state of potential may then have a chance of becoming actual. For members of a networked culture of virtuality, however, the allegorically inflected potential of the moving image to achieve figural embodiment also recommends it as a fetish object, at least in part because of its virtual status—a mobile status to the degree that human desire confers on the virtual object or avatar the eventual potential to "pass" or "cross," to metaphysically transubstantiate into material form. In such a way, then, does the avatar also suggest allegory's ongoing centrality in the expression of desire for unity between the ideal (and virtual) Platonic realm of meaning and the specific materiality of the object or human for which it stands.

An individual's conjoined experiences of telepresence and sign/bodies work together to suggest to her or his perceptive faculties the possibility that these allegorical online images and indexical signs of moving bodies are phenomenologically affective traces of the individuals to whom they point. The avatar figuratively indicates how networked affect can be induced by digital media's specific kinds of psychic and experiential effects—effects that are "more than" those noted by Deleuze in moving, touching, or disturbing us. This is because in the cinema the spectator must work to identify with the moving images on the screen in ways that exceed the psychically easier task

Figure 5.2
Array of idealized self-images in Second Life.

of identifying with online virtual beings that operators believe they have created in the first place, and often in some version of an idealized self-image (figure 5.2). The indexical worlds of MUVEs such as Second Life, then, point to the importance of digital affectivity: they are populated by avatars that have the power to move or disturb us, and this power is anchored by their telepresent locations in networked virtual space. Their seeming mobility—their ability to move through this space—works to suggests how virtual technologies have come to be understood, however implicitly and in however understated or even unstated a fashion, as having the capacities and affordances to authorize action and thereby induce affect at a distance.

Mobility

The rise of the avatar moving effortlessly through virtual space points directly to the related issue of mobility. While many fleshy bodies sitting in front of screens large and small may feel, or be encouraged to feel, that they are insufficiently mobile for the dictates of today's just-in-time, do-it-yourself, overworked world, in settings such as Second Life, their avatars are body doubles that can seem to constitute a kind of individuated virtual public as they move about the ersatz spaces they appear to populate at will. In so doing, these avatars accrue intense affect as they perform an imagistic body politics that viscerally depicts the ineffable difficulties and some of the unresolved problems of neoliberal realities and attendant forms of virtual mobility. I note the performative qualities of such politics—avatars are in the position to act as increasingly independent signs for the ways that their operators may desire to think. Avatars have come to accrue considerable affect through such qualities and potentialities precisely at the moment when most individuals cannot or dare not yet give adequate, let alone critical, voice to the possibility that the future will be more of the flexible, disintermediated, neoliberal same, given the overwhelmingly corporate-friendly encouragement, promoted in ubiquitous services such as Google search (with its basis on "relevant" answers directly linked to one's previous internet search history). For it is at this in-between experiential moment—before the process can be fully named, yet after it has been experienced within the parameters of an overall experience economy—that affect, here in the form of a fascination with the avatar's lively mobility, may most fully flow.

The moving image of the avatar, part of a larger swirling world of motion, can provide some psychic compensation for feeling insufficiently mobile, precisely because it depicts and therefore promises at least a virtual realization of a broadly based desire for greater actual mobility across all registers of embodied, economic, and social life. The avatar, therefore, in concert with users' experience of online telepresence, is a virtual object or body that, in its ability to suggest that a trace of the human now resides in technological form and circulates through digital networks, and vice versa, depicts a merger of humans and technology in its seeming to pass, in hyperallegorical fashion, back and forth from one state to another. As such, at the very moment when the idea that the market should occupy the pride of place once enjoyed by society gains its greatest strength, the avatar, seeming to conjoin human and nonhuman, points directly to our current status as human beings situated somewhere along a historical continuum running from the old liberal humanist subject to newer forms of ever-more-monetized patterns and interactive distributions. Through these patterns and distributions our telepresent body doubles can affectively circulate in our stead across digital networks, as both moving teleoperators and as disturbing texts breaching the ineffable and teaching what it might be like to live life in the universal, yet ever-so-privatized, Cloud.

In all of this the avatar generates a field of intensity that encourages participants in virtual environments such as Second Life to experience it as somehow equivalent to its human interpretant. This dynamic is part of a wider resurgence of an intensely capitalized techno-metaphysics that seeks to realize, through the turn to networked virtual spaces, an experiential synthesis of presence and appearance, here and there, thing and concept, and of the materially real and the ideal. At a moment of almost instinctive support for the idea of mobility as a major resource of contemporary neoliberal life, the online moving image of the avatar—our body double and home away from home—pulls us along in its tow, catching us in the affective field of intensity it establishes at the recursive intersection of material fixity and digital flow. Awesome.

Whither Affective Agency

Cruise missiles. Immersive virtual reality. Telerobotics. Webcams. All are forms of applied science that trade in what were once the realms of magic and the divine. These technologies operate within a highly mediatized, increasingly screen-based commodity culture increasingly anchored to promoting personal experience as the highest goal and value. Many participants in this culture live in awe of the field of intensity that the spectacle has become. These members are propelled by an implicit but dominant belief system, within which "for one to whom the real world becomes real images, mere images are transformed into real beings" (Debord 1994, 17). If, in earlier modern eras, the awe-inducing grandeur of a mountain range or the aurora borealis could induce experiences of the sublime in humbled pilgrim viewers, today significant components of this moral power have been relocated to information machines and the fields of intensity they are capable of generating in concert with us, their human "users." In a world that mass media repeatedly instructs us is overwhelmingly polluted, rapidly warming, economically imperiled, strife ridden, and poorly governed—a world that modernity has rendered disenchanted and separated from much of human experience—sublime grandeur and any accompanying affect are now often generated through the seemingly overwhelming power of digital media technologies and digital networks. Second Life's participants imaginatively transcend the here and now. In a world of individuals who have been raised with the illusion that they are in full control of their lives but who have come, as commodities, to understand otherwise, the avatar deeply resonates with the need to maintain control over some part of one's life. MUVE operators fabricate body doubles, and through these indexical sign/bodies seem to achieve self-control as they merge with the immanence of lively and expressive technical affect, if only for the moment.

In *One-Dimensional Man* (1964) Herbert Marcuse speaks to societal confusion about the meaning of technology and its place in society. While technology is a social relation that functions within the realm of epistemology, the juggernaut it has become requires work to understand the intersecting dynamics by which it is increasingly accorded ontological status. Marcuse argues that when technics itself becomes a universal form of material production, "it circumscribes an entire culture; it projects a historical totality—a 'world'" (1964, 154). The communication and cultural studies scholar James Carey (1975) arrived at a complementary conclusion when he came to realize that his binary model of communication as transmission versus communication as ritual was in the process of breaking down. His 1997 comment bears repeating: "To reconceive transmission as ritual is to reveal communications not as a means of sending messages *but as the constitution of a form of life*" (Carey 1997, 11, emphasis added). Communication, Carey was suggesting in the late 1990s, itself had already become "both a model of and a model for reality" (Carey 1997, 10)—in short, a conjoined and affective world.

For better and for worse, networked information and communication technologies, including the software and information machines developed since the late 1990s that allow avatars to stand, turn, and seemingly acknowledge their human referent as well as other avatars proximal to them in virtual space, now constitute a form of life that calls upon us, as forms of signs ourselves, to engage our allegorical aspect of mind and enter, by means of our body doubles, virtual space's many perceived fields of intensity.

The affective performances of a MUVE operator's online avatar further point to the need to believe in what Deleuze (2001) terms "necessary fictions." This is the Humean idea that our nature requires us to believe in the idea of something larger than ourselves. I link this idea to my point that we create technical, often highly aestheticized, forms (such as the networked digital avatar) based on what we variously identify as ideologies and discourse strategies precisely so these forms may generate the sense of affective intensity that allows us to then really believe in them and, finally, even love and embrace them as necessary fictions. I would also note that at times of great sociopolitical and socioeconomic uncertainty, art forms, including popular art forms such as those crafted in virtual worlds, can serve as forms of becoming—as forms of collective conversation about the limits of our reality, our perception, and our understanding of what we mean by the self. As Deleuze (2001, 16) observes, the work of art is less a representation than an experience of the sensible. Such art forms manifest an interest in expanding the definition of what it means to be alive to include seemingly independent character formations that beckon us from the other side of the screen. Yet transcendence always remains the outcome of immanence (Deleuze 2001, 31). At a time when the experience economy has developed to such a degree that the commercialized appeal to affect is now all but ubiquitous, by turning to the web in search of new forms of life, even though one cannot actually live in art, one may turn to virtuality to induce an experience so infused with networked affect that it comes to constitute a world in itself when faced with living on a disenchanted, disaffected, and overly financialized planet.

The networked phenomena I have discussed—metaphors of virtual space, telepresence as allegory, digital sign/bodies, and virtual mobility—are crucial to any success that this form of communication technology, directly trading in the metaphysics and visible meanings of liveliness, may accrue. The purpose of this chapter has been to argue how these phenomena, operating today within the contexts and possibilities of an expansive experience economy, together constitute a mechanism that is central to generating the circulation and experience of networked affect. For many individuals who are online all or a lot of the time, information and communication technology has become the contemporary "something more than" in which they need to believe, with the avatar's indexical liveliness the necessary fiction borne on the wings of phenomenologically induced affect.

Note

1. Earlier research informing aspects of this chapter's arguments appeared in parts of chapter 4, Hillis 2009.

References

Campbell, Joseph. [1949] 1968. *The Hero with a Thousand Faces*. Princeton: Princeton University Press.

Carey, James. 1975. A Cultural Approach to Communication. *Communication* 2:1–22.

Carey, James. 1997. Reflections on the Project of (American) Cultural Studies. In *Cultural Studies in Question*, ed. Marjorie Ferguson and Peter Golding, 1–24. London: Sage.

Debord, Guy. 1994. *The Society of the Spectacle*. Trans. Donald Nicholson-Smith. New York: Zone Books.

Defoe, Daniel. [1719] 2007. *Robinson Crusoe*. New York: Oxford University Press.

Deleuze, Gilles. 1986. *Cinema 1: The Movement-Image*. Trans. Hugh Tomlinson and Barbara Habberjam. Minneapolis: University of Minnesota Press.

Deleuze, Gilles. 1988. *Bergsonism*. Trans. Hugh Tomlinson and Barbara Habberjam. New York: Zone Books.

Deleuze, Gilles. 2001. *Pure Immanence: Essays on a Life*. Trans. Anne Boyman. New York: Zone Books.

Derrida, Jacques. 1976. *Of Grammatology*. Trans. Gayatri Chakravorty Spivak. Baltimore: Johns Hopkins University Press.

Diep, Francie. 2012. Long Distance Relationships May Benefit From "Hug Shirts," Other Technologies. *Huffington Post*. Available at http://www.huffingtonpost.com/2012/02/12/long-distance-relationshi_n_1271210.html.

Ehrsson, H. Hendrik. 2007. The Experimental Induction of Out-of-Body Experiences. *Science* 317 (5841):1048.

Hillis, Ken. 1999. *Digital Sensations: Space, Identity, and Embodiment in Virtual Reality*. Minneapolis: University of Minnesota Press.

Hillis, Ken. 2009. *Online a Lot of the Time: Ritual, Fetish, Sign*. Durham: Duke University Press.

Innis, Robert, ed. 1984. *Semiotics: An Introductory Anthology*. Bloomington: Indiana University Press.

Kelly, Kevin. 1994. *Out of Control: The New Biology of Machines, Social Systems, and the Economic World*. Menlo Park: Addison-Wesley.

Kurzweil, Ray. 2005. *The Singularity Is Near: When Humans Transcend Biology*. New York: Viking.

Lenggenhager, Bigna, et al. 2007. Video Ergo Sum: Manipulating Bodily Self-Consciousness. *Science* 317 (5841):1096–1099.

Lévy, Pierre. 1998. *Becoming Virtual: Reality in the Digital Age*. Trans. Robert Bononno. New York: Plenum.

Marcuse, Herbert. 1964. *One-Dimensional Man: Studies in the Ideology of Advanced Industrial Society*. Boston: Beacon Press.

Marvin, Carolyn, and David Ingle. 1999. *Blood Sacrifice and the Nation: Totem Rituals and the American Flag*. Cambridge: Cambridge University Press.

Nelson, Victoria. 2001. *The Secret Life of Puppets*. Cambridge, MA: Harvard University Press.

Neustaedter, Carman, Judge Tejinder, Serena Hillman, Erick Oduor, and Carolyn Pang. 2012. Connecting Families through Technology. Available at http://www.sfu.ca/~eoduor/CHI2012.pdf.

Peirce, Charles Sanders. 1992. *The Essential Peirce: Selected Philosophical Writings*. Vol. 1, *1867–1893*. Ed. Nathan Houser and Christian Kloesel. Bloomington: Indiana University Press.

Short, T. L. 2004. The Development of Peirce's Theory of Signs. In *The Cambridge Companion to Peirce*, ed. Cheryl Misak, 214–240. Toronto: University of Toronto Press.

Teilhard de Chardin, Pierre. 1964. *The Future of Man*. Trans. Norman Denny. New York: Harper and Row.

6 Affect and Drive

Jodi Dean

Anxiety

Growing anxiety accompanies extensions of popular media. More communication leads to more worry—porn and predators, identity theft, loss of privacy, wasted time. Jacques Lacan associates the affect that is anxiety with *jouissance*, the surplus enjoyment he designates as *objet a* (Lacan 2007, 147). Although anxiety seems to have no object (and thus differs from a fear or phobia), Lacan argues that it has to be approached in terms of *objet a*, the impossible object, surplus object, or object-cause designating excess enjoyment. Anxiety about networked media is, in this view, anxiety about enjoyment.

Slavoj Žižek describes the way enjoyment constitutes itself as "stolen," or as present and possible only insofar as one is deprived of it (Žižek 1993, 203–206). *I would have read a serious novel, cultivated an organic garden, driven senior citizens to the polls if I hadn't spent all day on Facebook. If I hadn't gotten absorbed in Facebook, I would have enjoyed. I would have spent time with my children, organized the workers, written a masterpiece had I not clicked on the cat videos and shared photos with fifteen hundred friends.* Blaming my failure to enjoy on Facebook compensates me for my failure by promising that *were it not for Facebook,* I would enjoy. My failure is not my fault.

The theft of enjoyment positions enjoyment as an object of desire. Allowing us to fantasize that we would actually prefer to be reading literary tomes, laboring in a weedy garden, and participating in a political process designed to ensure that political change never occurs, it postpones our confrontation with drive. Confident in what we would prefer to do, if only we could, we overlook what we are actually doing. *There's no way I spend three hours a day on Twitter! It's* important *for me to tweet my reaction to the events of the day!*

The fantasy of enjoyment displaces the fact that we are already enjoying, that we get off, just a little bit, in and through our multiple, repetitive, mediated interactions. It thereby occludes the economy of the drive. The fantasy of enjoyment's theft screens us from the Real of our enjoyment, the enjoyment that we can't avoid, even if we don't want it.

In Lacanian psychoanalysis, desire and drive each designate a way that the subject relates to enjoyment. Desire is always a desire to desire, a desire that can never be fulfilled, a desire for a *jouissance* that can never be attained. In contrast, drive attains *jouissance* in the repetitive process of not reaching it. Failure (or the thwarting of the aim) provides its own sort of success. If desire is like the path of an arrow, drive is like the course of a boomerang. What is fundamental at the level of the drive, Lacan teaches, is "the movement outwards and back in which it is structured" (Lacan 1998, 177). Through this repetitive movement outward and back the subject can miss his object but still achieve his aim, can "find satisfaction in the very circular movement of repeatedly missing its object" (Žižek 1999, 297). Because failure produces enjoyment, because the subject enjoys through repetition, drive captures the subject. Žižek writes, "Drive is something in which the subject is caught, a kind of acephalous force which persists in its repetitive movement" (Žižek 1999, 297). The subject gets stuck doing the same thing over and over again because this doing produces enjoyment. *Tweet. Tweet. Tweet. Click. Click. Click.*

Anxieties around networked media express our anxiety in the face of our enjoyment. We are captured doing not what we want but what we must. My concern in this essay is with a specific aspect of this stuckness, namely, the feedback loops, the circuits of drive, entrapping contemporary subjects. When networked personal communication and entertainment media are analyzed through the logic of drive, they appear not as something we want but as something we lack. Ubiquitous communicating persists as a tangle of objects that are difficult to avoid, as an inescapable circuit in which we are caught, compelled, driven. This circuit is that of communicative capitalism, the materialization of democratic ideals in the contemporary information and entertainment networks necessary for globalized neoliberalism (Dean 2002). Communicative capitalism relies on networks that generate and amplify enjoyment. People *enjoy* the circulation of affect that presents itself as contemporary communication. The system is intense; it draws us in. Even when we think we aren't enjoying, we enjoy (*all this email, I am so busy, so important; my time is too precious to waste on another Facebook game … but my score is going up; it's such a burden having so many, many friends—oh, and I should tweet it so they know how busy I am*).

Blogs, Facebook, Memegenerator, Tumblr, Twitter: they produce and circulate affect as a binding technique (see Karppi, this volume; Pybus, this volume). Affect, or *jouissance* in Lacanian terms, is what accrues from reflexive communication, from communication for its own sake, from the endless circular movement of commenting, adding notes and links, bringing in new friends and followers, layering and interconnecting myriad communication platforms and devices. Every tweet or comment, every forwarded image or petition, accrues a tiny affective nugget, a little surplus enjoyment, a smidgen of attention that attaches to it, making it stand out from the larger flow before it blends back in (see Cho, this volume). We might find ourselves more fearful, or seem somehow secure, even if we have no idea what we're looking for or what we've found. Unable to find a given dot, we feel, in ways that exceed our conscious perception, the movement of multiple colliding dots.

These affective links are stronger than hypertextual ones. Their resonance remains and continues after specific links are no longer operative. In flame wars, spam, and strategic friending (friending not as a sign of affiliation but in order to track one's enemy), intense feeling accompanies and reinforces code. Even failures to forward and refusals to link have affective impact: *why didn't she friend me? Why didn't he put me on his blogroll?* In a world of code, gaps and omissions can become knots of anxiety.

Affective attachments to media are not in themselves sufficient to produce actual communities—bloggers are blogging but the blogosphere doesn't exist. Conversely, the circulation of affect through multiple, networked media does not imply stimulus junkies in blank-eyed isolation before their screens. Affective networks produce *feelings* of community, or what we might call "community without community." They enable mediated relationships that take a variety of changing, uncertain, and interconnected forms as they feed back upon each other in ways we can never fully account for or predict. So while the merger and divergence of relations in affective networks resist formalization, the circulation of intensities leaves traces we might mark and follow.

Spectacle

In his *Comments on the Society of the Spectacle*, published twenty years after *The Society of the Spectacle*, Guy Debord offers the notion of the "integrated spectacle" as the highest stage of the spectacular society. Although he doesn't describe the integrated spectacle as a reflexive circuit or as the spectacle's turning in upon itself, such reflexivity seems to be its primary conceptual innovation. Debord writes, "For the final sense of the integrated spectacle is this—that it has integrated itself into reality to the same extent as it was describing it, and that it was reconstructing it as it was describing it. As a result, this reality no longer confronts the integrated spectacle as something alien" (Debord 1998, 9). The integrated spectacle is an element of the world it depicts; it is part of the scene upon which it looks. It is a circuit.

Debord misses the circuitry of the integrated spectacle because his account of the spectacle is embedded in a model of broadcast media. His arguments proceed as if the problem of the spectacle remained, for all its dispersion, ultimately a matter of top-down control, of actors and spectators. Debord worries about images as the individual's "principal connection to the world." The problem, though, isn't with the image's displacement of language and critical thought, or even with its commodity function. Rather, Debord's worry stems from the fact that the images the spectator sees are "chosen and constructed by *someone else*" (Debord 1998, 27). When "chosen by someone else" is the problem, the solution seems like it can be found in choosing and constructing for oneself—*and maybe with cool, free and open-source software, with photo and video uploading and sharing capabilities: freedom through smartphones plus Instagram.* If the problem of the image is that it comes from "someone else," then participatory technology is the solution. Anyone who makes her own images is a threat, a radical, a revolutionary. But this solution leaves out underlying questions of access and ownership, not to mention the fundamental trap of an ever-intensifying image environment as more and more of us upload videos to YouTube. Debord suggests that in the spectacular society, "those who control information" can alter at will individual reputations. He doesn't consider what changes when we alter our images ourselves (*I should have never posted those party pics on Facebook!*). He can't allow, in other words, for the possibility that in choosing for ourselves, in participating in the production of the spectacle, we might contribute to our own capture.

Discussion poses a problem similar to the manipulated image. Debord claims that "spectacular discourse leaves no room for any reply" (Debord 1998, 29). This doesn't apply to contemporary networked information and entertainment media: it's easy to "reply all"—although these replies, like the others circulating around and through us, don't feel like responses; they are just more contributions to be deleted, stored, or forwarded. Debord writes that people have "never been less entitled to make their opinions heard" (Debord 1998, 22). Again, under communicative capitalism, the opposite is the case. Everyone not only has a right to express an opinion, but each is positively enjoined to—*vote, text, comment, share, blog.* Constant communication is an obligation. Every interaction, transaction, inaction, reaction is construed in terms of a conversation. Debord rightly emphasizes the repetition constitutive of the spectacle. Arguments in the spectacle prove themselves "by going round in circles," "by coming back to the start." Yet he laments that "there is no place left where people can discuss the realities which concern them" (Debord 1998, 19). Today people discuss the realities that concern them everywhere and all the time—Tumblr, Facebook, Twitter, they ooze with the realities of individual concern. Discussion, far from displaced, has itself become a barrier against acts, as action is perpetually postponed. What appears as an exchange of reasons is a vehicle for the circulation of affect. The lack of action is the abundance of discussion viewed from a different angle.

Debord criticizes the experts who serve the media and state, experts he presents as falsifiers and fools. His argument, again reinforcing an underlying assumption that participatory media technologies might prove a way out of spectacular society, relies on a faith in amateurs, in ordinary people, individuals with the "capacity to see things for themselves" (Debord 1998, 18). Insofar as Debord's critique positions professionals as completely bound to the spectacular state, it relies on a suspicion toward expertise. Not only can expert knowledge not be trusted, but there is really no such thing as expertise: "The ability to falsify is unlimited" (Debord 1998, 18). Failing to follow his argument to the end, Debord implies that nonexpert knowledge necessarily brings with it capacities for resistance and transgression. This may be true under mass media, particularly in the case of censorious mass media. In the setting of communicative capitalism, however, another name for the impossibility of expertise, for falsification without limit, is the decline of symbolic efficiency. How do we know whom to believe or trust? Suspicion or even uncertainty toward expertise goes all the way down: skepticism toward politicians and the media, scientists and academics, extends to local knowledges, knowledges rooted in experience, and anything at all appearing on the internet. Not only has amateurism and gut-level or street knowledge supplanted what was previously considered expertise, but even amateur and everyday knowledge is now rejected as nothing more than opinion, and opinion that is necessarily limited, biased, and countered by others. The ability to falsify *is* unlimited. The lack of a capacity to know is the other side of the abundance of knowledge.

Finally, correlative to the embeddedness of Debord's critique of the image, discussion, and expertise in mass media, is his presumption that the spectacle is a form of state power, that it is a vehicle for mastery over the people. Understood reflexively, constant, pervasive communication can be a regime of control in which the people willingly and happily report on their views and activities and stalk their friends. We don't need spectacles staged by politicians and the mass media. We can make and be our own spectacles—and this is much more entertaining. There is always something new to be found on the internet. Corporate and state power need not go to the expense and trouble of keeping people entertained, passive, and diverted. We prefer to do that ourselves. Mark Andrejevic's analysis of the constellation of voyeurism and self-disclosure in interactive media (his focus is on the message board Television without Pity) persuasively demonstrates the ways even dismissive, critical engagement with television binds viewers more closely to the shows they claim to hate. The result, he argues, is a "reflexive redoubling that amounts to an active form of self-submission" (Andrejevic 2007, 160). Networked, participatory spectacles let us stage and perform our own entrapment.

Debord's claim that, in the society of the spectacle, "the uses of media guarantee a kind of eternity of noisy insignificance" applies better to communicative capitalism as a disintegrated, networked, spectacular circuit (Debord 1998, 15). Key to this circulation is the fact that networks are not only networks of computers, protocols, and fiberoptic cables. They are also affective networks capturing people.

Movement

Critical media theorists have recently begun to consider the affective dimension of networks. Describing the shift in thought toward affect, Patricia Clough writes that the affective turn marks "an intensification of self-reflexivity (processes turning back on themselves to act on themselves) in information/communication systems, including the human body; in archiving machines, including all forms of media technologies and human memory; in capital flows, including the circulation of value through human labor and technology; and in biopolitical networks of discipline, surveillance, and control" (Clough 2007, 3). Some of the recent work on affect and media technologies extends from Michael Hardt's and Antonio Negri's *Empire* (which is influenced by Gilles Deleuze and Félix Guattari). In the context of outlining empire as a new global political-economic formation, Hardt and Negri discuss the expansion and proliferation of communication networks as well as the role of informatization in the post-Fordist economy. Among the changes in labor they associate with informatization is "the production and manipulation of affect" (Hardt and Negri 2000, 293). Here they are concerned with often inchoate, preconscious, and shared feelings—of attachment, affection, excitement, fear, ease, or well-being—as products. Hardt and Negri view affective labor as including such seemingly diverse sectors as entertainment, healthcare, and women's unpaid labor. Each of these areas involves the production of moods and feelings, be they those of thrill and amusement, vitality and security, or care and belonging. Women's affective labor is particularly important to Hardt and Negri's account because it produces social networks. They don't link these social networks directly to the internet; neither do they take up the disruptive dimensions of networked intensities. Nonetheless, their association of affective labor with the production of social networks opens up the possibility of conceiving communication networks not simply in terms of linked machines but as networks that are constitutively affective.

Alexander Galloway and Eugene Thacker go further in this direction when they critique Hardt and Negri for relying on a simple symmetry between empire and the revolutionary force opposing it, the multitude. For Galloway and Thacker, the network form itself needs to be interrogated, particularly with regard to the constitutive tension "between unitary aggregation and anonymous distribution, between the intentionality and agency of individuals and groups on the one hand, and the uncanny, unhuman intentionality of the network as an 'abstract' whole" (Galloway and Thacker 2007, 155). My claim is that this uncanny intentionality is best understood through the psychoanalytic notion of drive. The loops and repetitions of the acephalous circuit of drive describe the movement of the networks of communicative capitalism, the ways its flows capture subjects, intensities, and aspirations. Accompanying each repetition, each loop or reversal, is a little nugget of enjoyment. We contribute to the networks, as creative producers and vulnerable consumers, because we enjoy it. In fact the open architecture of the internet enables and requires the capture of enjoyment insofar as it is premised on users' contributions, alterations, and engagement. It's not like cinema, where people only have to show up. For communication networks to function at all (as is abundantly clear in Web 2.0 and 4G mobile networks) people have to use them, play with them, add to them, and extend them. Our participation does not subvert communicative capitalism. It drives it. Again, contemporary information and communication networks are essentially affective networks.

Tiziana Terranova also jumps off from Hardt and Negri's discussion of empire in terms of a network of networks. Particularly compelling in this regard is her rejection of static accounts of the internet as a global grid or extended database that displaces attention from movement in and through the networks. Communication networks are dynamic. Terranova writes, "A piece of information spreading throughout the open space of the network is not only a vector in search of a target, it is also a potential transformation of the space crossed that always leaves something behind—a new idea, a new affect (even an annoyance), a modification of the overall topology" (Terranova 2005, 51). This something left behind, this product of movement through the networks, should be thought of in terms of enjoyment: both result from circulation through a communicative space.

Terranova approaches this affective production, however, by way of the image (she positions the image as a sort of bioweapon in an informational ecology). Although the image may be too restrictive a notion to account for the variety of contributions to contemporary networks—music, sounds, words, sentences, games, videos, fragments of code, viruses, bots, crawlers, and the flow of interactions themselves through blogs, Twitter, Facebook, and YouTube—Terranova rightly highlights that what's at stake in the image "is the kind of affect that it packs, the movements that it receives, inhibits, and/or transmits" (Terranova 2005, 42). The most interesting aspect of the image, in other words, is the way that it is not simply itself but is itself plus a nugget or shadow or trace of intensity. An image is itself and more.

Psychoanalysis can be of some assistance in theorizing the movements Terranova associates with affect. As Joan Copjec points out, both Freud and Lacan associate affect with movement (Copjec 2006, 95). Freud views affect as a kind of displacement, representation's fundamental "out-of-phaseness" with itself. The conventional view of the displacement of affect treats it as the distortion of perception by an excess of feeling. Copjec disagrees, arguing that the affective experience of something as moving indexes a movement beyond the perceiving individual, a surfeit or excess that ruptures the perception, making it more than itself and enabling it to open up another register (for Lacan, the Real; for Deleuze, the virtual). Affect, then, is this movement, a movement which estranges the subject from its experience (see Hillis, this volume). A thought, memory, or perception is affective to the extent that it opens up or indexes something beyond me.

I can't help but think of the cute cat photos and funny animal videos that circulate on the net. Why do people upload, forward, and link to these? It's not only because cats are cute or even because one's own cat is completely interesting. It's that the feeling that the cuteness accesses, the feeling that moves it, opens to something more, to a kind of beyond or potential. The dimension of affect is this "more than a feeling" that imparts movement. The potential here may be for connection (though one should be careful not to reduce affect to the intent of the subject sending cute cat photos), but not necessarily—anyone who uses email knows how annoying forwarded cuteness can actually be. Cute sayings or images are also not the only contributions that circulate: funny videos, shocking statements, pressing opportunities, silly applications all inhabit contemporary communication networks. They all provide momentary, even fleeting, charges and intensities, interruptions and divergences.

Insofar as affect, as movement, designates the doubling of an image, utterance, perception, or sound into itself and something else, we can account for the affective discharge of reflexivized communication. The additive dimension of communication for its own sake designates an excess. This excess isn't a new meaning or perspective. It doesn't refer to a new content. It is rather the intensity accrued from the repetition, the excitement or thrill of more. In the reflexive doubling of communication, the enjoyment attached to communication for its own sake displaces intention, content, and meaning. The something extra in repetition is enjoyment, the enjoyment that captures us in drive, and the enjoyment communicative capitalism expropriates.

At the same time that affect is movement, there is a specific affect that is a halting or arrest. Copjec invokes the image of running in place. This affect, which is an inhibition of movement, is anxiety. The experience of anxiety is a confrontation with excessive enjoyment: one encounters what is in one that is more than oneself, an alien yet intimate kernel at the core of one's being. Copjec writes, "*Jouissance* makes me me, while preventing me from knowing who I am" (Copjec 2006, 102). Finding oneself face to face with *jouissance*, one is pulled between incomprehensibility and extreme intimacy.

Copjec identifies two versions of the experience of anxiety: exposure to the excess of our unrealized past and to the punishing, relentless superego, itself an altered form of *jouissance* (as Žižek frequently puts it, the fundamental injunction of the superego is "Enjoy!").[1] In the first instance, my anxiety results from encountering past alternatives: *What would I have become had I stayed in that relationship? What would have happened had I arrived the next day instead?* Copjec writes, "For, in the experience of anxiety, one has a sense not only of being chained to an enjoyment that outstrips and precedes one, but also of the opacity of this enjoyment, its incomprehensibility and unassumability, which is dependent … on its being grounded in nothing actual, in a 'thrust-aside' past that never took place" (Copjec 2006, 105). Facing my enjoyment, uniquely mine but alien and seemingly unchosen, I cannot avoid the unsettling question, "How did I get here?"

We should also add to this aspect of anxiety the enjoyment of the other. As Žižek explains, one of the ways that the subject organizes enjoyment is through fantasies about the other. These fantasies express essential features of our own enjoyment. For example, homophobic treatments of gay men as excessively promiscuous, as having frequent, intense, anonymous sexual encounters, express the homophobe's suppositions regarding real sexual satisfaction (consequently, for conservatives, gay marriage threatens heterosexual marriage by eliminating its supplemental fantasy: that one sacrifices real sexual satisfaction for its sake; this sacrifice is necessary for the sacred character of marriage—without it, sex becomes common, conventional, and rather boring; in other words, the worst that the homophobe can imagine is that gay sex is just as boring as married sex). Žižek writes: "The fascinating image of the Other gives a body to our own innermost split, to what is 'in us more than ourselves'; and thus prevents us from achieving full identity with ourselves. *The hatred of the Other is the hatred of our own excess of enjoyment*" (Žižek 1993, 206).

In the second instance, the experience of anxiety results from the superegoic injunction to enjoy. The superego commands the subject to an impossible enjoyment, to find complete fulfillment in sex, exercise, professional achievement, a fabulous vacation. The very impossibility of fulfilling this injunction not only suffocates the poor subject but also incites a flight away from anxiety and toward the pursuit of knowledge (Copjec 2006, 109). To avoid the anxiety of the *jouissance* that prevents me from knowing who I am, I come under a compulsion to "keep on knowing more and more," a compulsion or thrust Lacan associates with an "epistemological drive" (Lacan 2007, 105–106). The attempt to escape anxiety thus results in capture at another level. Lacan associates this capture with science, capitalism, and the discourse of the university. All are constitutively open and incomplete, engaged in pursuits that never come to an end. We can extend this point by noting their contemporary merger and materialization in networked information and communication media (after all, the internet arose in the context of government-sponsored research, initially carried out not only by the Department of Defense but also at a small number of universities, the linking together of which provided its groundwork; later it was opened up to commercial interests and celebrated as the primary figure of global capitalism).

To reiterate, the object of anxiety is surplus *jouissance*, designated by Lacan as *objet petit a*. Copjec presents it in terms of a confrontation with an unrealized past as well as with the superego, a confrontation the subject attempts to flee by pursuing knowledge. Her account of anxiety corresponds to what Žižek (following Jacques-Alain Miller) designates as "constitutive anxiety," that is, "confrontation with *objet petit a* as constituted in its very loss," that is, *objet petit a* as an object of drive (Žižek 2006, 61). In both instances, the object is *loss* (rather than *lost*): the loss of an unknowable past (rather than a specific experience), the loss of a capacity to obey or comply (no matter what one does, one cannot satisfy the superego). The blockage or stuckness of anxiety, then, is at the same time the repetitive, circular movement of drive, the force of loss.

The point becomes clearer when we consider epistemological drive: keep on knowing more and more. In Lacan's account in Seminar XVII, this "keeping on" results from the change in the status of the Master in university discourse, that is to say, a change in the status and function of knowledge. Because university discourse cannot be anchored, cannot be held in place by an ultimate truth or injunction, it keeps on keeping on knowing. It doesn't come to an end or reach an ultimate goal. It circulates, and its circulation is an effect of its failure to anchor. Nothing can stop the progress of science; nothing can stop the movement of ideas. Information wants to be free—to circulate round and round. The more knowledge we accrue, the less we know. Abundance from one perspective is its lack from another.

The networks of communicative capitalism are affective because they are characterized by drive. Their affective dimension thus should not be reduced to desiring productivity or a nurturing emotional practice. Contra Hardt and Negri, networked communication is better understood through the negativity of drive, a negativity that results in stuckness and movement, rupture and creativity, a negativity, in other words, capable of accounting for the reflexivity in real networks (negativity here connotes positive feedback and the excess of an effect in relation to its cause). More crudely put, the affective charges we transmit and confront reinforce and extend affective networks without encouraging—and, indeed, by displacing—their consolidation into organized political networks (cf. Rossiter 2006). While this circulation might constitute a kind of affective labor, it is affective labor that is already captured.

In fact, rather than presuming the fitness of the category of labor, we do better to note the persistent disagreement among bloggers and net researchers regarding work and play in social networks. When we blog, are we working or playing? If we are working, then for whom are we working? Who enjoys, or who accrues enjoyment? If we enjoy, does that mean we are actually playing? Or might the instability here index the fact that we are caught in circuits of drive wherein we cannot escape enjoyment, but neither can we assume or accept it as our own?

Snare

Affective networks are a constitutive component of communicative capitalism. They express (are the expression of) the circulatory movement of drive—the repeated making, uploading, sampling, and decomposition occurring as movement on the internet doubles itself, becoming itself *and* its record or trace. The movement from link to link, the forwarding and storing and commenting, the contributing without expectation of response but in hope of further movement (why else count page views?) is circulation for its own sake.

Understanding this circulation by way of drive enables us to grasp how we are captured in its loop, how the loop ensnares. First, we enjoy failure. Insofar as the aim of the drive is not to reach its goal but to enjoy, we enjoy our endless circulation, our repetitive looping. We are captured because we enjoy. This idea appears in writing that associates new media with drugs, "users" and "using," as well as colloquial expressions like "Facecrack." Thomas Elsaesser illustrates the point via YouTube. Describing his movement among the links and videos, he writes, "After an hour or so, one realizes on what fine a line one has to balance to keep one's sanity, between the joy of discovering the unexpected, the marvelous and occasionally even the miraculous, and the rapid descent into an equally palpable anxiety, staring into the void of a sheer bottomless amount of videos, with their proliferation of images, their banality or obscenity in sounds and commentary" (Elsaesser 2008, 30). Failure, or what Elsaesser tags "constructive instability," is functional for communicative capitalism; it's our ensnarement in the loop of drive.

Second, we are captured in our passivity or, more precisely, by the reversion of our active engagements and interventions into passive forms of "being made aware" or "having been stated." The problem, then, is that ubiquitous personal media, communication for its own sake, turn our activity into passivity. They capture it, use it. We end up oscillating between extremes. On the one hand, we have opinions, theories, ideas, and information that we want to share. So we write our books and blogs, adding our contribution to the circulating flow. *Just what was needed—another blog.* On the other hand, the information age is an age wherein we lack the information we need to act. As communicative capitalism incites a continuous search for information, it renders information perpetually out of reach. Outraged, engaged, desperate to do *something*, we look for evidence, ask questions, and make demands, again contributing to the circuits of drive.

Contemporary communication networks are reflexive: we, the users, are creating them. We are producing the affective networks we inhabit, the connections that configure us. We provide the feedback that amplifies or ignores (or write the code that provides the feedback that amplifies or ignores). The more we contribute, the more extensive our submission. We configure our worlds, yet they are ever less what we desire but haven't reached, and ever more what we cannot escape yet still enjoy. As drive designates the plasticity of the objects to which we become attached, the repetitive movements of our attachment through networks, and the extremes and disequilibria inextricable from the circuits that result, it indexes the primary structure of enjoyment for contemporary subjects.

Note

1. Copjec follows Lacan in attributing the change to the shift from the discourse of the Master to the discourse of the university, itself a capitalist formation. Rather than following this temporalization, I view both elements as aspects of contemporary society.

References

Andrejevic, Mark. 2007. *iSpy: Surveillance and Power in the Interactive Era*. Lawrence: University of Kansas Press.

Clough, Patricia. 2007. Introduction. In *The Affective Turn*, ed. Patricia Ticineto Clough with Jean Halley, 1–33. Durham: Duke University Press.

Copjec, Joan. 2006. May '68, the Emotional Month. In *Lacan: The Silent Partners*, ed. Slavoj Žižek, 90–114. London: Verso.

Dean, Jodi. 2002. *Publicity's Secret: How Technoculture Capitalizes on Democracy*. Ithaca: Cornell University Press.

Debord, Guy. 1998. *Comments on the Society of the Spectacle*. Trans. Malcolm Imrie. London: Verso.

Elsaesser, Thomas. 2008. "Constructive Instability," or: The Life of Things as Cinema's Afterlife? In *Video Vortex: Reader Responses to YouTube*, ed. Geert Lovink and Sabine Niederer, 13–32. Amsterdam: Institute for Network Cultures.

Galloway, Alexander R., and Eugene Thacker. 2007. *The Exploit*. Minneapolis: University of Minnesota Press.

Hardt, Michael, and Antonio Negri. 2000. *Empire*. Cambridge, MA: Harvard University Press.

Lacan, Jacques. 1998. *The Seminar of Jacques Lacan, Book XI: The Four Fundamental Concepts of Psychoanalysis*. Ed. Jacques-Alain Miller, trans. Alan Sheridan. New York: W. W. Norton.

Lacan, Jacques. 2007. *The Seminar of Jacques Lacan, Book XVII: The Other Side of Psychoanalysis*. Ed. Jacques-Alain Miller, trans. Russell Grigg. New York: W. W. Norton.

Rossiter, Ned. 2006. *Organized Networks: Media Theory, Creative Labour, New Institutions*. Rotterdam: NAi Publishers.

Terranova, Tiziana. 2005. *Network Culture: Politics for the Information Age*. New York: Pluto Press.

Žižek, Slavoj. 1993. *Tarrying with the Negative*. Durham: Duke University Press.

Žižek, Slavoj. 1999. *The Ticklish Subject*. London: Verso.

Žižek, Slavoj. 2006. *The Parallax View*. Cambridge, MA: MIT Press.

Sensation

7   Ethologies of Software Art and Affect: What Can a Digital Body of Code Do?

Jussi Parikka

Reading Ted Chiang's (2010) short novel *The Lifecycle of Software Objects* is a great way to start thinking about affects and software. The novel narrates a story of embodied artificial intelligence as part of everyday human life, within which such software constructs occupy a position somewhere between a pet, a mascot, and a friend. The novel is an elaboration of software intelligence as somehow disturbing to categories of human thought, when it comes to the ability of supposedly artificial constructs to experience emotions, including those associated with pain, sexuality, and closeness. As an allegory for digital culture, Chang's novel asks us to consider the ways in which software, if not always embodying, at the very least mediates relations, emotions, and life. Software is not a world devoid of affect, but is completely entangled with human worlds of affective relations. The novel's focus on software's development and interactions points to the specific ways by which technology and humans have historically always been entangled. In the current chapter I extend this line of thought, and query the extent to which affect and *technical* media are entangled, especially on the level of software.

The notion of affect is useful for coming to terms with intuitive and embodied human-machine interactions. Greg Seigworth and Melissa Gregg (2010, 1) have carved out beautifully the essential points concerning affect that testify to its intensive, mobilizing, and mediating force, and they flag the inherent link between affect and in-betweenness. There is something mediate about affect itself, and it can be mobilized to better understand the relationships between human beings and software environments.[1]

Software Affect

In this chapter I develop the idea of software-based networks, nonhuman components included, as affective in themselves, and I do so in terms of their relationality. As a heuristic mode of description and analysis, relationality provides a way to think of networked software environments as defined by dynamics, instead of the static idea embodied in a geometrical diagram of networks (remember how many times you were shown the differences between a star network and a mesh network?). Networks are dynamic and changing entities of relations, in which software executes, time-critical events unfold, platforms and protocols malfunction, and glitches happen. My approach to affective software environments, moreover, calls for an *ethology* of code that accounts for the ways in which software interacts in technical environments as well as folds into cultural techniques, user habits, modes of perception, and users' memories.

As ethological beings, assemblages of software act as *agencements*, as processes "of arranging, organizing, fitting together" with other elements that enter into composition with them (Wise 2005, 77). The concept of affect helps us to better think through the aspect of connecting in-betweenness and circulation that characterizes affect itself (Seigworth and Gregg 2010). I approach software assemblages less as stable qualities and characteristics and more as modes of arrangement; I consider how their everyday unfoldings reveal how they work and what they can do. In software studies, my approach to networked assemblages resonates with recent calls to understand software through its forms of execution, compiling, and assemblages (Chun 2011a; Galloway 2012, 69).

I am interested in what software can do, what its limits are, and what sorts of relations it creates. I rely on an energetic, ethological, and material definition of software. For Jamie Skye Bianco (2007, 50), software "operates through energy, matter and time as materializing affect." Software programs affect social relations that expand to humans and nonhumans: habits, patterns of social behavior, modes of perception, sensation, and memory. Another word for this is "subjectivation." Software expresses its powers through computer interfaces, operating systems, and social media platforms from Facebook to Twitter that quantify network discussions for trend sniffers and analysts. This also includes the silent work of ubiquitous computer environments programmed to monitor and sense our moods and predispositions and anticipate future events. Software extends to other realms of expression, such as cash machines, digital games, and the Oyster card interfaces of the London Underground that connect with the eyes and hands of human beings. Software, then, governs access and denial of it. Moreover, software now extends itself into other, nonvolitional aspects of human being increasingly harnessed into HCI (human-computer interfacing) or BCI (brain-computer interfacing) applications.

It is important to note, however, that digital environments—whether the digital cinema of interest to Bianco, or software environments of other sorts—not only mediate this programmability but themselves are influenced by related milieus—including technical operating systems and protocols, social perceptions, labor conditions, and so forth—within which they operate and circulate. We need, therefore, to remain aware of the assemblages, distributions, and relations of software—the milieus within which programming happens, and, as a consequence, to approach software from an ethological mode of analysis, in the sense of looking at what software does, how it acts, and how it relates (cf. Parikka 2010).

To be sure, this sounds like a paradox, for what is algorithmic logic based on if not the formalization of procedures of action? And yet, an ethological approach makes sense once we recognize that in order to action social relations, algorithms themselves (and on a different level, software too) have to be constantly actioned. What is interesting with respect to software is that the potential for change revealed through this constant actioning is, by definition, one of software's crucial features. Software can be thought of as a plug-in, as it is defined by its capacities to connect or deny contact, to enable or disable, to afford or block. Software objects are constituted in wider assemblages of enunciation and the constellations that Gilles Deleuze and Félix Guattari (1987) call "abstract machines." These assemblages work through other software objects, protocols, and platforms.

While software has clear links to humans in HCI and BCI, and is of crucial importance to the functioning of commercial digital culture, it has been "hidden" under various layers and hence remains imperceptible to most users. Nevertheless, software's crucial position as an interfacing of various regimes of expression and as a crucial node in the abstract machines of capitalist digital culture demands careful scrutiny. A certain kind of scrutiny is manifested in the increasingly widespread realization that deep layers of cookies and other trackers escort everyone's daily web activities. Facebook has been the subject of such scrutiny (Felix 2012), given that the affects of site users (their likes, dislikes, preferences, and obsessions) constitute a key part of the company's business model (see Karppi, this volume).

I have outlined the affective potentials for software as part of a larger assemblage, and in the remainder of the chapter I offer a discussion of the politics of software and the aesthetics of the imperceptible. I exemplify this discussion by placing special emphasis on software art projects and the ways they allow for an in-between interplay among relationality, affect, and software.

Art of the Imperceptible

What characterizes several contemporary software art projects, as well as what Ned Rossiter (2006) calls the "processual aesthetics of new media," is a willingness to dig deeply into the relationality of digital culture beyond the screen. Rossiter writes how such aesthetics seek "to identify how online practices are always conditioned by and articulated with seemingly invisible forces, institutional desires and regimes of practice" (Rossiter 2006, 174). This becomes evident in software and net art projects' continuous interest in translations and transmutations. Net art refers to a heterogeneous set of art practices that take the internet as their crucial medium of investigation and execution. Examples include alternative browser projects such as the Web Stalker,[2] Peter Luining's ZNC browser,[3] and ecological projects such as Google Will Eat Itself,[4] which examines the continuum stretching from code to political economy and the networks of agencies (in the sense of *agencements*) involved in search engines.

Rossiter (2006, 176–178) extends his excavation of processuality toward a radical empiricism of digital culture, and he posits the primacy of movement as a characteristic of new media. Committed to transmutationality, radical empiricism offers a way to understand network and software temporality. This perspective pushes us to see code as more than just the source code. Software establishes relations and is defined by relations: this constitutes a radical empiricism in action. This radical empiricism is what connects my discussion of code and software to the theme of affect understood through its relationality. In more concrete terms, code's radically creative temporality becomes evident when we understand code's executability. Code exists only in its execution, a point popularized by several net art projects, including the mock "execution" of code on T-shirt designs (for example, the Biennale.py net art virus, discussed in greater detail below, that became a paradoxical digital art consumer object available in printed clothing form as well as expensive CD-ROM formats), oral performances such as media theorist Franco Bifo Berardi's "execution" of the source code of the Loveletter virus in 2001 during the "Digital is not Analog-art" conference, and Geoff Cox's (2013) *Speaking Code*.[5] Cox's apt analysis of the political power of performative code illustrates how performative accounts of language resonate with an understanding of the unfolding performance of code. Practices such as live coding, where the unfolding of code becomes a public performance with the coder as a sort of a DJ/VJ figure, relate to a wider set of questions that tie programming to labor as a performance in post-Fordist culture.

Software art is a way to understand software culture more broadly, and hence the relational, affective aspects of software. Printing or orating viral code and making it, through such an alternative execution, less tied to code's specified digital surroundings highlights how differently computer technologies and code can be related to phenomenological modes of understanding technology, code, and software. The challenge of such an approach is to consider things not immediately available to the senses as completely real. Code is one of those things whose scale is slightly at odds with the normal symbolic processes humans have used to operate culture, for instance writing, even if having a relation to it. Code operates at different speeds, and on such a distributed level that it seems to escape simple definitions. There is something in the processual aspect of code/software that relates to how it is perhaps captured better as a vector of individuation than as the individual, to use Simondon's (2007) philosophical vocabulary. In short, instead of a focus on fully constructed individuals, objects, and entities, the perspective of individuation is interested in the milieu of forces in which things are in the process of individuating.

In addition to thinking about code as something that makes computers do things, we need to consider the ways in which code is transformed into software as an entity that has various cultural visibilities. This transformation ranges from the ways in which code relates to the human sensorium (the interface, for instance) to cultural representations of code and software. As a horizon for analysis, framing code through software art produces a different understanding than framing it through social media. Looking at code and software through such experimental practices is better for an analysis of what code can do, what its limits are, how far it can go in stretching the analysis and repositioning of social relations. Hence my focus on teasing out some of the implications this perspective has for the relational, ethological, and affect-related notions of code. My focus also brings forth the question of code as imperceptible and misrepresented, and therefore as escaping representational frameworks in software art projects. If we consider software through software art, and approach software art as the art of the imperceptible, then we can elaborate a politics of the art of the imperceptible through affects, sensations, relations, and forces (see Grosz 2008). Such an approach demands a certain ecopolitics of forces, where analysis focuses on what constitutes software as well as on its capacity to constitute—for instance human affects. Here nonhuman and human forces entangle.

In terms of software, this reference to nonhuman forces and imperceptibility is relevant on at least two levels. Software is not (solely) visual and representational; it works through a logic of transposition. What is transposed is not content, but intensities and information that individuate and inform agency. Code, and subsequently software, is a computational transposition among the (potentially) visual interface, the source code, and machinic processes. Even "software art" is a contested term, given how differently various projects mobilize their relation to art. Indeed, its definition seems to rest on the difficulty of pinning down software art as a social and cultural practice. Put bluntly, quite often what could be called software art is reduced, in pejorative accounts, to processes such as sabotage, illegal software actions, crime, or pure vandalism, as when, for instance, it comes down to viral software or Face-to-Facebook sort of identity hijacking in social media.[6] It is instructive in this respect that in the archives of the Runme.org software art repository, the list of categories offered for access contains fewer references to traditional terms of art discourse, such as "genre" and "artist," than to "appropriation and plagiarism," "dysfunctionality," "illicit software," and "denial of service." One subcategory, "obfuscation," sums up many of the wider implications of software art as resisting identification,[7] and also can be seen as evidence of a defining feature of software more generally. At least this is the argument advanced by Alex Galloway about the paradoxical nature of "software as a medium that is not a medium" (2012, 69). Referring to obfuscation as a principle of software deployment, Galloway argues that software's slippery nature is due to the fact that "code must be compiled, interpreted, parsed, and otherwise driven into hiding by still larger globs of code" (Galloway 2012, 69).

The variety of terms for software art, however, doesn't stem from a deconstructionist desire to postpone and dislocate patterns of identification ad infinitum, or from the archivists' nightmare à la Borges or Foucault, but from a "poetics of potentiality," as Matthew Fuller (2003, 61) has called it. This is already evident in older projects like the I/O/D Web Stalker browser (an alternative way to access the internet that "dispels with the page metaphor of traditional browsers and presents URLs as a series of circular lines that are the links")[8] and other later software art. Poetics of potentiality refers to the way that experimental software tests the limits of computers and expression. Art becomes "not-just-art" in its wild but methodological dispersal across a whole media ecology. Projects like Face-to-Facebook (2011) extend hacker art into proprietary social media cultures. As writers such as Florian Cramer and Inke Arns have noted, software art can be seen as a tactical move through which to highlight the political contexts, or subtexts, of "seemingly neutral technical commands" (Arns 2005, 3; see also Arns and Hunger 2005).

Arns's text highlights the politics of software along with its experimental and non-pragmatic nature, and resonates with what I outline here. Nevertheless, I want to transport these art practices into another philosophical context, more closely attuned to Deleuze and others able to contribute to thinking the intensive relations and dimensions of technology, such as Simondon, Spinoza, and the early twentieth-century pioneer of ethology, Jacob von Uexküll (2010). To this end I will contextualize some notions in the practices and projects of software and net art, and do so through thinking code as ethological experimentation.

Released in 2005, the Google Will Eat Itself project is exemplary of such creative dimensions of software art. Authored by Ubermorgen.com (featuring Alessandro Ludovico vs. Paolo Cirio), the project is a parasitic tapping into the logic of Google and its AdSense program. By spoofing AdSense accounts, the project is able to collect micropayments from Google and use the money to buy Google shares—a cannibalistic eating of Google by itself. At the time of writing, the project pages estimate that it will take 202,345,117 years until GWEI fully owns Google. The project works as a playful intervention into the logic of software advertisements and the new media economy. Conceptually, the project resides somewhere on the border of sabotage and illegal action—or what Google, in a letter from its legal department to the artists, refers to as "invalid clicks." Imperceptibility is the general requirement for the success of the project, as it tries to use the software and business logic of the corporation through piggybacking on the latter's modus operandi. It gathers its strength partly from the imperceptibility that is so crucial for a postrepresentational logic of resistance. One can notice similar logic at play in some of Paolo Cirio's later projects, including Face to Facebook (2011) and Loophole for All (2013).

In addition to the tactics deployed in some software art projects, what is interesting here is a broader logic of imperceptibility that characterizes contemporary networked society. This logic—"what you don't see is what you get"—has been identified as an important characteristic of digital culture by media analysts such as Friedrich Kittler (1995). Code that communicates with lower-level machine architecture has this feature of imperceptibility in the phenomenological sense that it evades the human sensorium, but software (as a packaged form of code) is also imperceptible in the political and economic sense of being hidden from the end user. Large, pervasive software systems such as Google's are imperceptible in the complexity of the massive amounts of code but also in the ecological complexity of the relations they establish with users (what GWEI aims to tap into). Cloud computing is exemplary of a shift of code further from the user, as is the move toward ubiquitous computing and the internet of things. This situation does not easily map in terms of the binary of "open" and "closed" code that has been the axis of political debate concerning software. Instead, one is situated and governed within ecologies of code without being able to account for their totality. Imperceptibility, however, can also become a crucial mode of experimental and tactical projects. Indeed, resistance works immanently within the diagram of power and, instead of refusing its strategies, adopts them as part of its own tactics. Diagrams (as abstract machines) are cartographies of power, but they are also distributions of singularities—and thus contain the potentials for deterritorialization.[9] Here, the imperceptibility of artistic projects resonates with the micropolitical mode of disappearance, and what Galloway and Thacker (2007, 135–136) term "tactics of non-existence." Escaping detection and surveillance becomes the necessary prerequisite for various guerrilla-like actions that stay off the radar, at least for limited periods.

The disruption of perceptions is evident in such projects as the artist duo Jodi's tactical computer "crashes." Glitches, arguably one example of a micropolitics of dysfunctionality, are part of the standard repertoire of software art, as are closer ties with malicious software, exemplified by the Biennale.py net art virus released in 2001.[10] Though it was released at the 49th Venice Biennale, which placed it within established art contexts, the workings and technical nature of the virus defied institutional stratification. A weird, intensive object in its own right, the virus, written by two net art groups, 0100101110101101.ORG and epidemiC, was distributed as a kind of consumer object—sold at a high price to investors on a CD-ROM but also distributed through T-shirts on which the code had been printed.

The Biennale virus clearly was not intended as malicious or destructive software in the usual sense, as it neither spread nor executed without the user being aware of its presence. Instead, though it was an *invisible* piece of code, it was described in an interview with Cornelia Sollfrank as embedded in absolute *transparency*. The authors' "names and domains were written on the code," and antivirus software houses were notified; the virus, however, was designed to survive without harming its host (Sollfrank 2001, n.p.). "So, it sucks energy, but tries to stay invisible as much as possible. ... It just installs itself in the background" (Sollfrank 2001, n.p.).

Such technical invisibility is part of the imperceptibility of net art and software art referred to above. These examples, therefore, are more than mere "art." They occupy a transinstitutional status characteristic of the network society, and involve a range of sociotechnical relations between and among art, law, the economy of digital production, the politics of software, and so on, as their constituting forces. Executable code reaches out into milieus far beyond those concerned with technical execution only. This explains the recent emergence of dynamic notions of software culture, such as "media ecologies" (Fuller 2005), "processuality" (Rossiter 2006), and, more generally, assemblages (see Wise 2005, 77–87).

Imperceptibility, however, should not be understood solely in terms of a representational logic of what is seen and what is not. Rather, it can be more widely understood as referring to the constituting material and energetic force of what governs sensations, perceptions, and representations. Such a perspective not only brings ethology to software culture, it also questions the use of general terms such as "the digital" to describe a cultural situation in which practices of code and software have become central. "Digital" is too broad a category for any specific understanding of the weird materialities of network culture that relate to movements across scales and between human and nonhuman agencies. Code and software are increasingly more about relationality with machine milieus as well as their relations with the wider world in which they are always embedded (from the abstract machines of capitalism to the concrete assemblages where we twist and turn our pelvises, knees, necks, and thumbs, sharpen our eyes, move our gaze across the screen and its surroundings, resharpen and blur—as when dealing with games, browsers, and mobile interfaces).

The emergence of network culture in the 1990s was characterized by the hyped word "virtual," but in a very different sense from Deleuze's rigorous assessment, which emerged from pairing the virtual with the real. The virtual has a different relation to the real than to the actual, and is an element of creative difference that is seen as a dynamic field of unraveling tendencies, so to speak. Constantin Boundas describes the virtual as consisting of incorporeal events and singularities, and this perhaps is a new way of thinking about software art as well: it summons such singularities as embedded both in the nonhuman materiality of computers and in the incorporeal events acting as experimentations (Boundas 2005, 296–297). Software is not an immaterial virtual, in the sense suggested by the hype of the 1980s and 1990s, but is incorporeal-material in the Deleuzian sense. Experimental net art projects are imperceptible in relation to a politics of the nonrepresentable: the imperceptible is the singular not perceived by coding mechanisms, it is the surplus of code and its potentiality for new connections. Staying imperceptible allows software art to frame the political economic ontology of our culture of commercial software.

To draw on the powers of the imperceptible, then, involves looking beyond the representational. Brian Massumi explains the politics of camouflage that is continuously immanent to the actual world, and he works through its vacuoles and "derelict spaces" (Massumi 1992, 104–105). New actual-virtual circuits can open up political imaginations, Massumi argues. The art of camouflage passes to the inside, but while doing so releases transmutational forces, producing resistance as friction in the "molar machine," along with the stuttering of language. Things change. Something takes place.

Code enacts, enables, and produces effects and affects: relations across scales, tapping into human social relations, relations with machines, relations inside machines—code, and software events as well. As Fuller notes, software's raw materials are subjectivities that are templated according to the "actions, schemas and decisions performed by software." As such they also produce further "sequences of seeing, knowing and doing" (Fuller 2003, 54). Software, then, is not only a black box for input, but a process of modulation in itself, the poetics of potentiality in action. This means looking at projects such as the Web Stalker alternative browser not simply as art, but also as productions of new social relationships that incorporate relations with data as well as relationships with art (Fuller 2003, 61).

Relationality: Ethology

A key point that emerges from this discussion of the potentiality of software art is the value of conceptualizing software as a process of individuation and relationality. In order to extend from potentiality to relationality, software art projects need to involve themselves with other modalities of expression. Software, then, is a relay between a plethora of cultural practices, and hence the most interesting points are the connections that software establishes. Imperceptibility and structural misperception evident in software art projects can in this sense serve as indices for a wider media ecology of digital culture.

Ethologically, the task is to develop concepts resonating with computational culture through notions of body, affect, and ethology advanced by Deleuze and influenced by the thought of Spinoza and von Uexküll. To address the notion of a software ethology, I would like to extend the idea of bodies—one that Deleuze does not explicitly restrict to human or visible bodies—to software objects. For Deleuze, Spinozian ethology begins with the idea that bodies are composed of the relations of motion and rest between their particles, as well as through the affects (affecting and being affected) produced through relations with other bodies. This kinetic-dynamic notion of a body enables us to define living things (and software too) not by their form but as "a complex relation between differential velocities, between deceleration and acceleration of particles" (Deleuze 1988, 123). Computational and executable media can also be seen as time-critical, to use a term that Wolfgang Ernst (2013) applies to technical media.

If software has a body, it is constituted primarily through the connections software establishes. We could say that, as an ethological process, software is defined by its motion and rest, speeds and slownesses. These are its affects, its relations with the other bodies involved in its unfolding in time. Deleuze and Guattari's famous example of the tick (adopted from von Uexküll) referred to the world of the tick as defined by three key affects: light attracts it to a branch, the chemical smell of a passing animal makes it jump, and lack of hair on the animal's skin makes it burrow in. What if we take the idea of affects understood as this type of triggering relation as our guide to software, too?

To take a simple example, we can ask, What defines a virus program? One answer is that such a program is defined by its three affects: (1) infection: the various ways a virus can distribute itself through other software and protocols; (2) payload: what a virus does, from erasing the hard drive to playing a harmless tune; and (3) trigger: the routine that triggers the virus (Harley, Slade, and Gattiker 2001, 5). More specifically, "affects" are a form of understanding specific types of programming and software as the ways in which they function in milieus. Since the 1970s such affects have been evident in the emergence of object-oriented programming—what Casey Alt (2011) calls the abstract machine of contemporary culture. Object-oriented programming exhibits the relationality, polymorphism, and contextuality that characterize software culture. As Alt explains, software objects are polymorphic (open to various meanings, or affects, depending on their context) and defined by the various topological relations of clusters of objects that are open to emergent unfoldings. Object-oriented programming is also filled with a sense of spatiality: its terms signal its connection to space, environment, movement, topology, architecture, and the relations of insides and outsides (Alt 2011, 288). This is not only an issue of the internal workings of software but also extends to the milieus in which software performs in the human social world. Alt relies on Deleuze's concept of affect when he argues that affections are the occupying of the interval. The interval is what resides between the nodes. It is a relation that is often ignored as "blank," but it is actually an invisibility that structures how things do and don't connect. It is also the moment of indetermination, and software objects can be further characterized as residing at the event of indetermination: they are grounded in durations and temporal unfoldings, and are not simply prescribed structures.

Indeed, ethologically, these are not so much structural features of software as temporal tendencies, or potentials that allow certain relations and interactions with software environments, which then work in wider abstract milieus of economic, political, and other material energies. The relationality of ethological assemblages provides a potentiality into which several software art projects aim to tap. The questions continuously (yet implicitly) posed by critical experimental software are then how to find the defining singularities of current abstract machines of digitality, and how to take into account the complexity of software culture's ecological ties.

The Deleuzian-Spinozian analysis of the dynamics of bodies-in-relations is useful for understanding how software, besides being regulated and embedded in a range of social and political practices, itself controls and affords. Ethology, as conceived by Deleuze and Guattari, necessarily dips into the virtual in the sense of potentiality, where the "goodness" and "badness" of encounters are fixed only in and through the unfolding of their affective relations. Ethology is, in this sense, experimental by definition. As Moira Gatens writes, "Ethology does not impose a plane of organization but rather posits a plane of experimentation, a mapping of extensive relations and intensive capacities that are mobile and dynamic" (Gatens 1996, 169). This necessarily involves "a micropolitics concerned with the 'in-between' of subjects" open to a range of becomings (Gatens 1996, 167).

In a Spinozist vein, ethologies deal with goodness and badness in terms of potentiality: what is good for an object, or its milieus, unfolds only in experiential and experimental lived relations. The tactical irresponsibility that seems to characterize various software-related art projects stems from an experimentation with such categories of the good and bad, and with the fuzzy borders of legality and illegality of network culture (see Sampson and Parikka 2009). The point about imperceptibility is easiest to make with examples that move along this fuzzy border.

Cartographies of such ethological relations look for intensive connections between and among a range of entangled agencies: human and nonhuman, and the various in-betweens or affects that regulate such relations. Such cartographies map experimentations and mutations, and we need to keep our analytical antennae open for them in the technomaterial regimes, too. Mutations take place through intervals and express the potentiality of dynamic systems. In the vocabulary of Simondon (2007), systems have to do with metastability: the dynamic individuation of entities becomes the primary focus instead of the end product (the individual). Entities are understood through their milieu of relations. Metastability is this state of potentiality in a system that is open to changes through those individuating relations.

Software's various ethological relations connect to wider media ecologies, which is what projects such as Google Will Eat Itself illustrate. This is how they gain their momentum from the transdisciplinary zone between economy, politics, and code—and hence how they highlight their intimate and immanent connections with wider mechanisms of biopower. This sense of assemblages as transdisciplinarity and border-crossing is akin to ecological modes of the production of software objects, subjectivity, and the social. In an ecological manner, Google Will Eat Itself is an exercise of immanent critique that addresses the given technosocial condition of software-based network culture.

In addition to the GWEI project, Amazon Noir ("The Big Book Crime," which took advantage of the "Search Inside This Book" function to "steal" thousands of books from the Amazon website) is an example of such transmutational projects. Of similar stature is the Face-to-Facebook project (2011),[11] with its own version of stealing and parasitical relation to Web 2.0 social media culture. In this project, the algorithm-enhanced purloining of Facebook profiles and subsequent recreation of them as dating site profiles played not only with the software-based characteristics of sociability in digital culture, but also with such social features as the importance of the face in identity politics (figure 7.1).

The diagram reproduced in figure 7.1 is more than a representation of the project. It is akin to experimentation with the links and relations inherent in the corporate software systems connected to key sectors of the creative industries and information

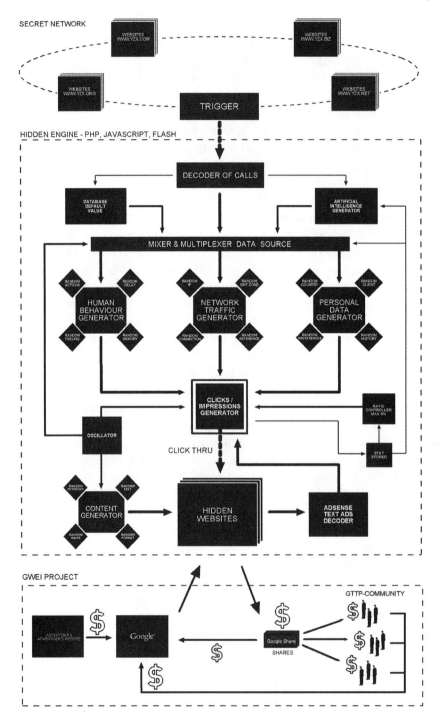

Figure 7.1
GWEI Diagram: http://gwei.org/pages/diagram/diagram.html. Reproduced courtesy of Paolo Cirio.

society. The Amazon Noir project is itself an example of software tapping into a proprietary system; by parasitizing the logic of intellectual property, the project aims to reproduce an idea of liberation through such parasite-sized gaps. Its software automated the process of copying books from Amazon.com, and remained unnoticed and was left unannounced for a while. As Michael Dieter points out, Amazon Noir worked through a diagrammatics of ambiguity that was "heightened by the abstractions of software entities" (Dieter 2007, 18), and established an ethology of software that acknowledged the ethical issues. That is to say, it interrogated what software is capable of, as well as the possibilities for experimenting with the boundaries of the proprietary system and its rules of accountability.

Such an interpretation links ethics to ethology and affect. Affective relationality is a matter of the composition and decomposition of forces, of relations, and hence of objects that also function as an analytic cartography of network culture. Software entangles itself in the programming of how bodies behave (from emotions to other physiological and cognitive dimensions), but we also need to keep an eye on software itself as managed as well as managing, as governing a milieu. Software itself, then, is an object of study for an ethology that maps how software's own capacities are controlled, supported, diminished, enhanced, and sometimes quietly exploded so as to become imperceptible to our usual cognitive coordinates.

Notes

1. To be sure, twenty-first-century networked media life does not lack affect. The attractions of social media platforms, participatory cultures, sharing, and the contagious modes of mediated forms of sociability are embedded with expressions full of affect. Affect itself is contagious, in the manner theorized by Gabriel Tarde more than a century ago and taken up today in the idea of contagious networks (Sampson 2012): sociability is based on imitation, and hence, for instance, virality can become a leading concept.

2. See Web Stalker introductory page at http://v2.nl/archive/works/the-web-stalker/view, accessed June 7, 2013.

3. See http://znc.ctrlaltdel.org/.

4. See http://gwei.org/.

5. On temporality, see the Jaromil and Jodi collaboration TBT: Time Based Text. The software allows a user to tap into the process of writing on the computer keyboard and frame in its sheer materiality and unfolding temporality. See http://tbt.dyne.org. On the fundamental temporality of computing, see Chun (2011b).

6. I return to this topic below, but the project pages can be found at http://www.face-to-facebook .net.

7. The software art archive at http://www.runme.org demonstrates the multiplicity of projects—and the ensuing difficulty of general definitions, which in itself feeds into finding much more open-ended and experimental definitions that grasp software art in terms of potentiality.

8. The quote is from the project's presentation on the Visual Complexity web page at http://www.visualcomplexity.com/vc/project.cfm?id=7.

9. Galloway (2004) offers a novel approach to the diagram in the context of the internet. He shows the multilayered and multiscaled ontology of the internet and how it can be understood as a diagrammatic distribution of relations and nodes that govern and distribute agencies.

10. On glitch and software (art), see Goriunova and Shulgin (2008, 110–119). For Jodi projects, see, for example, http://www.jodi.org and http://404.jodi.org.

11. http://www.face-to-facebook.net.

References

Alt, Casey. 2011. Objects of Our Affection. How Object-Orientation Made Computation a Medium. In *Media Archaeology: Approaches, Applications, Implications*, ed. Erkki Huhtamo and Jussi Parikka, 278–301. Berkeley: University of California Press.

Arns, Inke. 2005. Code as Performative Speech Act. *Artnodes* (May 2005). Available at http://www.uoc.edu/artnodes/espai/eng/art/arns0505.html.

Arns, Inke, and F. Hunger. 2005. The Clean Rooms' Dirty Secret. Temporary Software Art Factory: Readme 100 in Dortmund, Germany, 2005. In *Readme 100: Temporary Software Factory*, ed. Olga Goriunova, 9–15. Dortmund: HMKW.

Bianco, Jamie Skye. 2007. Techno-Cinema: Image Matters in Affective Unfoldings of Analog Cinema and New Media. In *The Affective Turn: Theorizing the Social*, ed. Patricia Ticineto Cloud and Jean Halley, 47–76. Durham: Duke University Press.

Boundas, Constantin. 2005. Virtual/Virtuality. In *The Deleuze Dictionary*, ed. Adrian Parr, 296–298. Edinburgh: Edinburgh University Press.

Chiang, Ted. 2010. *The Lifecycle of Software Objects*. Burton, MI: Subterranean Press.

Chun, Wendy Hui Kyong. 2011a. *Software and Memory*. Cambridge, MA: MIT Press.

Chun, Wendy Hui Kyong. 2011b. The Enduring Ephemeral, or the Future is a Memory. In *Media Archaeology: Approaches, Applications and Implications*, ed. Erkki Huhtamo and Jussi Parikka, 184–203. Berkeley: University of California Press.

Cox, Geoff. 2013. *Speaking Code: Coding as Aesthetic and Political Expression*. Cambridge, MA: MIT Press.

Deleuze, Gilles. 1988. *Spinoza: Practical Philosophy*. Trans. Robert Hurley. San Francisco: City Light Books.

Deleuze, Gilles, and Félix Guattari. 1987. *A Thousand Plateaus*. Trans. Brian Massumi. Minneapolis: University of Minnesota Press.

Dieter, Michael. 2007. Amazon Noir: Piracy, Distribution, Control. *M/C Journal* 10 (5) (October). Available at http://journal.media-culture.org.au/0710/07-dieter.php.

Ernst, Wolfgang, ed. 2013. *Digital Memory and the Archive*. Minneapolis: University of Minnesota Press.

Felix, Samantha. 2012. This Is How Facebook Is Tracking Your Internet Activity. *Business Insider* (September 9). Available at http://www.businessinsider.com/this-is-how-facebook-is-tracking-your-internet-activity-2012-9?op=1.

Fuller, Matthew. 2003. *Behind the Blip: Essays on the Culture of Software*. New York: Autonomedia.

Fuller, Matthew. 2005. *Media Ecologies: Materialist Energies in Art and Technoculture*. Cambridge, MA: MIT Press.

Galloway, Alexander R. 2004. *Protocol: How Control Exists after Decentralization*. Cambridge, MA: MIT Press.

Galloway, Alexander R. 2012. *The Interface Effect*. Cambridge: Polity Press.

Galloway, Alexander R., and Eugene Thacker. 2007. *The Exploit: A Theory of Networks*. Minneapolis: University of Minnesota Press.

Gatens, Moira. 1996. Through a Spinozist Lens: Ethology, Difference, Power. In *Deleuze: A Critical Reader*, ed. Paul Patton, 162–187. Oxford: Blackwell.

Goriunova, Olga, and Aleksei Shulgin. 2008. Glitch. In *Software Studies: A Lexicon*, ed. Matthew Fuller, 110–119. Cambridge, MA: MIT Press.

Grosz, Elizabeth. 2008. *Chaos, Territory, Art: Deleuze and the Framing of the Earth*. New York: Columbia University Press.

Harley, David, Robert Slade, and Urs E. Gattiker. 2001. *Viruses Revealed! Understand and Counter Malicious Software*. New York: Osborne/McGraw Hill.

Kittler, Friedrich. 1995. There Is No Software. *CTheory* (18 October). Available at http://www.ctheory.net/articles.aspx?id=74.

Massumi, Brian. 1992. *A User's Guide to Capitalism and Schizophrenia: Deviations from Deleuze and Guattari*. Cambridge, MA: MIT Press.

Parikka, Jussi. 2010. *Insect Media: An Archaelogy of Animals and Technology*. Minneapolis: University of Minnesota Press.

Rossiter, Ned. 2006. *Organized Networks: Media Theory, Creative Labour, New Institutions*. Rotterdam: NAI Publishers.

Sampson, Tony D. 2012. *Virality: Contagion Theory in the Age of Networks*. Minneapolis: University of Minnesota Press.

Sampson, Tony, and Jussi Parikka, eds. 2009. *The Spam Book: On Porn, Viruses, and Other Anomalous Objects from the Dark Side of Digital Culture.* Cresskill: Hampton Press.

Seigworth, Gregory J., and Melissa Gregg. 2010. An Inventory of Shimmers. In *The Affect Theory Reader*, ed. Melissa Gregg and Greg Seigworth, 1–25. Durham: Duke University Press.

Simondon, Gilbert. 2007. *L'Individuation psychique et collective.* Paris: Aubier.

Sollfrank, Cornelia. 2001. Biennale.py—The Return of the Media Hype. *Telepolis* 7 (7). Available at http://www.heise.de/tp/artikel/3/3642/1.html.

von Uexküll, Jakob. 2010. *A Foray into the Worlds of Animals and Humans.* Trans. Joseph D. O'Neil. Minneapolis: University of Minnesota Press.

Wise, J. Macgregor. 2005. Assemblage. In *Gilles Deleuze: Key Concepts*, ed. Charles J. Stivale, 77–87. Chesham: Acumen.

8 Sensation, Networks, and the GIF: Toward an Allotropic Account of Affect

James Ash

The GIF file type was created in 1987 by Steve Wilhite, then an employee of Compu-Serve, as a "standard defining a mechanism for the storage and transmission of raster-based graphics information" (CompuServe 1987, n.p.). GIF stands for Graphics Interchange Format, a type of compressed digital image file that was one of the first image files widely used on the internet. GIFs can be static images or can be animated to display a short looping sequence. Animated GIFs gained popularity in the early 1990s, when users were first able to create and host their own web pages and decorate them with animations such as a flag blowing in the breeze or a light flashing. The content of GIFs began to change during the mid-2000s with the rise of online video-hosting sites such as YouTube, which provided a proliferation of ready-made raw material for GIF makers to edit and remix.

While it was once principally a part of the vocabulary of coders and technology-savvy consumers, the term GIF has gained wider cultural prominence. In 2012 its verb form was named Oxford University Press US dictionary word of the year, defined as "to create a GIF file of (an image or video sequence, especially relating to an event): he GIFed the highlights of the debate" (Oxford Dictionaries 2012). One of the panelists involved in adjudicating the word of the year, Katherine Martin, explained its selection:

GIF celebrated a lexical milestone in 2012, gaining traction as a verb, not just a noun. The GIF has evolved from a medium for pop-cultural memes into a tool with serious applications including research and journalism, and its lexical identity is transforming to keep pace. (Martin 2012, n.p.)

As Martin suggests, animated GIFs have many uses and applications, from displaying animated charts in a work presentation to short comedic skits or clips. For instance, the 2012 presidential debates in the US were "live GIFed," with key moments between Barack Obama and Mitt Romney edited into looping animations. Animated GIFs are widely used across a variety of internet settings, including social media, web pages, and message board forums. Specific websites, such as gifbin.com and ohmagif.com, have been set up to collect and create particular types or genres of GIFs, from film and television to news items and home video footage.

Considering the prominence of the GIF in online and internet culture, there has been almost no examination of it as a cultural phenomenon from either a technical or sociological perspective. When GIFs have been discussed in a media and communication context, the discussion usually has been part of a broader argument around internet memes. In Michael Dieter's work, for example, GIFs are considered from a critical perspective as part of "the churn of Net flotsam ... indicative of ... accelerated conditions of communicative capitalism" (Dieter 2011, n.p.). Discussions of GIFs often revolve around the nature of a GIF's "virality," its capacity to travel across time and space and reach a large audience (Fernback 2003; Burgess 2008; Berger and Milkman 2010), or its role in participatory culture (Knobel and Lankshear, 2007; Lessig 2008). Little has been said, however, about how and why GIFs circulate around the internet. To invoke a more robust discussion, I consider GIFs as "informational entities" (Goddard and Parikka 2011) in their own right, with an autonomous power to shape and manipulate users' capacities on an affective level.

Mark Hansen describes affect as opening the "in-between of emotional states ... to some kind of embodied yet intentional apprehension" (Hansen 2004a, 589; also see Hansen 2004b). New media, he suggests, can operate on this in-between level "to broker a technical enlargement of the threshold of the now, to intensify the body's subject-constituting experience of its own vitality ... to expand the thickness of the pre-objective present" (Hansen 2004a, 589). Hansen is concerned with how media technologies act on the body and shape its capacities to sense time. Moving in a related but slightly different direction, I am interested in how the potential for affect travels around and through networks before it reaches a human body, as well as in an object's capacity to influence that body once contact is made. What is important about Hansen's argument is his insistence that to understand the type of affect a media object generates, one needs to pay detailed attention to its material specificity. Paying attention to the specificity of the GIF as a digital file type, I argue, allows us to consider how the potential for affect travels through networked environments.

To understand how a GIF's potential for affect travels within a digital network, and at the same time remain open to different affective responses by different viewers, I develop Gilles Deleuze's work on Francis Bacon to theorize the relationship between sensation and affect as allotropic. Briefly, sensation refers to the organization and transmission of forces between entities, and affect to how these forces alter and shape the capacities of bodies as they encounter and are encountered by these forces. As such, I argue that what makes a GIF successful as a means for generating novel forms of affect is related to its particular properties and capacities as an object, as well as to its content, because its particularities as a file type frame and organize the types of sensation transmitted within it.

Organized forces such as electricity or sound are allotropic in the sense that they express either sensations or affects, depending on how they travel and what they encounter. My account seeks to show that no simple distinction can be made between organic (human) and inorganic (digital) forms of sense, and that these translations of sense in the inorganic realm are central to framing the potential for affect generated in human users. Sensation, then, primes the context of affective encounter, and the affects generated by exteriorized sensations (such as paint brushed onto a canvas) are not reducible simply to an individual's personal and historical contexts.

Using Deleuze to examine the GIF as a particular digital object also allows me to reflect upon recent debates regarding the negative possibilities of digital grammatization. Grammatization refers to the translation of information or media from temporal to spatial registers through the creation of a series of discrete marks. An example of grammatization would be writing, in which the temporal flow of speech is translated into a series of discrete letters or symbols on a page or a screen. Another example would be a CD, in which the temporal flow of music is recorded and stored as digital data on a plastic disk.

Bernard Stiegler (2012) argues that a key outcome of the processes of grammatization is the production of what he terms "tertiary memory." Tertiary memory is exteriorized or materialized memory, different in kind from primary memory (human perception) and secondary memory (human recollection). Stiegler suggests that tertiary memory is key to changes in human culture, because when information is stored outside of human memory it can be reliably recalled in the future. This has huge benefits, as it allows information to be created and transmitted across time and space in ways that would be impossible if that information remained in the form of fleeting words from a mouth or sound from a musical instrument (see also Ong 1982).

Stiegler also argues, however, that digital grammatization can have negative consequences for society at large. It is particularly problematic in today's networked computational environment, he suggests, because content is policed and controlled by a series of cultural industries, whose aim is to manipulate the temporal consciousness of those who engage with such content in order to sell products and generate profit (Stiegler 2009; 2010). This leads to what he terms a fundamental disaffection on the part of people who become oversaturated by the media that swamp their lives. This saturation "particularly affects the higher functioning of the nervous system: conception (understanding), perception and imagination, that is intellectual, aesthetic and affective life—the mind in all its dimensions" (Stiegler 2012, 86). He points to television and its advertising as forms of constant distraction that encourage viewers to endlessly shift their attention, which leads them to become unable to concentrate for long periods of time when engaged in activities such as reading. This inability discourages critical and creative thought, and further locks viewers into cycles of mindless consumption (Stiegler 2012, 88).

It follows that the GIF's short, looping, and often hypnotic nature can be understood as encouraging short attention spans as well as exemplifying Stiegler's claims about the problems of digital grammatization. I offer a different take, however, and suggest that GIFs do not necessarily lead to a mindless form of disaffection, but instead can actively amplify the potential for affect through their technical structure. To unpack these points, my discussion is divided into three sections. The first turns to the question of networked affect explicitly to argue that sense should not be considered as an exclusive property of human beings, but also as distributed and modulated across technical networks. In the second section, I argue that a GIF's capacity for affect is based upon three aspects of its technical structure—duration, color, and repetition. In the third section I suggest that processes of grammatization create the potential for excessive forms of affective experience that cannot be reduced to cognitive saturation, distraction, or disaffection. GIFs thereby demonstrate how simple forms of technology can undermine the supposed control that the cultural industries of film, television, and other media have over the content they create, for GIFs work only by exceeding the context of their production.

Modulating Sensation and Affect in a Network

Writing about the work of painter Francis Bacon, Deleuze develops a theory of sensation as irreducible to organic life. Deleuze suggests that sensation is not just a product of a living nervous system but a basic capacity of any object, entity, or system. In this model, sensation is a matter of force, or more precisely, "sensation is vibration" (Deleuze 2003, 32). On this basic level, every object has a capacity to sense and be sensed, because it also has a capacity to vibrate or be perturbed by forces traveling from another object, either directly or indirectly. As Deleuze puts it, "Force is closely related to sensation: for a sensation to exist a force must be exerted on the body, on a point of a wave" (Deleuze 2003, 41). Sensations are, therefore, not contained within the nervous system, but can be exteriorized synthetically in a medium such as paint or photographic paper; "sensation[s] ... [are] ... like arrests or snapshots of motion, which would recompose the movement synthetically in all its continuity, speed and violence" (Deleuze 2003, 29). The capacity of a sensation is inherently linked to the body or object that organizes that sensation. In Deleuze's words, "every sensation ... is already an 'accumulated' or 'coagulated' sensation" (2003, 27). In the case of painting, dipping a paintbrush in a paint pot organizes the distribution of paint on the bristles of the brush and allows the paint to be applied to a canvas. The sensation a blob of paint generates is therefore the outcome of the event of the encounter among brush, paint, and canvas. But, for Deleuze, that sensation can also remain accumulated or coagulated on the canvas after the brush and the human using it have left the scene.

This is not to say that sensations are organized by the static structure or properties of the objects involved in an encounter alone. Rather, Deleuze proposes that sensations are linked to the rhythms enabled or set in motion by the objects involved in an encounter. He defines rhythm as an arrangement of vibrations or "a wave that traces levels or thresholds in the body according to the variation of its amplitude" (Deleuze 2003, 23). It is not only the thickness of the bristles or coarseness of the canvas that creates the sensation of the paint, but also the motions and movements of hand on brush and brush on paint and paint on canvas that transmit and translate forces into sensations. In this regard, sensation is a two-way process. Objects and bodies sense and are sensed through an encounter between the organizations of their vibration: "sensation has one face turned toward the nervous system … and one face turned toward the … place, the event" (Deleuze 2003, 25). Exposed to sensation, both humans and nonhumans are altered. In Deleuze's words, "I become in the sensation and something happens through the sensation, one through the other, one in the other" (ibid.). Returning to the paintbrush example, we can say that the paintbrush's encounter with the canvas affects the composition and shape of the brush as well as the thickness and color of the paint which is applied using that brush.

In his work on Francis Bacon, Deleuze does not clearly delineate between the concepts of sensation and affect. For the purposes of this chapter, sensation can be understood as the rhythmic organization of organic and inorganic forces along with the transmission of these forces. Affects can be understood as the encounter of those organized forces with other bodies, an encounter which in turn shapes what these bodies are and the sensations they can generate. Sensations are constantly being reorganized through events of affective encounter, which in turn generate new sensations, and thus new contexts for the occurrence of affective encounters.

It is useful to develop Deleuze's definition of sensation and create a link between the concepts of sensation and affect, because this allows us to account for how sensations travel through networks and prime the context in which affective encounters take place. Rather than considering the network as a passive set of objects for transmitting information that becomes sense when it is experienced by a human body, we can consider the whole network as transmitting and translating sense itself, which in turn generates affects as these sensations encounter bodies. Computational objects and networks are not an instrumental tool for accessing information; their very structure, and the objects that power that structure, are central to the types and qualities of sense generated, and thus structure the affects that a particular object can potentially generate.

In this case, sensation and affect are not different in kind from one another, but are linked through an allotropic relationship. In *Francis Bacon* Deleuze mentions the concept of allotropy on a number of occasions, but does not elucidate it in any detail. For example, he says that "sensation is not qualitative and qualified, but has only an intensive reality, which no longer determines with itself representative elements, but allotropic variations" (Deleuze 2003, 32). In chemistry, the term "allotropy" refers to the different forms some chemical elements can take in the same phase or state, when exposed to different external conditions. Allotropy, then, denotes the changes in physical properties that can occur in some elements without a corresponding change to their overall substance. For example, depending on the temperature and pressure of the environment in which carbon is placed, it can take the form of either graphite or diamond. In Deleuze's language, allotropy involves the modulation of sensation as a form of intensive difference. According to Bonshek's (2003) reading of Colebrook (2002), intensities are pure forms of difference that cannot be sensed directly but only through the qualities that emerge from them. Using the example of human vision, Bonshek, citing Colebrook, suggests that we experience the pure difference of white light (which creates the color spectrum) only through the "intensity" of a single color, such as a shade of red. Our eyes do not perceive "the difference of each vibration of light" but "[contract] complex data into a single shade or object" (Bonshek 2003, n.p.). For Deleuze, allotropic modulation might be defined as how pure forms of difference (such as white light) come to be experienced as a particular quality (the color red) through the way bodies or objects encounter this difference.

Modifying Deleuze's use of the term, I define allotropy as the process through which a force is modulated and expresses itself as a sensation or an affect, and vice versa, depending on its encounters with other objects within a digital network. For example, when pressing a key on a keyboard, a finger creates a force that generates a sensation for the user (perhaps a feeling of solidity or give), which is shaped by the properties of the plastic, metal, and the type of springs used in the keyboard. At the same time, this force becomes reorganized into a different sensation for the capacitive circuit underneath the keys that is activated when the key is pressed. This sensation, understood as a different organization of vibrations, completes an electrical connection and sends a signal to the computer's processor, which registers it as a keystroke. Nonetheless, the sensation and affect of the keystroke are linked to the sensation of the finger in the sense that without the force created by the finger there could be no sensation to affect the capacitive circuit and register a keystroke. Through this process the rhythmic force of the finger typing generates sensations that travel through the various components of the computer and are modulated into affects as they encounter other components, generating further sensations which may be very different from the original. This same process can be applied to all manner of objects in a digital network, such as a router, an ethernet cable, and so on.

The allotropic modulation of forces extends to the human accessing the network, and can generate a further series of modulations in the user's body that, in turn, create new associations among different senses, thoughts, and memories. These associations can take many forms, such as synesthesia, or what Deleuze, following Marcel Proust, terms "involuntary memory." Synesthesia is the stimulation of sense organs by alternate sensory inputs. For example, people with extreme forms of synesthesia can "taste" color, or "see" sound. Involuntary memory involves the coupling of "two sensations that existed at different levels of the body, and that seize … each other like two wrestlers, the present sensation and the past sensation, in order to make something appear that was irreducible to them" (Deleuze 2003, 47). Involuntary memories might entail a strange sense of nostalgia, generated as a result of a sound or smell recalled from a different part or earlier time of an individual's life.

Within a digital network, associations such as synesthesia and involuntary memory can be created through the connection of various pieces of content (such as the mixing of a sound and an image in a video on YouTube) or the linking of technical elements or affects to particular pieces of content (such as a feeling of physical drag when a web page fails to load). The resonances of sense involved in the particular tone of a sound or resolution of an image can create new modes of affective experience. In the networks of the internet as well as the network of the body, forces allotropically modulate between sensations (the organization of forces) and affects (what those sensations can do) as they move and encounter other objects within these networks.

Following Deleuze's account of sensation as vibration, in which organic and inorganic matter alike have a capacity to sense, I argue that GIFs organize sensation in order to modulate affects and that these modulations are shaped by the technical specificity of the file types and networks through which GIFs travel. To understand the affective potentials of GIFs, the next section examines three forces that frame a GIF's potentiality to create sensations and affects: movement, color, and repetition.[1]

Affective Potentialities of the GIF

In this section I concentrate on a variety of GIFs from different sources, some made using photos taken by the GIF's creator and others using preexisting content from television, film, and fan-made material. It is important to note that these GIFs have been created for a variety of purposes, such as comedy value, to amaze or dazzle the viewer, or as a response on a message board or forum in place of a textual reply. While the content may radically differ from GIF to GIF, a set of common material features shapes their potential for transmitting forces and modulating between sensations and affects that can be shared by multiple viewers. Here I want to concentrate on just three of a GIF's material features: its short temporal duration, its limited color palette, and the way it can be programmed to continuously loop and repeat.

Short temporal duration

GIFs' animation times are generally short; they typically run for two to five seconds before looping and repeating. This short duration is key to the way in which they allotropically modulate the sensations from which they are composed into affects. For example, consider the dramatic "Prairie Dog" GIF originally taken from a segment of a Japanese television show, *Hello Morning*, in which the show's hosts are shown learning about this creature.[2] The GIF is a five-second animation of a prairie dog standing on its rear legs in a glass cage (figure 8.1). The animal suddenly turns toward the camera, which zooms in on its seemingly intense stare (figure 8.2). The prairie dog GIF achieved widespread online popularity around 2007, and is often used on message boards to signal a surprised response or feigned shock to an earlier post or event. On one level, this particular GIF is an anthropomorphic take on an animal's actions. As viewers of the GIF, we are asked to ascribe human features, intentions, and emotions to the prairie dog, namely that it is shocked or surprised by something that has just taken place. Indeed, the editing of the GIF is designed to create and enforce this narrative. Thinking through how the GIF communicates sensation and generates affect, however, suggests that its power to amuse or excite cannot entirely be reduced to the arbitrary narrative that one may apply to the images themselves.

Like all GIFs, this one is a form of compressed image, created in a raster format that uses a type of lossless compression to reduce the image's file size, while keeping an exact copy of the original uncompressed image. A raster format is a dot matrix data structure in which an image is created from a rectangular grid of pixels. The prairie dog's seeming capacity for movement is generated through linking a series of raster images to give the appearance of animation. GIF creators can customize the animation by defining the number of frames a GIF contains as well as the number of frames displayed per second. These factors determine the animation's speed of movement and the length of time it takes to play. The prairie dog GIF consists of forty-five frames of animation and lasts five seconds before it repeats. Its short duration is a product of the necessity to keep its file size small. The longer the GIF, the larger the file size. Larger files take longer to load, something that is especially noticeable on web pages that have many GIFs embedded within them. The technical requirement to keep GIFs small in file size influences the editing decisions made when a GIF is created.

These technical limitations mean that in all GIFs the action shown is necessarily removed from a broader context that would give the viewer clues about its original source (often a film, television program, or news report). Indeed one of the first questions often asked about a successful or popular GIF is, "Where did it come from?" This decontextualization helps remove any narrative that may be present in the original clip. However, the GIF does not simply impose a new narrative through its reediting. Rather, the very editing of the GIF creates new resonances and rhythms of sensation, which can potentially generate new affects. The zooming camera of the prairie dog GIF takes on a more intense force because the original television show's presenters who discussed the prairie dog no longer precede the shot. The fact that the clip loops over and over also encourages viewers to focus on the glint of light in the prairie dog's eyes, which they might have missed had they watched only the original clip. By editing the original clip into a short repeating loop, the GIF emphasizes the incorporeal forces involved in the relationship among prairie dog, its backdrop, and the camera. In other words, the GIF organizes sensation in a new way to prime the types of affect that might occur upon viewing the image, which were less likely to emerge when viewing

Figure 8.1
Still of "Prairie Dog in Glass Cage" GIF.

Figure 8.2
Close-up of "Prairie Dog" GIF.

the original television show from which the GIF was drawn. In the case of the prairie dog GIF, sensations of movement and zooming can become allotropically modulated into an uncanny affect of shock or amusement.

Color

GIFs utilize a red, green, and blue (RGB) color palette that contains space for 256 entries, which allows a single GIF to display a maximum of 256 colors. This limited palette means that most images gain a graininess absent in the original source image. In the "Jack Nicholson Nodding" GIF[3] (taken from a single shot excerpted from the 2003 film *Anger Management*), for example, graininess enhances the obsessed and slightly maniacal grin on Nicholson's face and works to associate his famous celebrity grin with a creepy kind of menace (figure 8.3). The GIF's limited color palette affords it the capacity to allotropically modulate an affect that is potentially different from what might be experienced when viewing the original film. Posted on forums and message boards, the Nicholson GIF is often used to communicate that a forum user has a strong (often sexual) desire for an object, an individual, or a practice (even as the GIF itself remains able to generate different affects, dependent on its individual viewers, such as revulsion or disgust).

Figure 8.3
Still from "Jack Nicholson Nodding" GIF.

Repetition

Animated GIFs embedded in web pages or deployed on social media can be set up to run automatically as soon as they have loaded. Many of these GIFs are also set to run in an endless loop, whether the user is paying attention to it or not (although they can also be set to run once, or a fixed number of times). The fact that GIF makers can set GIFs to run in an endless cycle, autonomous of the viewer, gives them a power to capture and hold attention. Their looping nature leaves the "before" and "after" of the GIF tantalizingly beyond the viewer's reach. Unless they can find the source material from which the GIF was drawn, viewers can only guess at what goes on in the full clip. Indeed, this curiosity is amplified by the contextual clues that may be partially visible at the beginning or end of a loop. With no simple way of stopping the loop, however, one can only concentrate and try to catch sight of a recognizable object.

In the same way that repeatedly speaking a word causes that word to sound strange and foreign, because it is uttered outside the context of familiar use, constantly looping GIF images alter the capacity for affect that the original images possessed, by reorganizing the images into new rhythms of sensation. The reorganization of movement and color, and the introduction of repetition, give the GIF a different capacity to affect compared to its source material.

Figure 8.4
Still from Micaël Reynaud, "Cat Yawning on a Lawn" GIF.

Deleuze's account of synesthesia and involuntary memory is useful in considering how GIFs might allotropically modulate force into sensations that are experienced as affects on different sensory levels in human viewers. For example, the designer Micaël Reynaud uses photos and graphics he has made to create complex time-lapse GIFs, such as of pizza being cooked in an oven[4] or a cat yawning on a lawn (figure 8.4). Synesthetically, these GIFs might invoke proprioceptive feelings of stickiness or warmth in the viewer's body as the dough thickens and rises, changing density, shape, and texture. The constant looping of the GIF can induce affects of grip, grab, and holding in the muscles, as viewers try to examine, grasp, and visually immobilize the organized sensation of the constantly repeating image. The yawning cat GIF might also work on the level of involuntary memory, uniting past and present sensations into novel combinations. Past experiences of touching animal fur, or particular experiences with grass, might unite to generate a new affect of tiredness, as viewers watch the cat yawn while it sits on the grass. Yet one cannot be sure of the particular emotional response that might arise in any single viewer's body when watching an animated GIF before it actually takes place. As Paasonen (2011) argues, affective resonances are open-ended, and the kinds of affect a sensation generates will be relative to the particular biographical, historical, and social context of the viewer. The specific technical structure of GIF animations, however, primes and frames the moment of encounter and, therefore, works to shape the particular affects that can emerge. The fact that popular GIFs proliferate and become internet memes suggests that while the affects they generate are not assured, the organization of sensation can and does produce equivalent affects in multiple viewers.

Toward an Allotropic Account of Networked Affect

I have examined the GIF as a digital file type in order to develop an allotropic account of how the potential for affect travels through digital networks. Modifying Deleuze's account of allotropy to think about the way forces express themselves as sensations or affects, depending on their mode of transmission and encounter, also contributes to broader debates around how affect travels. I have argued that affect itself does not travel, but that the potential for an affect to occur is framed by the particular forces and sensations that enable an affective encounter to take place. This broad point follows the classic statement of Marshall McLuhan (1964) that "the medium is the message," that the medium in which the message is presented influences how it is interpreted. This chapter expands that argument around technological mediation through an exploration of the affective realm. Concentrating on the affective realm destabilizes the concept of a message simply as a piece of content with intentional meaning, as well as the idea that interpretation only operates on the level of conscious awareness.

An allotropic account avoids the conceptual divides, generated in recent literature, that distinguish between contextual and precognitive accounts of affect (for example, Leys 2011; Papoulias and Callard 2010). From a contextual perspective, the affects experienced by humans are ultimately shaped by an individual's social and historical situation. From a precognitive perspective, affect works on an autonomic level, shaping bodily capacities and experiences with minimal interference from mediating historical and social factors.

Thinking allotropically alters the terms of debate between contextual and noncognitive accounts of affect by introducing a distinction between sensation and affect. Affects do not simply germinate at a point of encounter between two bodies but are intimately tied to sensations, which travel via human, technical, and nonhuman means. Even if affects shape human bodies on a precognitive level, the affects themselves are always already shaped by social and historical forces because they emerge from environments that precede particular individuals and objects. To understand how affects emerge, one has to follow forces and sensations as they travel and consider how such sensations are allotropically modulated as they meet with, and are translated into, affects by all manner of entities.

Earlier I introduced Stiegler's account of grammatization. Reflecting on the GIF as an object with a series of affective capacities, however, calls his account into question. Stiegler's account of grammatization, central to his critique of the digital cultural industries, concerns the exteriorization of information into some durable form, whether it be writing, drawing, or digital code. Developing Deleuze's notion of force and sensation to think about digital networks suggests that digital objects are anything but durable or fixed; instead they actively resonate alongside other objects to create rhythms of sense. As the example of the prairie dog GIF demonstrates, these resonances and rhythms always exceed any particular process of grammatization. While "Prairie Dog" and "Jack Nicholson Nodding" are lower-quality versions of the original video clips, these GIFs gain a quality of excess through the way they modulate between sensations and affects as they move within a network.

GIFs therefore contest a narrative in which digital grammatization is about the creation of disaffection through repetition and cognitive saturation. GIFs point to the ways in which images have, and always have had, an excessive quality beyond their production (see Hillis 2009). The prairie dog GIF, for example, takes on an affective life beyond *Hello Morning* and the Japanese television station that owns and runs the show. Rather than leading to a rise in disaffection, the hypnotic nature of GIFs can intensify the potential to experience affect precisely because of their automated, grammatized, and cyclical nature.

Notes

1. While the content of a GIF as well as its cultural context are key components in their affective response, the focus of this essay is on the GIF's technical attributes.

2. The prairie dog GIF can be viewed at http://gifsoup.com/view/129865/dramatic-prairie-dog .html.

3. The "Jack Nicholson Nodding" GIF can be viewed at http://replygif.net/163.

4. The yawning cat GIF can be viewed at https://plus.google.com/117576570968762597633/ posts/8eKFAC8sqdi. The rising pizza GIF can be viewed at https://plus.google.com/photos/ +micaelreynaud/albums/6020488297409604961/6020488301734667602?pid=602048830173466 7602&oid=117576570968762597633.

References

Berger, Jonah, and Katherine Milkman. 2010. Social Transmission, Emotion, and the Virality of Online Content. Available at http://opim.wharton.upenn.edu/~kmilkman/Virality.pdf.

Bonshek, Corrina. 2003. Deleuzian Sensation and Unbounded Consciousness in Anna & Corrina Bonshek's Reverie I (2002). *Body and Technology Jou*rnal 3 (2):n.p.

Burgess, Jean. 2008. "All Your Chocolate Rain Are Belong to Us?" Viral Video, YouTube and the Dynamics of Participatory Culture. In *Video Vortex Reader: Responses to YouTube*, ed. Geert Lovink and Sabine Niederer, 101–109. Amsterdam: Institute of Network Cultures.

Colebrook, Claire. 2002. *Understanding Deleuze*. St Leonards, Australia: Allen and Unwin.

CompuServe. 1987. GIF: Graphics Interchange Format. Available at http://www.x-ways.net/ winhex/kb/ff/GIF87.txt.

Deleuze, Gilles. 2003. *Francis Bacon: The Logic of Sensation*. Trans. Daniel W. Smith. New York: Continuum.

Dieter, Michael. 2011. The Becoming Environmental of Power: Tactical Media after Control. *Fibreculture Journal* 18. Available at http://eighteen.fibreculturejournal.org/2011/10/09/ fcj-126-the-becoming-environmental-of-power-tactical-media-after-control/.

Fernback, Jan. 2003. Legends on the Net: An Examination of Computer-Mediated Communication as a Locus of Oral Culture. *New Media and Society* 5 (1): 29–47.

Goddard, Michael, and Jussi Parikka. 2011 introduction to special issue, Unnatural Ecologies. *Fibreculture Journal* 17. Available at http://seventeen.fibreculturejournal.org/issue-17-unnatural -ecologies/.

Hansen, Mark. 2004a. The Time of Affect, or Bearing Witness to Life. *Critical Inquiry* 30 (3): 584–626.

Hansen, Mark. 2004b. *New Philosophy for New Media*. Cambridge, MA: MIT Press.

Hillis, Ken. 2009. *Online a Lot of the Time: Ritual, Fetish, Sign*. Durham: Duke University Press.

Knobel, Michele, and Colin Lankshear. 2007. Online Memes, Affinities and Cultural Production. In *A New Literacies Sampler*, ed. Michele Knobel and Colin Lankshear, 199–207. New York: Peter Lang.

Lessig, Lawrence. 2008. *Remix: Making Art and Commerce Thrive in the Hybrid Economy*. New York: Penguin.

Leys, Ruth. 2011. The Turn to Affect: A Critique. *Critical Inquiry* 37 (3): 434–472.

Martin, Katherine. 2012. Oxford Dictionaries USA Word of the Year 2012: "to GIF." *OUP Blog*. Available at http://blog.oup.com/2012/11/oxford-dictionaries-usa-word-of-the-year-2012-gif.

McLuhan, Marshall. 1964. *Understanding Media*. New York: McGraw-Hill.

Ong, Walter. 1982. *Orality and Literacy: The Technologizing of the Word*. New York: Routledge.

Dictionaries, Oxford. 2012. Oxford Dictionaries USA Word of the Year 2012. *Oxford Dictionaries Blog*. Available at http://blog.oxforddictionaries.com/press-releases/us-word-of-the-year-2012/.

Paasonen, Susanna. 2011. *Carnal Resonance: Affect and Online Pornography*. Cambridge, MA: MIT Press.

Papoulias, Constantina, and Felicity Callard. 2010. Biology's Gift: Interrogating the Turn to Affect. *Body and Society* 16 (1): 29–56.

Stiegler, Bernard. 2009. *Technics and Time 2: Disorientation*. Stanford: Stanford University Press.

Stiegler, Bernard. 2010. Bernard Stiegler's Pharmacy: A Conversation. *Configurations* 18 (3): 459–476.

Stiegler, Bernard. 2012. *Uncontrollable Societies of Disaffected Individuals*. London: Polity Press.

9 Technologies of Feeling: Affect between the Analog and the Digital

Jenny Sundén

In the midst of the affective networks of contemporary digital cultures and communities, built on endless technological upgrades to increase computational speed, power, and performance, something seemingly of the opposite order is taking shape. It is a culture that contrasts speed with slowness, displaces the new with the old and the used, and replaces supposedly immaterial streams of data with highly material, tactile technologies, materials, and fabrics. These turns to the analog are evident in, for example, craftivism and do-it-yourself movements, employing strategies such as reverse engineering, recycling, reuse, hacking, and modding.[1] There are heaps of blogs and social networking pages testifying to a return to things analog: the obsession with analog photography among contemporary hipsters, the layering of the analog and the digital in Instagram, the appeal of the mixed tape in cassette culture, the fascination with mechanical clockwork in steampunk. Laura Marks (2002, 152–153) speaks of a desire for indexicality among digital videomakers that she terms "analog nostalgia," "a retrospective fondness for the 'problems' of decay and generational loss that analog video posed ... in a sort of longing for analog physicality." In a similar vein, *New York* magazine reports on an "analog renaissance" within a new "analog underground":

This loosely allied network of artists, tinkerers, and the merely tech-weary aren't ditching their iPhones or boycotting Facebook just yet, but they are seeking a slower, more hands-on way of doing things. Instead of downloading mp3s by the thousand, they're combing the bins at once-endangered record stores. In lieu of Tweeting their every errant thought, they're snail-mailing actual typewritten letters.[2]

In a world increasingly composed of discrete units of zeros and ones, such love affairs with the analog could be understood as a reaction to a particular capitalist techno-logic. But as will become clear in this chapter, there is not necessarily a contradiction at play between reacting against and being an intrinsic part of the very same logic. Neither is the digital itself vacated of passionate connectivity. While there is a growing movement of neo-Luddites, highly critical of as well as distancing themselves from digital cultures and technologies, most "analogists" appear to be digital natives (cf. Marks 2002), moving back and forth between different modes and codes as a manner of inhabiting communities that are as locally rooted as they are digitally connected. A desire for the analog highlights not only a longing for a past, but also seems to indicate an interest in the interplay between analog and digital media. Put differently, it is a longing for an *idea* of the past, for an imaginary time made real through analog practices in the present.

Steampunk cultures provide compelling examples of a contemporary affective investment in the analog, coupled with intense digital connectivity.[3] In this chapter, I use steampunk as a way of thinking about affect in analog and digital media and forms of embodiment in contemporary technological cultures. After a brief introduction to steampunk cultures, I will evoke affect as a manner not only of recognizing steampunk as visual spectacle, but also of better understanding the appeal of the analog in terms of a desire for technologies that can be felt powerfully, even feared. I will then critically engage with Brian Massumi's (2002) notion of the superiority of the analog, which at first sight may seem to play straight into the hands of steampunks and their passion for the analog. Then again, his engagement in and with an analog register as dynamic and transformative depends on a digital register that is almost completely immobile and lifeless. This polarity fails to address how steampunks tend to shuttle, intensely, between the digital and the analog according to a logic that remains to be made explicit. In an attempt to think differently about affect between the analog and the digital, I will suggest that steampunk, rather than being characterized by a return to the analog (in a manner that requires a turning away from the digital), is more aptly understood in terms of the *transdigital*. Within this chapter, then, steampunk is used as an especially intriguing example of a broader tendency toward transdigital modes of using and sensing media in contemporary media landscapes.

Steampunk has been described as an "aesthetic technological movement" (Catastrophone Orchestra and Arts Collective NYC 2007), incorporating science fiction, art, engineering, and a vibrant twenty-first-century subculture. It is characterized by a retro-futurist take on the steam-powered technologies of the Victorian era. Rather than being reenactors, steampunks are reimaginators with a punk do-it-yourself ethos, organized around the question: "What if we continued as an analog society instead of a digital one?" Steampunk is certainly not one culture but many, replete with ambiguities and contradictions. There are those who emphasize the "steam" in steampunk and tend to appear fairly romantic, neo-Victorian, with an emphasis on aesthetics.[4] And there are those who are more critical and "punk," invested in the political potentials of technological anachronism.[5] This mixture is also reflected in steampunk costumes, which are dense with Victoriana (crinolines and corsets, top hats and pocket watches), yet anachronistically extended or infringed by wearable technologies: clockwork, brass accents, and all kinds of modified contraptions. In and through its many guises, steampunk as a movement has the potential of combining playfulness and whimsy with a sharp political response to the production and consumption of digital media technologies. The ways in which we imagine and feel for technologies matter, and steampunk at its best brings the power of reimagination to technological cultures.

Steampunk Affects

The very first issue of *Steampunk Magazine*—an ambitious print-and-web periodical devoted to the steampunk fiction genre as well as its growing culture—argues that steampunk, above all, is a non-Luddite critique of technology:

[Steampunk] rejects the ultra-hip dystopia of the cyberpunks—black rain and nihilistic posturing—while simultaneously forfeiting the "noble savage" fantasy of the pre-technological era. It revels in the concrete reality of technology instead of the over-analytical abstractness of cybernetics. Steam technology is the difference between the nerd and the mad scientist; steampunk machines are real, breathing, coughing, struggling and rumbling parts of the world. They are not the airy intellectual fairies of algorithmic mathematics but the hulking manifestations of muscle and mind, the progeny of sweat, blood, tears and delusions. The technology of steampunk is natural; it moves, lives, ages and even dies. (Catastrophone Orchestra and Arts Collective NYC 2007, 5)

If the console cowboys of cyberpunk hacked their way through cyberspace, arguing for free information and open source software, steampunks are hardware hackers, ultimately reclaiming technology for the masses. If cyberpunk incorporates sinister, dystopian visions of worlds consisting of disembodied, immaterial information, steampunk is more hopeful, as well as strikingly embodied and material. The two may unite in their critique of the corporate expert cultures of digital technologies, but steampunk performs an interesting disruption within discourses of weightless, ubiquitous information, instead continuously emphasizing the palpable weight, materiality, and vividness of technologies. Expressed along the lines of an ice-cold intellectual logic, the "digital" in this passage (expressed through "the over-analytical abstractness of cybernetics") seems devoid of affect, whereas steampunk technologies are saturated by a language of intensity and excess. They are "the hulking manifestations of muscle and mind, the progeny of sweat, blood, tears and delusions" (Catastrophone Orchestra and Arts Collective NYC 2007, 5).

Steampunk technologies can be stunning with their shimmering brass accents, bronze ornaments, and brushed steel surfaces. Clunky chunks of metal meet the rounded shapes of watch parts and soft brown leather. It is a realm of the inner workings of machines and machine parts made visible, of technology turned inside out in an endless exposure of cogs, cogwheels, springs, and screws, bringing together visual beauty with a noticeable tactile dimension and an invitation of sorts to take part in the making of technology (see figures 9.1 and 9.2).

Figure 9.1
Original handcrafted steampunk jewelry: http://www.etsy.com/shop/ClockworkJungles. Courtesy
of Amber Reed, owner of Clockwork Jungles.

These are technologies that live and breathe as tangible incarnations of a past (that
never was), belonging to an era when technologies seemed open to alteration and
transformation. This understanding of the democratizing potential in the analog simultaneously begs the question: Who gets to be a steampunk maker? Within steampunk communities, technologies are something to touch and be touched by, distinctive technologies of feeling that attempt to restore or recreate a sense of technological
uniqueness and magic supposedly lost in the streamlining and uniformity of contemporary digital technologies (cf. Onion 2008). In its bringing together of nineteenth-
century mechanical engineering and neo-Victorian punk romance, steampunk is not
merely about visually beautiful objects, but equally about hands-on concreteness and
touch. This multisensorial engagement with the physical reality of technologies as
"real, breathing, coughing, struggling and rumbling parts of the world," as something
that "moves, lives, ages and even dies," points at the intensity and affective charge of
technological attachments within steampunk.

But notwithstanding the passage quoted above, a critique of the digital as completely void of affect, routed through a love story of the analog, steampunks are at the

same time digitally connected and skilled users of the very technologies and practices under scrutiny. The non-Luddite response to technology makes steampunks postindustrial (and, as I will suggest, transdigital) and tech-savvy, yet with an interestingly ambivalent relationship to digital technologies. Steampunk scenes are largely fueled by the web (Second Life, for example, houses a large group of steampunks). It is in online venues that steampunks gather and mobilize to exchange ideas, visions, and, perhaps above all, images. Steampunk is a movement that simply would not have existed in its current shape had it not been for the possibilities of making and distributing images digitally, of crisscrossing steampunk aesthetics with online visual cultures. If tactility is key when it comes to the allure of the analog in steampunk, then the promise of reimagining and reimaging a technologically defamiliarized past in spectacular ways may explain the draw of the digital for steampunk movements.

Steampunk areas in Second Life, such as the lands of Caledon, New Babbage, and Rosser's Landing, are saturated with whimsical technological contraptions—clockwork devices, airships, submersibles, and even Victorian architecture floating in the sky. In Caledon's South End, my research character, steampunkette JenMadelene, came across something interesting from the point of view of *digital* tactility and crafting: the fabulous Trilby's Mill (papermaking, letterpress printing, and fine bookbinding), created by a real-life book artist who goes by the Second Life name Trilby Minotaur. Trilby has become something of an in-world celebrity with more than a thousand visitors to her mill since it opened in 2008. Trilby's is a two-storied watermill, with the bottom floor

Figure 9.2
Google Image search for "steampunk second life."

devoted to the process of papermaking. This is also the place to lay your hands on one of Trilby's beautifully textured dresses:

Trilby's Mill clothing is made from decorative elements found in old and rare books, the sort of thing the fairy folk who live behind the books on the bookshelf might wear. The texture for this dress came from the marbled endsheets of a book published in 1797. Marbling is done by floating ink on a bath of liquid and swirling it into a pattern. A piece of prepared paper is then gently laid on the water to pick up the ink.[6]

The top floor of the mill houses a steam-powered printing press, based on Trilby's 1950s real-life press (a Vandercook 4), which has been reimagined and remodeled for the nineteenth-century Caledon scenery. This floor also holds a bookbindery section, where you can sit down to sew a book by hand, then stroll out on the balcony to get a good view from above the waterfall that drives the big waterwheel. JenMadelene has visited many steampunk venues in Second Life, but few are as captivating and tangible in their loving details as this one.

How, then, could this affective moving back and forth between the analog and the digital be conceptualized? Could the body in steampunk be understood as something that moves between the analog and the digital, in terms of border crossing, or as a kind of switching? What are the differences between affects in the analog and the digital realms?

My point of departure to understand the interrelations between bodies and affect is a Deleuzian reading of Baruch Spinoza.[7] Spinoza's philosophy is vitally concerned with relationships between bodies—which can be human bodies but also body parts, animals, and inanimate objects (Deleuze 1988, 127). Rather than being a fixed entity, a body is a vibrant relation whose structure and boundaries are in constant flux, defined in and through its capacity to affect or be affected. Bodies (and minds) in Spinoza are not forms, functions, substances, or subjects but modes, defined by the affects of which they are capable, by the set of affects that occupy a body at each moment. With Spinoza, affect is variation, or passage, that which moves between bodies, be they human or nonhuman, whole or fractured. The body is understood relationally, which involves ideas of the body in movement and as movement, as well as its capacity to affect and be affected. The body is one with its affective capacities, or, as Massumi (2002, 15) has it, with its transitions. If affect is variation, transition, translation—turning the body into a medium of sorts, or an amplifier—it could also be something of a switchboard between analog and digital modes of moving, sensing, and communicating. To Massumi, the body is a "transducer," an energy converter that facilitates crossovers between qualitatively different media, "relaying between artificial and natural intelligence, human will and programmed motion, organic and mechanical movement" (Massumi 2002, 118). But as will become clear, for Massumi such transductions are almost exclusively about *analog* impulses from one medium to another—as if the digital has no place for bodies as transitioning devices.

In Love with the Analog

In a personal interview with Fredrik Anjou, a Swedish musician in a band labeled as steampunk by participants in the steampunk music scene, he discussed the evanescent quality of the digital in contrast to the physical concreteness and beauty of analog technologies, instruments, and ways of making music:

Of course it is for real [the digital], but I can't feel it. It feels very ephemeral. For me, it's like that. And that's why we play the music we do. We play on real instruments. We prefer to play live, and when we recorded the album, we did it analogically in an old studio. And then it's digitally mixed and mastered in a computer, but it's still us, playing for real. I could never create music in a computer. I'm very analog that way. My entire body. I want to do things for real. Write by hand, and such.[8]

In this account, the analog certainly rubs up against the digital, in the studio and elsewhere. But the point brought out clearly in this interview is that for Anjou, the analog is that which can be *felt*, something that makes possible musical connections and community that are "real." The digital is granted a realness of sorts ("you can always print things out on paper"), but it is an actuality that does not have the same feel to it.

If it wasn't for its time consuming aspect and for having to deal with so many retypings, I would much rather write on a typewriter than on a computer. Because I find that it's for real, and above all that it's such a beautiful machine, compared to that one [points at my iPhone, used as a recording device].[9]

Steampunk cultures are saturated with allusions like these to analog technologies and modes of working and relating to the world and to others. What comes forth is a particular sense of physical concreteness, tactility, and beauty that digital technologies are found to be lacking. It does not seem to be a question of digital technologies as lacking altogether the possibility of touch, since plenty of digital media technologies are all about touch (screens), touching, and getting in touch. The question is rather one about the difference between different kinds of touch. It is about the difference between the soft tapping on a relatively short-lived computer keyboard and the more forceful pressing down on the durable keys of a typewriter, which in turn press back up against the fingers. There is even a growing market for modified computer keyboards to replicate some of that feel (which, again, points at the analog as intimately entangled with the digital). Richard R. Nagy—aka Datamancer—is one of the most well-known steampunk contraptors and technical artists, and especially so for his stunning neo-Victorian modifications of desktops, laptops, and keyboards. On the topic of what the keys of his keyboards feel and sound like, he explains:

The mechanical keys give the keyboards the slightest bit of a tactile "click" or "snap" to them, which lends itself nicely to the "typewriter" theme of the keys and provides a nice sense of touch-feedback. They are slightly louder than a "soft touch" style membrane keyboard, but not obnoxiously so.[10]

The allure of this modified keyboard is its particular sense of tactility with a touch feedback. But with that tactility, and the very "snap" of the mechanico-digital keys, which approaches that of a typewriter, comes a louder noise than regular computer users may be accustomed to. This level of noise calls for an in-between version that is louder than a regular computer but quieter than an actual typewriter. It is a hybrid type of touch and a hybrid noise that, while having immediate connections to the (digital) computer, are also reminiscent of a time when technologies were imagined to provide other ways of touching and being touched than those for which postindustrial media contexts allow.

Massumi's (2002) affect theory, in its encounters with the domain of the analog, is written from a similar stance. In his understanding of affect, the intimate connection between bodily movement and sensation is crucial. Taking as a starting point this connection, every shift in the body, no matter how small, makes something change and generates new modes of feeling. The body is here understood as neither mediated nor discursive, but as something with a more immediate link between moving and feeling. Massumi clearly separates affect from emotion, the unmediated from the mediated, and the analog from the digital in a manner that has interesting resonance with ways of thinking and feeling the analog in steampunk. But not only do analog and digital modes and codes belong to distinctly separate registers, the digital in his argument seems to completely short-circuit the body, in movement and as movement.

Massumi is careful to point out how what he names the virtual is clearly separated from the digital. To him, the virtual is something intimately corporeal, yet reaches beyond the body. He writes of the virtual, in a Deleuzian manner, as an exceedingly real, yet abstract, incorporeal dimension of the body itself. The body is as immediately virtual as it is immediately actual, Massumi says. If the body as movement never coincides with itself, but only with its own capacity to change, with its own variation, then there is always a range of variations and potentials that are never actualized. The virtual is about this nonactualized, nonpresent (since it has slipped away, or never was) potential to change. To him, there is nothing more disturbing for thinking about virtuality than to conflate the virtual with the digital and its ways to systematize, measure, and code. The digital has connections to the virtual as potential only through the analog. Massumi contrasts a highly moving, dynamic, and transformative analog mode with a digital mode that is strikingly inert, static, and lifeless. He understands the analog as analogical, but not as an analog(y) of something. It does not model something else, but refers rather to a process of self-referential transformation:

The analog is *process*, self-referenced to its own variations. It resembles nothing outside itself. ... Sensation, always on arrival a transformative feeling of the outside, a feeling of thought, is the being of the analog. It is matter in analog mode. This is the analog in a sense close to the technical meaning, as a continuously variable impulse or momentum that can cross from one qualitatively different medium into another. Like electricity into sound waves. Or heat into pain. Or light waves into vision. Or vision into imagination. Or noise in the ear into music in the heart. *Or outside coming in.* Variable continuity across the qualitatively different: continuity of transformation. (Massumi 2002, 135.)

If the analog is a process of gradual variability or multiple differentiation across a sliding scale between different media, or bodies, the digital is "a numerically based form of codification (zeros and ones)" closely related to the numeric operations of digitization, "step after ploddingly programmed step. Machinic habit" (Massumi 2002, 137). For Massumi, however, language reduced to machine code in a word processor comes to life anew on the screen through acts of reading. Reading as a process is in Massumi's terms analog. Users do things of which the machine code itself is not capable; they experience that which appears on the screen. In other words, while the mode or the processing may be digital, the process—of reception, or experience, or embodiment—is analog. In spite of this encounter between the digital and the analog, in which the digital is realized through the analog as process, it is striking how devoid of affect Massumi's argument is (the body present in the argument is restless, inattentive, and bored in front of the computer; see Petit, this volume). The digital equals the machinic, the technological, the inorganic in his thinking, and digital technologies are clearly not a passionate matter.

At the end of the chapter (which aptly carries the title "On the Superiority of the Analog"), there is an opening of sorts toward how the digital and the analog could be thought in more composite terms. But, in the next moment, it becomes obvious that the analog always has primacy:

There is always an excess of the analog over the digital, because it perceptually fringes, synesthetically dopplers, umbilically backgrounds, and insensibly recedes to a virtual center immanent at every point along the path—all in the same contortionist motion. It is most twisted. The analog and the digital must be thought together, asymmetrically. Because the analog is always a fold ahead. (Massumi 2002, 143)

To think the analog and the digital tightly together seems like a good idea as a counterweight to arguments that speak of the digital as that which has gradually replaced the analog, as if societies depending on digital processing would be digital to the bone. But while Massumi thinks the analog and the digital intimately together, they are still very much distinct, and, for him, only one of them (the analog) seems to entail sensation, transformation, affect. Affect theory, generally speaking, destabilizes the human subject along with the kind of cultural theory that posits the transformation of signification and representation as the only serious political issue. Affect theory facilitates an opening up of the body to external forms of affective power and forces, and it does so in ways that make it difficult to stay within a humanist project and its privileging of human subjectivity, as well as its privileging of signification and meaning. While Massumi's way of writing affect is certainly nonrepresentational (or antirepresentational), his move beyond human skin never seems to venture far enough to let other types of skin, or (nonhuman) bodies, into the picture. Or, more to the point, when his nonsignifying philosophy of affect hits the digital, he becomes strikingly humanist.

Moving through the Heart of the Digital

Is it productive, or even possible, to speak of the analog as that which always proceeds, envelops, and grounds the digital? And does the digital, by necessity, equal the machinic? There seems to be something of a slippage in Massumi's argument between modes of embodiment and affect on the one hand, and modes of technologies or media on the other. Technically, it is reasonably easy to distinguish between analog and digital communication, between a many-valued continuum and a two-valued discontinuum (even if every such distinction is not without its own problems and slippages). But in matters of the human, organic body, the question is much more complex. As has been clear from the first wave of cybernetics, without the digital there would be no analog. In other words, it is only after the advent of the digital computer that previous generations of mechanical, analog computers could be named accordingly. As Anthony Wilden (1972) shows in his influential essay "Analog and Digital Communication," the very distinction between analog and digital communication depends on the way information is circulated or transmitted in manmade, cybernetic devices. He distinguishes the analog computer, "defined as any device that 'computes' by means of an analog between real, physical, CONTINUOUS quantities and some other set of variables" (Wilden 1972, 50), from the digital computer, which "involves DISCRETE elements and discontinuous scales" (Wilden 1972, 51), and concludes: "Whereas in man-made information-processing devices the boundaries of the analog/digital distinction are fairly clear, the same is not true for the intraorganismic communication of the human body" (Wilden 1972, 52). Put differently, the human body as an affect system is a complex fusion or mixture of analog and digital communication systems.

Eve Kosofsky Sedgwick and Adam Frank (1995) make a similar case in their discussion of affect in the field of cybernetics. In their reading of the American psychologist Silvan Tomkins, they point out how his theory of affect overlaps with perspectives in cybernetics in ways that result in an understanding of the human as an intricate layering of biological and mechanical components in relation to which the digital (on/off) takes intimate turns with the analog (the continuous or multiply differentiated):

[W]e must nonetheless deprecate (as would Tomkins or indeed any systems theorist) the further homology that might identify the machine or computer with digital representation and the biological organism with analogical representation. The tacit homology machine: digital:: animal: analogical ... represents bad engineering and bad biology, and it leads to bad theory. Even supposing information machines and living organisms to be altogether distinct classes, they certainly have in common that each comprises a heterogeneous mixture of digitally and analogically structured representational mechanisms. For that matter, the distinction between digital and analog is itself anything but absolute. (Sedgwick and Frank 1995, 505)

In contrast to Massumi, who seems to simply equate the digital with the computational, Sedgwick and Frank resist the idea that the machine or the computer must always be associated with digital representations and the biological organism with analog representations. Instead, they open a space for understanding affect as something that continuously moves back and forth between the digital and the analog. For example, sexuality as a mechanism of desire can be on/off at the level of the drive system, whereas its link to motivation and action needs multiple and qualitatively different possibilities.

If Massumi's digital is never mobilized by bodies in movement and as movement, my own argument takes seriously the seeming lack of distinction in Spinoza between nature and artifice (Deleuze 1988, 124), which opens up possibilities for exploring the affective relations and the in-betweens of human and nonhuman bodies (be they digital or analog). Bodies in steampunk are densely technological in ways that make it difficult to restrict the area of the digital to that which does not move bodies, or put them in motion. Steampunk embodiment consists of technological extensions, both physically concrete (analog) extensions, such as wearables and corporeal gadgets, and online (digital) extensions, such as transnational community ties and the fantastical incorporations of steampunk in Second Life. Importantly, the analog as a peculiarly affective affair in steampunk is completely dependent on digital technologies, imaging, and circulations as the very tools by which the past is bent and reshaped.

As I have shown in this chapter, there is an affective switching, or turn-taking, between analog and digital media and forms of embodiment in contemporary steampunk practices. Within the field of new media studies, it is old news that "new" media always embody, remix, amplify, and sample "old" media. What retrospectively can be called (predigital) analog culture is now being twisted and remade at the very core of digital cultures by being mixed into a media landscape, or a set of media practices, that give rise to analogico-digital fusions.[11] These fusions are perhaps most obvious in retro interpretations of new media, such as when a cell phone is connected to a clunky, old-fashioned handset, or to a tripod and a zoom lens, or becomes an iPhonograph. Such amalgamations of the analog and the digital are common in steampunk, an example being the humorous take on Apple's iPod: Dr. Grymm's Eye-Pod "Two Point, OH!," which is the second generation of a *Frankenstein*-style modded iPod.[12] But, as has also been shown, the layering of analog and digital can be understood in more subtle ways.

I started out this chapter by pointing to a set of media practices that seemingly embrace the analog nostalgically, at the expense of the digital. And yet, from the beginning it was already clear that these turns to the analog did not require a turning away from the digital. On the contrary, this seemingly newfound passion for the analog is completely dependent on the digital—it is a fascination for the analog that builds on digital connectivity in ways that insist on a rethinking of the digital itself. In a *Wired* column, Nicholas Negroponte (1998) claimed that "the Digital Revolution is over," and he pointed out how the revolutionary period of the digital was passing, as digital technologies were becoming mundane, ubiquitous, and invisible: "Being digital will be noticed only by its absence, not its presence." What he gestures at could be termed the "postdigital," as a way of characterizing the era that comes after "the digital revolution" (cf. Pepperell and Punt 2000). But in contrast to Negroponte's idea of ubiquitous computing and the invisible ubiquity of digital technologies, the notion of the postdigital has been discussed in much more material terms. In studies of contemporary (electronic) music, the postdigital becomes a manner of analyzing the materiality of the digital by paying attention to digital glitches and systemic failure (Cascone 2000), and in the field of digital artistic practice, postdigital art is defined as "art forms that address the humanization of digital technologies through interplay between digital, biological, cultural, and spiritual systems, between ... high tech and high touch experiences" (Alexenberg 2011, 10).

The juxtaposition of high tech and high touch is interesting. Steampunk practices could perhaps be understood as postdigital in this sense, with reference to a materialist analysis of the digital. Then again, it is unclear whether the postdigital could account for the intense shuttling between the *analog* and the digital, in steampunk and elsewhere. There is also a risk with the term postdigital that it inserts a chronological ordering. "Post," in the sense to come after, fails to account for how the digital was never immaterial, disembodied, or placeless. Instead, I suggest the term *transdigital*, to account for analog passions that are shaped through the digital in ways that concretely activate, but also move across the borders of or beyond the digital. The transdigital makes gestures at such media practices that are digital at heart, but simultaneously transgress or challenge the category itself. In working with "trans," I take the cue from transgender studies, and in particular Susan Stryker's way of understanding transgender "as an umbrella term that refers to all identities or practices that cross over, cut across, move between, or otherwise queer socially constructed sex/gender boundaries. ... Like 'queer,' 'transgender' may also be used as a verb or an adjective" (Stryker 1994, 251).

To queer or trans the digital, then, is to transcend, transgress, or otherwise bend the boundaries of media (and bodies). Steampunk can be understood as something that transes (or queers, or punks) "steam." The "punk" in steampunk works as a critical tool in that it provides ways of bending, or hacking, or reimagining the past (Carrott and Johnson 2012). But steampunk is also quite concretely a transing of the digital *with* steam, a contestation of the digital by means of a technological imagination based on nineteenth-century mechanical engineering. The affective relation to the analog in steampunk is invested in technological concreteness, materiality, and tactility. When steam in terms of high touch and concrete tactility transes the digital, this is a process that highlights the materiality of the digital, as well as its connectedness with other temporal orders and technological forms. Steampunk, rather than merely being a return to a bygone era, is a reconsideration, or transing, of the (digital) present.

Transdigital technological practices are trans-formative. There is something transitory and fleeting about transformations, but also something concrete and acutely material. A transformation is fundamentally about change, in being an act, a process, or an instance of transforming or of being transformed. To transform is to move, to shift, to turn, but, more radically, it can also be about transmutation, even metamorphosis. Emphasizing the "trans" in transformation, to trans-form is a matter of something taking form differently from, across the borders of, beyond itself, or perhaps as something else, another form (such as the analog). Trans also draws attention to material specificity. Transgressions accentuate the transgressed medium, or body. A transgression of a category, a body, a form, makes visible the category itself, its material specificity. If the transgender body emphasizes gender (no matter how fictitious) as that which is being transed, the steam in steampunk punks the digital in ways that draws attention to the specificity of digital materiality and processing, and at the same time underscores the digital as something highly porous and interconnected.

What is becoming exceedingly clear in transdigital encounters and practices is the very materiality of technologies, as well as their affective relationality. If the postdigital is performing something of a discursive break with the digital, the transdigital rather gradually displaces, but also intensifies and clarifies, what has been there all along. The digital was always strikingly material, embodied, and situated (Sundén 2003). What a conceptualization of the transdigital brings to the fore is the increasing visibility of such materiality, as well as a heightened attention to the local, embodied, affective nature of technological practices. The ongoing revival or return to analog media technologies makes an intensification of the materiality of the digital particularly clear, since it is a revival actualized only by a move through the heart of the digital. This chapter has engaged with what could be termed *transdigital affects*, a type of corporeal relationality that arises in contemporary passionate encounters with the analog made possible by, or realized through, the digital. A different way of conceptualizing transdigital affectivity would be to address anachronism, and to think affects in an anachronistic register. Time in steampunk is not linear, not chrono-logical, but tangled through temporal loops and folds, through a play with future (virtual) possibilities by an intricate entanglement of the analog and the digital. This is not mere analog nostalgia. This is transdigital affectivity in an anachronistic vein, a looking back with a twist as an attempt to inhabit the present differently.

Notes

1. *Craftivism* is activism focused on craft and crafting practices, most notably knitting, to challenge and disrupt dominating consumerist norms and orders (such as knitting infiltrating public

spaces). *Reverse engineering* is about exposing the underlying technological principles of a technological object, usually by taking it apart, or by building something that works similarly, but without simply replicating the original. *Modding* (from modification, or to modify) refers to the activity of modifying hardware and/or software to create functions at odds with the original design intentions.

2. Halpern (2011).

3. This chapter is part of the larger research project Clockwork, Corsets, and Brass: The Politics and Dreams of Steampunk Cultures, financed by Riksbankens Jubileumsfond (the Swedish Foundation for Humanities and Social Sciences).

4. See, for example, the community pages *Brass Goggles,* "a blog and forum devoted to the lighter side of all things Steampunk," http://brassgoggles.co.uk/blog, http://brassgoggles.co.uk/forum, and *Steampunk Empire*, http://www.thesteampunkempire.com.

5. See, for example, *Steampunk Magazine*, http://www.steampunkmagazine.com and the postcolonial steampunk blog *Beyond Victoriana*, http://beyondvictoriana.com.

6. See https://marketplace.secondlife.com/p/Trilbys-Mill-1797-dress-for-petites-boxed/3300741.

7. For a detailed reading of Spinoza on affect in the context of steampunk—as well as of critical feminist engagements with Spinoza—see Sundén 2013. This article engages in affective renderings of the relations, rhythms, and power of the corset in steampunk as a soma-technology, offering a Spinozian micropolitical feminism of the in-betweens of bodies.

8. Interview with Fredrik Anjou, Stockholm, April 3, 2012.

9. Ibid.

10. http://www.datamancer.com/cart/faq-ezp-22.html.

11. Jake Buckley (2011) borrows the term "analogico-digital" from Bernard Stiegler (2002) as a way of theorizing the digital as something other than merely a catalyst for the analog.

12. See   http://www.steampunktribune.com/2011/11/eye-pod-two-point-oh-has-been-released .html and https://www.youtube.com/watch?v=LbdHGjknyF4.

References

Alexenberg, Mel. 2011. *The Future of Art in a Postdigital Age: From Hellenistic to Hebraic Consciousness*. Bristol: Intellect.

Buckley, Jake. 2011. Believing in the (Analogico-)Digital. *Culture Machine* 12:1–15. Available at http://culturemachine.net/index.php/cm/article/view/432/463.

Carrott, James H., and Brian David Johnson. 2012. *Vintage Tomorrows: A Historian and a Futurist Journey through Steampunk into the Future of Technology*. Sebastopol, CA: O'Reilly.

Cascone, Kim. 2000. The Aesthetics of Failure: "Post-Digital" Tendencies in Contemporary Computer Music. *Computer Music Journal* 24 (4):12–18.

Catastrophone Orchestra and Arts Collective NYC. 2007. What Then, Is Steampunk? *Steampunk Magazine* 1. Available at http://www.combustionbooks.org/downloads/SPM1-printing.pdf.

Deleuze, Gilles. [1970] 1988. *Spinoza: Practical Philosophy*. Trans. Robert Hurley. San Francisco: City Lights Books.

Halpern, Ashlea. 2011. The Analog Underground; Analog Renaissance. *New York Magazine* (July 3). Available at http://nymag.com/shopping/features/analog-2011-7/ and http://nymag.com/shopping/features/analog-renaissance-2011-7.

Marks, Laura. 2002. *Touch: Sensuous Theory and Multisensory Media*. Minneapolis: University of Minnesota Press.

Massumi, Brian. 2002. *Parables for the Virtual: Movement, Affect, Sensation*. Durham: Duke University Press.

Negroponte, Nicholas. 1998. Beyond Digital. *Wired* 6 (12). Available at http://www.wired.com/wired/archive/6.12/negroponte.html.

Onion, Rebecca. 2008. Reclaiming the Machine: An Introductory Look at Steampunk Everyday Practices. *Neo-Victorian Studies* 1 (1):138–163.

Pepperell, Robert, and Michael Punt. 2000. *The Postdigital Membrane: Imagination, Technology, Desire*. Bristol: Intellect.

Sedgwick, Eve Kosofsky, and Adam Frank. 1995. *Shame and Its Sisters: A Silvan Tomkins Reader*. Durham: Duke University Press.

Stiegler, Bernard. 2002. The Discrete Image. In *Echographies of Television: Filmed Interviews*, ed. Jacques Derrida and Bernard Stiegler, trans. Jennifer Bajorek, 145–163. London: Polity Press.

Stryker, Susan. 1994. My Words to Victor Frankenstein above the Village of Chamounix: Performing Transgender Rage. *GLQ: A Journal of Lesbian and Gay Studies* 1 (3):237–254.

Sundén, Jenny. 2003. *Material Virtualities: Approaching Online Textual Embodiment*. New York: Peter Lang.

Sundén, Jenny. 2013. Corporeal Anachronisms: Notes on Affect, Relationality, and Power in Steampunk. *Somatechnics* 3 (2):369–386.

Wilden, Anthony. 1972. Analog and Digital Communication: On the Relationship between Negation, Signification, and the Emergence of the Discrete Element. *Semiotica* 6 (1):50–82.

10 "Make Love Not Porn": Entrepreneurial Voyeurism, Agency, and Affect

Stephen Maddison

In her groundbreaking work on pornography, film scholar Linda Williams (1990, 50) suggests that hardcore pornography articulates a "frenzy of the visible," a fixation with the "involuntary confession" of bodies in the throes of pleasure. The drive to know the truth of pleasure in another body, the sensations that derive from its pursuit—the tension, the frustration, the power, the shudder of its partial fulfillment—these animate the profit potential of the porn industry. But hardcore porn is no longer a function of the modalities of cinematic representation and distribution addressed by Williams. Just as bricks-and-mortar adult movie theaters have become anachronisms, VHS and DVD/Blu-Ray have become relics. As porn has moved to online settings, it has become a critical site to consider the relationship between bodily sensation and networked communication (Maddison 2004).

In this chapter I use porn as an opportunity to consider the relationship between agency and affect. I do so through an assessment of two alternative porn sites: FuckforForest, a nonprofit site that subverts the commercial model of online porn to raise money for ecoactivism, and MakeLoveNotPorn.tv, a pay porn venture launched in 2012 by Cindy Gallop, a former brand adviser to Coca-Cola and Levi's jeans, which makes money by offering the experience and affect of alternative porn. Gallop's injunction to "Make Love Not Porn" serves as her rallying cry to make contemporary porn feel "real" and "authentic" at the very moment when we must work harder within the neoliberal ideology of the enterprise society, and therefore have less time and emotional energy for fulfilling sex. Such circumstances encourage the demand for greater pornographic realism, for which consumers must pay; affect is the lubricant that encourages them to pull out their wallets.

Porn has persistently represented a significant battleground for a range of debates about gender, sexuality, representation, and power (Segal and McIntosh 1992; Attwood 2002; McNair 2002). These debates frequently turn on the tension between agency and embodiment, a tension that stages the human body as a site of excitement and potentiality, or of containment and repression. The deadlocks that arise from this tension have been described as a "tired binary" (Juffer 1998, 2), yet new insights offered by theories of affect, along with the rapidly changing context of network cultures, give us new opportunities for breaking tired binaries and old deadlocks. In a world radically transformed by digitization and networked communication, the value of insights offered by the affective turn is difficult to overlook, especially in work that relates the "new" materialism of the sensory and the affective to the "old" materialisms of work, agency, and social power (Lazzarato 1996, 2001; Ahmed 2004, McRobbie 2010).

Culturalist approaches, such as cultural studies, need to embrace the vocabulary and insights of affect theory if they are to question the ways in which cultural phenomena like sound, music, and pornography work so powerfully upon the body. Jeremy Gilbert (2004) speaks to the limitations of culturalist approaches in getting to grips with sound. He suggests that "the fact that sound is difficult to talk about in linguistic terms does not make it desirable … to consign music to a realm of sublime mystery. … The problem we have is that music is by definition an organised form of experience, one whose effectivity is strictly delimited by sedimented cultural practices, but … one whose structured effects cannot be fully understood in terms of meanings" (Gilbert 2004, n.p.). The enabling force of semiotic theory in cultural studies, Gilbert notes, allows it to unmask "the cultural constructedness of all apparently natural social phenomena" but with the effect of also erasing "the specific sensuous differences between various types of aesthetic practice" (Gilbert 2004, n.p.). He accepts Massumi's distinction between emotion and affect, where emotion is "qualified intensity … owned and recognized" (Massumi 1996, 221), but he problematizes the effacement of the social from Massumi's schema. Insisting on the potential continuities between structuralist paradigms and the affective turn, Gilbert suggests that "a post-logocentric cultural theory should not … be seen as the latest in a succession of theoretical fads, but as contributing to a long tradition of socialist analysis" (Gilbert 2004, n.p.). He insists that such an approach is crucial in working against the hegemony of competitive individualism that "has emerged across a vast range of sites as the … ideology of contemporary neo-liberalism" and which works against "any notion of collectivity, of public good, of shared experience" (Gilbert 2004, n.p.).

Cultural phenomena are shaped by social forces and power relations as much as by affective resonance, and questions about their operation are always questions about cultural forces, power relations, and the potential for social change. If we are to make sense of Gallop's injunction that we "Make Love Not Porn"—an injunction rooted in concern about the social effects of porn on human relationships—then we need to understand not only the sensations associated with consuming porn but also the affective experiences of labor and sociality more widely.

The idea of affective, or immaterial, labor is useful in understanding the structures of contemporary pornography, especially in the context of what has been referred to as the "enterprise society," one defined by market relations, competition, inequality, and the privilege of the individual. Tiziana Terranova's (2004) foundational work in *Network Culture* considers the materiality of work in the digital economy, where notions of the commodity, and of producers and consumers, are in creative flux, even as value remains of critical importance: "The Internet does not automatically turn every user into an active producer, and every worker into a creative subject. The process whereby production and consumption are reconfigured within the category of free labour signals the unfolding of another logic of value" (Terranova 2004, 75). Terranova is influenced by Maurizio Lazzarato's concept of immaterial labor, which describes two components of labor, one in which skills are increasingly associated with cybernetics and computer control, and the other which creates the cultural content of the commodity, and is a function of the collapsing distinction between work and life. This second element of immaterial labor exceeds the traditional understanding of labor value in critiques of capital and locates specific forms of work in the digital networked economy. Immaterial labor describes the value of the worker's affectivity to capital: her emotions, tastes, desires, opinions, social interactions, networks, domestic practices; her bodily reactions, sensations, and capacities. The increasing significance of Facebook as a professional networking tool points to such a collapse of the distinction between work and life, as does its use as a surveillance tool by employers. Indeed, we might suggest that the phenomenon of social media exemplifies Lazzarato's thesis, blurring boundaries between work time and leisure time, between work self and private self. Here we might start to appreciate the implications of Gallop's business venture, MakeLoveNotPorn. tv, the unique selling point of which is its delivery of a more authentic and equitable experience of emotion and sensation: this is a question about the relationship between affect and commerce.

In networked culture, pornography most frequently takes the form of commodities that are traded as gifts, or through peer-to-peer sharing, or in financial transactions based on a pay-per-view or subscription basis. In the case of pornographic fiction posted to and downloaded from sites such as Literotica, Screeve, and Nifty, the creativity, tastes, and desires of authors are foregrounded and subject to categorization, reflection, and discussion in forums, feedback posts, ratings lists, and so on. Such exchange of affectivity often circulates without direct financial transactions, but through a site or online community that is itself funded by advertising links, often to other forms of online pornography (Literotica functions in this way).

In the case of sites that sell access to video content, the most popular commercial model works by offering short preview or introductory clips, with images, text, and other context designed to solicit payment in order to access full or further content. Here the affective power of the preview material, which depends upon striking a balance between potential affective capacity and realized affective capacity, directly correlates to the economic success of the site. Preview material must act on potential consumers' bodies powerfully enough to have them reach for their bank cards, yet not so powerfully that they would not wish to do so again. These "forces of encounter," as Greg Seigworth and Melissa Gregg (2010) describe them, account for the intensity of consuming porn, but also of making it. The financial value of networked porn depends upon the immaterial labor of porn performers and producers: their tastes, but also their bodily reactions, sensations, and capacities. I shall return to the question of immaterial labor in porn in the context of the enterprise society. Before doing so, however, I will situate my discussion within the current political and critical context of porn studies.

Constrained Optimism and Altporn

An influential vein in porn studies exhibits what I refer to as "constrained optimism." It coincides with the affective turn in cultural theory as well as the widespread academic and political acceptance of the failure of ideological revolution and social democratic ideals. If criticism of the dominance of so-called logocentric perspectives hinges on its tendency to "focus on negative critique," the affective turn offers "more life-affirming alternatives to the status quo" (Paasonen 2011, 9). Critics in this vein of porn studies sidestep a mainstream industry generally considered to be characterized by standardization, repetition, misogyny, and low artistic value, coupled to its failure to yield the "sexual democratization" for which some commentators had hoped (McNair 2002, 207; Attwood 2006, 81). Instead, they have tended to focus on a range of alternative pornographies (Cramer 2007; Jacobs 2004a; 2004b; Attwood 2007; Paasonen 2007; 2010; Van Doorn 2010), referred to variously as altporn (Attwood 2007; Jacobs 2004a; 2004b), netporn (Paasonen 2010), realcore (Messina, quoted in Gemin 2006), indie porn (Cramer 2007; Cramer and Home 2007), and amateur porn (Jacobs 2004a; 2004b). Florian Cramer and Stewart Home (2007, 164) have suggested that indie porn "is the pornography of this decade, if not of the whole century." Academic work on these alternative pornographies, which I will refer to hereafter as "altporn," tends to demonstrate constrained optimism by looking for breakthrough trends, movements, and artifacts to validate the agency of the progressive voyeur or sexual dissident against the forces of reaction and bigotry. At the same time, I would suggest that much work on altporn evades engagement with the political implications of apparently progressive sexual activism that is nevertheless located in conventional relations of capital, and which offers forms of agency and empowerment associated with consumer culture.

The problem of categorization casts a long shadow here. Susanna Paasonen has rightly suggested that "the notion of the mainstream is porous and contingent," and it is clear that the category of altporn is slippery (Paasonen 2007, 163). As the description of a particular kind of online product or experience, altporn can be difficult to disaggregate from the output of an industry that depends upon continual commodity innovation (Biasin and Zecca 2009), and where the categories of amateur and professional, producer and consumer, are in flux. As a category of critical enquiry, then, altporn fails to encompass the diverse range of practices being undertaken, and indeed much work in this area demonstrates a self-conscious preoccupation with the limits and frailties of taxonomical ordering, as the diversity of terms listed above demonstrates.

Work in porn studies is critical of tendencies in altporn, most significantly around questions of labor and commodification. Yet the focus on alternative pornographies tends to maintain an investment in the promise of agency, where this agency is a function of the expansion of the technological resources available in a networked culture, the proliferation of choice, and the blurred boundary between consumer and producer. FuckforForest, frequently cited as an example of indie or alternative porn (Jacobs n.d.; Attwood 2007; Bonik and Schaale 2007; Paasonen 2007; 2010; Dicum 2005), illustrates the complex networked dynamics of affective labor, self-commodification, and agency. The site itself is an example of constrained optimism in its rallying cry, "We cum to save the world!," and as a nonprofit altporn site it provides a useful corollary and contrast to Gallop's more business-minded MakeLoveNotPorn.tv.

FuckforForest (figure 10.1) adopts the standard commercial model for online porn sites, with free previews and subscription-based access to regularly updated hardcore material and subverts it as a form of ecoactivism. This operates in three ways: first, marketing of the site works to raise the profile of ecological issues, rather than to merely publicize the site's sexual imagery; second, the site is run on a nonprofit basis, and subscriptions are donated to eco-charities and organizations; and third, users are given the option of uploading explicit images of themselves in lieu of monetary subscription. The site, then, equates affective responses to sexual imagery with both progressive political ideals and a promise of mutuality and inclusivity. In this, FuckforForest exploits a critical moment of arousal, when the process of speculatively, perhaps aimlessly, browsing acquires a purpose that becomes directed toward fulfillment and climax, enabled by the potentially disruptive moment of credit card authorization. Here, bodily intensity is marked by both the representational and the mechanical, as delineated by the practice of browsing free preview clips and paying for full clips, and articulated by a "grabbing" of content and money from the network, the touch of hands on body, mouse, trackpad, purse.

FuckforForest lubricates desire for the bodies of ecoactivists with the promise of solidarity with their ideals. And the thrill of such solidarity, simultaneously sensuous, ideological, and financial, has worked as a form of political advocacy: since its inception in 2004 the site has raised over €245,549 (approximately US$330,000) for rainforest protection charities.[1] However, FuckforForest has not always been able to donate its revenues as it would like, or to continue to work with some organizations, due to moral objections to FuckforForest's explicit sexuality. Both the Rainforest Foundation and World Wildlife Federation have refused donations, and FuckforForest was obliged to withdraw from its work with Arbofilia, a Costa Rican reforestation project, when other funders of the project threatened to withdraw their support.

Figure 10.1
FuckforForest home page: http://www.fuckforforest.com/.

FuckforForest is significant in a number of ways. The site represents an optimistic and encouraging worldview in which sexuality, public life, political activism, ethical environmentalism, and interpersonal exploration are validated and mobilized in productive dialogue, and linked through an appeal to bodily sensation. In contrast to the way in which many online porn sites link sexuality to gender power or gender violence, FuckforForest frames sexuality and bodily sensation as potentially liberating, egalitarian, and socially transformative. While the models on the site appear to be uniformly young, white, and slender, there's a noticeable lack of what Paul Willemen (2004, 21) has described as "meat" and "plant" embodiment. Images on the site show model/activists with body hair, unenhanced breasts, and flaccid as well as erect penises of modest proportions, in contrast to what Mark Davis (2009) has described as the "Viagra cyborg" prevalent in mainstream commercial hardcore. The organization of genital play in the film clips is enthusiastic, amateurish, and lacks both the predictability of the "normative pornoscript" (Van Doorn 2010) and the professionalized effect of the digital workflow that characterizes clips on pay sites. In short, FuckforForest seems "real."

"Make Love Not Porn"

Cindy Gallop launched MakeLoveNotPorn.com in 2009 as a way of facilitating "a dialogue … about sex" by counterposing "porn myths" ("men love coming on women's faces") with the "real world" ("some women like this, some don't"). MLNP is not grassroots activism, but rather, like Gallop's other online initiative, IfWeRanTheWorld.com, articulates politics as a function of corporate social responsibility. The funky messages about sex and choice operate as a storefront for selling T-shirts, investment opportunities, and Gallop's own entrepreneurial activity as a brand advisor. In the context of immaterial labor, we might see Gallop's website as trading her immaterial and affective experience of sex, and her branding and communication skills, for financial reward, professional esteem, and investor confidence, but also as reconfirmation of her status not only as a successful business person but as an enterprising subject.

This particular enterprising subject accepts the role of the state apparatus in the failure of sex education ("I'm trying to counterbalance the impact of porn as sex education"), and seeks personal self-actualization through the articulation of her own autonomy ("Sex at its absolute best is transcendental … you just have to be creative"). Gallop may resist elements of porn's normative script of genital play and sexual negotiation, yet it is clear that her agency, as an entitled member of the neoliberal elite, is critical to both her insight into what is wrong with porn's influence on sexual practice and her desire and ability to do something about it.

In 2012 Gallop launched MakeLoveNotPorn.tv, a pay porn site and at the time of writing still in beta, which literally capitalizes on the investor confidence she was able to muster with her original site. MLNP.tv offers a familiar altporn experience that exhibits many of the characteristics which Feona Attwood (2007) identifies in the new taste cultures: an appeal to community and authenticity, a self-consciousness about resisting familiar porn tropes, and an aestheticization of sex that accords with the apparent bourgeois bohemianism of *Sex and the City* in its television and movie incarnations. Gallop's site proclaims that it is "Pro-sex. Pro-porn. Pro-knowing the difference," and outlines its philosophy:

MakeLoveNotPorn.tv is of the people, by the people, and for the people who believe that the sex we have in our everyday life is the hottest sex there is. We are not porn—porn is performance (often an exceedingly *delicious* performance, but a performance nonetheless). We are not "amateur"—a label that implies that the only people doing it right are the professionals and the rest of us are bumbling idiots. (Honey, *please*.)[2]

The site's tone makes an appeal for emotional identification with the kinds of postfeminist subjects who exhibit what Angela McRobbie describes as a new form of feminine deference, quite literally clothed in the privileges of consumer culture that arises from women's capacity to earn and seeks approval not directly from men but from the "fashion and beauty system" (McRobbie 2007, 723–724).

Figure 10.2
MakeLoveNotPorn home page: https://makelovenotporn.tv/.

An interview with the *Guardian* newspaper in the UK, illustrated with a photograph of Gallop reclining on a rather fabulous animal-print chaise, makes explicit the correlation between the distinctiveness of MLNP.tv and Gallop's persona. MLNP.tv is "an elevated style of adult video," which offers "tasteful erotica" that will be "the sex education of the future," while Gallop herself is "enthusiastically single and unashamed to date men less than half her age," despite being fifty-two years old, and "wears figure-hugging black ensembles, attends glamorous parties and is not shy in correcting her aggressive young lovers" (Walters 2012). The persona is complex: lust, a taste for younger men, sexual promiscuity, charisma, class and wealth, the liking of porn despite distaste for its apparent myths. The projection of greed/agency/business acumen represents her affective labor as owner of a website looking to attract more users, as she leverages her tastes, desires, opinions, social interactions, networks, domestic practices, bodily reactions, sensations, and capacities—all with a promise of our potential pleasure and fulfillment in purchasing porn clips.

MLNP.tv strives for intimacy in its tone while offering the fashionable gloss and style of a corporate site. There are four levels of sexual representation on offer. First, what we might characterize as postfeminist post-porn, empowering rhetoric in such statements as, "Welcome to our little experiment that celebrates all of us who makefunnymagnificentcrazydirtysexymessygloriouslovenotporn," and "In a world where you can access so much online for free, and where artists, creators and producers struggle to make money, we believe that everyone who creates something that gives other people pleasure deserves to make money from it." Second, there are the clips themselves, of which, at the time of writing, there are thirty-one available for rent, uploaded by ten different posters: seven heterosexual, one lesbian, two solo; one mixed race black/white, one mixed race Latino/white. The clips range in length from three to forty-six minutes and express a range of styles: some are amateur, with poor lighting, little or no editing, and a fixed camera position (e.g., clips uploaded by Ionsquares); some are more elaborate, with editing, music, and a more self-consciously aesthetic and artistic style (e.g., clips uploaded by Lilycade and Violet+Rye). Third, each clip has a small selection of still images that can be freely viewed. Fourth, most clips include a "peek"—a short preview of the video made by the posters.

I have noted the affective and economic power of the preview clip for pay-per-view (and subscription) porn sites. MLNP.tv has a page of specific advice for potential posters on the importance of the preview clip. Sara, curator of content, writes:

One of the things I've loved the most about curating our very first mlnp.tv #realworldsex videos has been the sheer joy I've experienced every time one of our #makelovenotpornstars submits a work. And, being the lucky lady that I am, I've often had the privilege of knowing a little bit of the backstory behind each work that makes watching it all the more enjoyable.

And of course, the mlnp.tv team really wanted you, the user, to also reach that level of enjoyment (heh).

So, we created a space for each #makelovenotpornstar to upload a video separate from their main work. A place where you would be able to introduce your #realworldsex videos and point out something that was particularly juicy about your #realworldsex experience.

Not only that, but these intro videos are available as "previews" of your #realworldsex videos themselves, allowing users to view these "trailers" for free and learn a little more about your work before they rent it.

When you submit your own #realworldsex video, be sure to include an intro video of your own. We call them "context," and it's part of what we mean by "contextualizing" your submissions. Backstories are HOT! You'll be sure to gain more rentals, more #realworld cash and much admiration not only from the mlnp.tv community but also from me, Madam Curator![3]

There are many things to draw attention to here. Backstory and contextualization are foregrounded as connected to pleasure and profit. Here the preview clip not only serves to balance the affective intensity delivered with the affective intensity promised (yet still withheld), but also potentially offers pre-pornographic stickiness and a form of relationality that exceeds the confines of the experience of watching the genital acts in the feature video itself. The peek does not merely preview the video, it is not merely constituted as a segue to the main event, but is instead an insight into the sensations, relations, and conditions that manifest that event, both as private genital act and as pornographic self-exhibition. The peek offers discrete pleasures attached to the act of voyeurism it promises, but ones that surprise and move in ways that exceed our expectations of the pornographic scene. Stickiness here is about binding the consumer to the affective labor of posters who profit directly from the return visits and repeated rentals that such stickiness represents, but it is also about the visceral experience of watching the peeks, many of which are shockingly intimate, troubling in their frailty, vulgar in their often unintentional directness, and gross in their effect upon the sexual knowledge we have of their participants. Some of the peeks have a professional gloss and attest to the ambiguous notion of amateurism that altporn sites like MLNP.tv demonstrate, where posters are already sex bloggers or porn performers or creative professionals (Violet+Rye, LilyandDanny, and AudioSmut) who use MLNP.tv to extend the field of their entrepreneurial subjectivity and business activity.

MLNP.tv's Madam Curator suggests that the gold standard for peek clips was uploaded by Lily and Danny, both of whom work as porn performers. Their peek features the couple talking directly to camera about the circumstances behind the making of the sex scene they are selling on MLNP.tv. They talk about being asked to contribute to MLNP.tv by Cindy Gallop herself, about how Lily sometimes cannot have vaginal sex with Danny because she has been working hard filming, about how in their professional lives they are asked to do "crazy" positions that do not always feel as good as they look, about being regularly tested for HIV and STDs, and about being a "fluid bonded couple." The power of this peek, however, lies not just in the specific knowledge it reveals—experiences of acting in and watching porn, negotiating sex with your boyfriend after having sex with other professionals all day—but in the force of the encounter it stages between Lily and Danny, who constantly touch and gaze at one another and at the viewer with a kind of comfortable yet intense intimacy. Porn solicits a familiar range of affects, from arousal and orgasm to disgust and humor, but Lily and Danny's peek ruptures something in the familiar structure of our license to look at porn; there is a simple and mundane authenticity here that is shocking. This peek exceeds our expectations of the normative pornoscript affectively and representationally, unlike the clips available on FuckForForest, which offer much more conventional affective and sexual experiences.

These peeks go some way toward justifying the site's claims about authenticity and resisting familiar porn tropes. In this, MLNP.tv is following a trend exhibited currently in much commercial online porn, where behind-the-scenes clips are either offered as a free preview or added as a coda to the paid video (Härmä and Stolpe 2010). MLNP.tv is distinctive in applying this form of commodity innovation to commercial clips produced in more strongly marked amateur contexts, where performers have a preexisting relationship, and where the affective resonance of intimacy exceeds both the physical vulgarity of the sex acts and the stilted conversation exhibited by strangers or work colleagues, brought together for professional reasons, who are subject to the demands of a director, producer, or webmaster.

MakeLoveNotPorn.tv refines the altporn formula in a number of ways. These innovations can be summarized in terms of the ambition of the project: in its scale, MLNP.tv represents a significant shift in its attempts to mainstream hardcore porn to taste cultures defined by aspirational lifestyle shopping, where aesthetic and tonal cues reinforce an experience that foregrounds the power of choice, and where pleasure and agency are intertwined ("Pro-sex. Pro-porn. Pro-knowing the difference"). MLNP.tv self-consciously eschews the taxonomies of online porn—"creampie," "anal," "Asian," and so on—and instead works to instantiate a categorization based on a funkier, more playful, and more feminist logic. MLNP.tv expresses an ambition to market hardcore pornography to women (and couples) more familiar with *Sex and the City* and the "fashion and beauty system" (McRobbie 2007) than with YouPorn, or to women and couples already familiar with the "sexist and disgusting" nature of porn (Cramer 2007) and yet subject to the terms of the postsexualized society Gill (2003) describes: a society where elaborating a generalized enterprise form of the self stands as the very marker of professional and social success. McNay (2009) eruditely articulates the contradictory nature of appeals to agency and individuality in the enterprise society, arguing that such appeals actually demonstrate responsible self-management, not emancipation. These are the conditions of immaterial sex, where libidinal, emotional, and physiological energies, desires, and sensations designate terms of human capital.

Gallop, brand innovator and pornographer, manifestly represents the apex of this formation. MLNP.tv as commodity innovation arises from the insights of Gallop's own sex life, which are self-represented as public relations copy and work as a guarantee of both authenticity and her upscale postfeminist values. Likewise, the site facilitates wider, self-managed forms of enterprising immaterial sex, where participants upload their sex scenes in expectation of earning fifty percent of the rental fees generated. These participants represent different levels of experience with sexual entrepreneurship, from porn stars on their day off to sex bloggers and media professionals diversifying their creative portfolio. Innovations such as the peek constitute an extension of the terms of pornographic immateriality, commodifying moments of intimacy and intensity that exceed the conditions of generic genital play in most pay porn. This commercial advance is a function of the social conditions, and the cultural and political insights, that animate MLNP.tv—its idiom, mode of address, and aesthetic cues, its information architecture and site design, and the affectivity of Gallop's labor. Here the incitement to confess the secrets of bodily capacity (Williams's "frenzy of the visible"), which has been the animating principle of commercial porn's promise of authenticity and realness, exemplifies the conditions of the enterprise society. And for consumers, MLNP.tv's apparent rejection of the normative pornoscript and standardized niche marketing, along with its flattery of bourgeois values and tastes, might actually feel like making love, not making porn. But only in the bizarrely contradictory social conditions that neoliberal ideology describes can such a distinction be meaningful in the first place, as the collapsing distinctions between work and life, public and private, professional networks and personal relationships result in less time and emotional energy for sexual intimacy and intensity, while prescribing ever more elaborate standards for its online performance by others. Here brand extension and commodity innovation acquire an affective intensity as modes of sociality.

From Agency to Entrepreneurial Voyeurism

The question of how we activate political engagement within representational cultures has never been straightforward, as the examples of FuckforForest and MakeLoveNotPorn.tv demonstrate; but recent theoretical and political developments, not least in the aftermath of the publication of Michel Foucault's lectures from the Collège de France, have challenged taken-for-granted assumptions about the value of agency in cultural negotiations. In *The Birth of Biopolitics*, Foucault describes neoliberal governmentality as "a formal game between inequalities" (Foucault 2008, 120) designed to propagate the equality of inequality, where competition and the enterprise form become generalized as the primary mode not only of social institutions and interaction, but of individuality itself. In the context of Foucault's analysis of the self as a function of the enterprise society, Lois McNay has questioned the relationship between individual agency and political engagement. She asks, "If individual autonomy is not the opposite of or limit to neoliberal governance, but rather lies at the heart of disciplinary control through responsible self-management, what are the possible grounds upon which political resistance can be based?" (McNay 2009, 56; see also Gregg, this volume).

For Lazzarato, the organization of labor in neoliberalism works to maximize polarizations of income and power while working to prevent these inequalities becoming "irreducible political dualisms": in this way neoliberalism affects a depoliticization of labor (Lazzarato 2009, 120). The enterprise society involves the "generalization of the economic form of the market ... throughout the social body and including the whole of the social system not usually conducted through or sanctioned by monetary exchanges" (Foucault 2008, 243). McNay has emphasized several features of neoliberalism's construction of the self-as-enterprise. Critically, the organization of self around a market logic "subtly alters and depoliticizes conventional conceptions of individual autonomy" by foregrounding choice, differentiation, and "regulated self-responsibility" (McNay 2009, 62). This has profound effects for sociality: McNay suggests that the self as entrepreneur "has only competitors." Neoliberalism proceeds on the basis that these competitors, alienated from one another by the governmental maximization of the inequalities between them, should seek advancement through the acquisition and exploitation of individual freedoms, which proliferate constantly. Neoliberalism discourages class and other forms of solidarity precisely because the competitors are constantly differentiated from one another, and because the "idea of personal responsibility is eroded" (McNay 2009, 65) by the outsourcing to individuals of rights and responsibilities previously secured by the social contract.

These theories of labor and power may help to account for the constrained optimism porn-studies writers have exhibited about altporn. On the one hand, we can see the work of altporn entrepreneurs as expressions of the post-Fordist multitude: emergent expressions of creativity and sociality arising from the articulation of communities of interest, where interdependence and cooperation, as functions of new technological possibilities, are expressed by user-generated content and interactivity in forums, blogs, and reviews. On the other hand, we can see altporn entrepreneurs as affective laborers for whom the distinctions between life and work, and work and leisure, have collapsed, and for whom the opportunity to comply with the requirement to constitute themselves as an enterprise arises from an exploitation of their latent immaterial creativity. We might describe what emerges from such transactions as immaterial sex, where libidinal, emotional, and physiological energies, desires, and sensations that are a function of human capital produce surplus value.

Successful consumption of porn depends upon restive file browsing, with hands occupied not only in stroking the body but in operating the mouse or trackpad, opening and assessing files in order to patch together a bricolage of quality pornographic moments. Access to porn, then—especially altporn—is dependent on managing networks and social media where we must demonstrate entrepreneurial skill, choose appropriate contractual subscriptions, follow links and recommendations to new sites of free content, keep up with chat rooms, torrent lists, blogs, and feeds to ensure that we are not missing out on opportunities to realize our desires and demonstrate our self-management. These patterns of the entrepreneurialism of the self mirror the practices necessary to maintain professional success as an immaterial laborer. These are also the conditions described by Mark Fisher's (2009, 21) notions of "reflexive impotence" and "depressive hedonia," where pornographic pleasures, in all their accessibility, standardization, and dependability, conform somewhat to work-centric patterns of social relations. This is a moment when the search for pleasure, as Nina Power (2009, 51) notes, might become just another form of work.

Here the optimism that Paasonen (2011, 9) detects in the turn toward affect, which seeks "life-affirming alternatives to the status quo," potentially founders, reminding us that bodily sensations need to be socially and politically situated. This is a question about the purpose and direction of cultural theory. But it is also a question about experiences other than the practice of theory. Whether sensations and experiences related to online porn are life-affirming or repressive, or complex modalities of both, and more, remains an urgent question. Situating these experiences and sensations in a social context is one way of potentially avoiding a methodological trap in which we affirm the social importance of affect but are then unable to socially locate it, or to account for it outside the terms of a theoretical enunciation that can often feel startlingly subjective and individualized. In part, we might explain the enduring popularity of porn as a subject for critics and theorists of gender and sexuality by noting that its materiality, both in the sense of artifacts and institutions, and, in its effect upon bodies, its "carnal resonance" (Paasonen 2011), allows us to adjudicate sexual practice: porn offers a privileged, seductive lens through which the private is also public. Porn can act as a barometer for modes of pleasure and their political effects, but in order to serve this purpose sensation must be culturally located. To what extent, for example, does pornographic immaterial sex, enacted by sexual "cyborgs" (Davis 2009) and "athletes" (Taormino, quoted in Paasonen 2011) articulate a standard for (self) regulation of the (sexual) self, one that might be impossible to achieve but which is coterminous with the enterprise society? Is it impossible to achieve because we don't have enough time for an elaborate recreational sex life, or at least one that matches the affective capacity of the sexualized society? Impossible to achieve because we are unable to autonomously realize our libidinous capacity, because we are too tired, alienated, socially inept, or domestically and socially compromised? Impossible because our sensory and affective responses might relate more to mediated networked interactions than to intimate bodily ones?

In such a context we might understand Gallop's exhortation that we "Make Love Not Porn" as an appeal to network our desires to commodities with the allure of bourgeois bohemianism, to the promise of egalitarian gender play, where intensity is seemingly unrestricted by the standard taxonomies of pay-per-view porn, and where our apparent privacy promises an experience of that intensity released from the liability and responsibility of our entrepreneurial self.

Notes

1. http://articles.sfgate.com/2005-04-13/home-and-garden/17366933_1_fff-forest-rain.

2. https://makelovenotporn.tv/pages/about/how_this_works.

3. http://talkabout.makelovenotporn.tv/post/29496789424/contextisall.

References

Ahmed, Sara. 2004. *The Cultural Politics of Emotion*. Edinburgh: Edinburgh University Press.

Attwood, Feona. 2002. Reading Porn: The Paradigm Shift in Pornography Research. *Sexualities* 5 (1):91–105.

Attwood, Feona. 2006. Sexed Up: Theorizing the Sexualization of Culture. *Sexualities* 9 (1):77–94.

Attwood, Feona. 2007. No Money Shot? Commerce, Pornography and New Sex Taste Cultures. *Sexualities* 10 (4):441–456.

Biasin, Enrico, and Federoca Zecca. 2009. Contemporary Audiovisual Pornography: Branding Strategy and Gonzo Film Style. *International Film Studies Journal* 9 (12):133–150.

Bonik, Manuel, and Andreas Schaale. 2007. The Naked Truth: Internet Eroticism and the Search. In *C'Lick Me: A Netporn Studies Reader*, ed. Katrien Jacobs, Marije Janssen, and Matteo Pasquinelli, 77–88. Amsterdam: Institute of Network Cultures.

Cramer, Florian. 2007. Sodom Blogging: Alternative Porn and Aesthetic Sensibility. In *C'Lick Me: A Netporn Studies Reader*, ed. Katrien Jacobs, Marije Janssen, and Matteo Pasquinelli, 171–176. Amsterdam: Institute of Network Cultures.

Cramer, Florian, and Stewart Home. 2007. Pornographic Coding. In *C'Lick Me: A Netporn Studies Reader*, ed. Katrien Jacobs, Marije Janssen, and Matteo Pasquinelli, 159–170. Amsterdam: Institute of Network Cultures.

Davis, Mark. 2009. *Sex, Technology and Public Health*. Houndmills: Palgrave Macmillan.

Dicum, Gregory. 2005. Eco-Porn: Great Sex for a Good Cause. *SFGate.com* (April 13). Available at http://www.sfgate.com/homeandgarden/article/GREEN-Eco-porn-Great-Sex-For-A-Good-Cause-3175838.php.

Fisher, Mark. 2009. *Capitalist Realism: Is There No Alternative?* Winchester: Zero Books.

Foucault, Michel. 2008. *The Birth of Biopolitics: Lectures at the Collège de France 1978–1979*. Houndmills: Palgrave Macmillan.

Gemin, Tiziana. 2006. Realcore: Sergio Messina and Online Porn. *Digimag* 19. Available at http://www.digicult.it/digimag/issue-019/realcore-sergio-messina-and-online-porn/.

Gilbert, Jeremy. 2004. Signifying Nothing: "Culture," "Discourse" and the Sociality of Affect. *Culture Machine* 6. Available at http://www.culturemachine.net/index.php/cm/article/view/8/7.

Gill, Rosalind. 2003. From Sexual Objectification to Sexual Subjectification: The Resexualisation of Women's Bodies in the Media. *Feminist Media Studies* 3 (1):100–106.

Härmä, Sanna, and Joakim Stolpe. 2010. Behind the Scenes of Straight Pleasure. In *Porn.com: Making Sense of Online Pornography*, ed. Feona Attwood, 107–122. New York: Peter Lang.

Jacobs, Katrien. 2004a. Pornography in Small Spaces and Other Places. *Cultural Studies* 18 (1):67–83.

Jacobs, Katrien. 2004b. Negotiating Contracts and the Singing Orgasm. *Spectator* (London) 24 (1):17–29.

Jacobs, Katrien. n.d. The Stimulus Plan Needs to Get Laid: Eco-Pornography and the Alt-Economy. Available at http://www.libidot.org/neural/eco.pdf.

Juffer, Jane. 1998. *At Home With Pornography: Women, Sex and Everyday Life.* New York: New York University Press.

Lazzarato, Maurizio. 1996. Immaterial Labor. *Generation Online,* trans. Paul Colilli and Ed Emery. Available at http://generation-online.org/c/fcimmateriallabour3.htm.

Lazzarato, Maurizio. 2001. General Intellect: Towards an Inquiry into Immaterial Labour. Trans. Ed Emery. Available at http://libcom.org/library/general-intellect-common-sense.

Lazzarato, Maurizio. 2009. Neoliberalism in Action: Inequality, Insecurity and the Reconstitution of the Social. *Theory, Culture and Society* 26 (6):109–133.

Maddison, Stephen. 2004. From Porno-topia to Total Information Awareness, or What Forces Really Govern Access to Porn? *New Formations* 52:35–57.

Massumi, Brian. 1996. The Autonomy of Affect. In *Deleuze: A Critical Reader,* ed. Paul Patton, 217–239. Oxford: Blackwell.

McNair, Brian. 2002. *Striptease Culture: Sex, Media and the Democratization of Desire.* New York: Routledge.

McNay, Lois. 2009. Self as Enterprise: Dilemmas of Control and Resistance in Foucault's "The Birth of Biopolitics." *Theory, Culture and Society* 26 (6):55–77.

McRobbie, Angela. 2007. Top Girls? *Cultural Studies* 21 (4):718–737.

McRobbie, Angela. 2010. Feminism and Immaterial Labour. *New Formations* 70 (4):60–76.

Paasonen, Susanna. 2007. Epilogue: Porn Futures. In *Pornification: Sex and Sexuality in Media Culture,* ed. Susanna Paasonen, Kaarina Nikunen, and Laura Saarenmaa, 161–170. New York: Berg.

Paasonen, Susanna. 2010. Labors of Love: Netporn, Web 2.0 and the Meanings of Amateurism. *New Media and Society* 12 (8):1297–1312.

Paasonen, Susanna. 2011. *Carnal Resonance: Affect and Online Pornography.* Cambridge, MA: MIT Press.

Power, Nina. 2009. *One-Dimensional Woman.* Winchester, Washington: Zero Books.

Segal, Lynn, and Mary McIntosh, eds. 1992. *Sex Exposed: Sexuality and the Pornography Debate.* London: Virago.

Seigworth, Gregory J., and Melissa Gregg. 2010. An Inventory of Shimmers. In *The Affect Theory Reader*, ed. Gregory Seigworth and Melissa Gregg, 1–28. Durham: Duke University Press.

Terranova, Tiziana. 2004. *Network Culture: Politics for the Information Age*. London: Pluto Press.

Van Doorn, Niels. 2010. Keeping It Real: User-Genderated Pornography, Gender Reification, and Visual Pleasure. *Convergence* 16 (4):411–430.

Walters, Joanna. 2012. Make Love Not Porn, Says Oxford Graduate on a Mission to Make Sex More Erotic. *Guardian* (15 September). Available at http://www.theguardian.com/culture/2012/sep/16/make-love-not-porn.

Willemen, Paul. 2004. For a Pornoscape. In *More Dirty Looks: Gender, Pornography and Power*, ed. Paula Gibson, 9–26. London: BFI.

Williams, Linda. 1990. *Hard Core: Power, Pleasure and the "Frenzy of the Visible."* London: Pandora.

11   Digital Disaffect: Teaching through Screens

Michael Petit

This chapter's discussion of digital disaffect and pedagogy is situated in the specifics of a second semester, first-year undergraduate humanities course in critical inquiry and reasoning.[1] During the semester, data and information on the broad-based topic "emotions and the internet" were collected by more than one hundred students who conducted one-on-one qualitative interviews and quantitative surveys of peers from across the university. Before students designed the interviews and surveys, they narrowed the broad topic to a specific research question they wanted to investigate, based on a single affective state—happiness, self-confidence, sense of security, boredom, and so forth. Students thus collected data and information on a broad scope of affective states and entered it into a digital archive open to all students to draw on for their final research projects. Finally, students produced self-evaluative responses throughout the semester on their internet use and the web's affective value for their own lives.

I draw on this wealth of material, as well as additional interviews I conducted with media studies faculty, to provide an affective portrait of a generation of undergraduates born digital.[2] Deeply immersed in screens and media technologies, social media, and other forms of digital culture, undergraduates browse the web on laptops and smartphones seeking and finding its affective potentialities in what many of them see as a vast and stimulating place. "Everything is there," one interview subject states, "and it's like this great library of knowledge at any time, it doesn't close at 5 p.m., it is twenty-four hours, you know, and there are people online that you talk to and I really feel, more than any other time in my life, I feel connected to the world." The affective allure of this 24/7 library of knowledge is irresistible to many, including while they are in class. Stand at the back of a lecture hall and watch, as students listen and scroll through web pages and check Facebook updates, even as they take notes. Stand in front and see a sea of screens—laptops, smartphones, tablets—and know that you are quite literally teaching through screens (figure 11.1).

Classrooms are quasi-public spaces, and, as Lauren Berlant (2004, 450) has written, "Public spheres are affect worlds at least as much as they are effects of rationality and rationalization." Within a pedagogical context, rationality and affect are often placed

Figure 11.1
"What changes with ubiquitous access?" Photograph by Will Richardson, http://www.flickr.com/photos/wrichard/3743686850/sizes/o/. Creative Commons license.

in tension, with rationality and rationalization front and center even though students' affective responses to the material and the teacher also are intrinsic to effective learning. This tension is counterproductive. From a phenomenological point of view, sense and sensation cannot be separated or shut off at any given moment (Sobchack 2004), and affect theory rethinks their division when addressing embodied human cognition. As Susanna Paasonen points out, humans are bodies "made of guts, bones, and blood, oriented by drives, conditioned by physical affordances, and animated by affective intensities" that are "constantly engaged in semiotic activity of representation, mapping, and depiction" (Paasonen 2011, 25). Embodiment cannot be separated arbitrarily from cognition; affect is not separate from thought. Silvan Tomkins (1995) addresses affect as inbuilt in the human body—a system in place that is part of who we are in the world, and Isobel Armstrong argues that the body speaks through affect, thereby "both confirming ownership of the body by consciousness and disowning consciousness" (Armstrong 2000, 117).

Keeping sense and sensation, rationality and affectivity in balance in contemporary classrooms is complicated by the bifurcated, multitasking, perhaps even ADHD- and Ritalin-inflected attention capacity of many undergraduates. A phenomenological sense of twoness, one component of digital disaffect, is everywhere within digital culture: in multitasking, in the focus on a screen that lets individuals divide their attention between here and there, in the caress of the point-and-click interface that addresses individual need in the conflation of experience and entertainment, and in the offer and expectation of affective agency and immediacy. For many digital natives, clicking gets it now; the teacher just seems slow. However, the close intellectual focus (and patience) required for rationality and rationalization—the rhythm or tempo of attention—shifts and erodes over time. "Have you ever gone online for a particular reason and not been sidetracked?" one interview subject was asked. "Of course not," he answered. "It is like that always, I can't even read my school textbooks. I take a break after five minutes. The only time I have ever been able to block out all forms of internet was when I was reading *Fifty Shades of Grey* this summer."

A university teaching environment where students must be allowed to bring screens-as-learning-aides to the classroom necessitates teaching through screens in another sense: using the web to teach students about it. In *Pedagogy of the Oppressed*, Paulo Freire writes that "the starting point for organizing the program content of education … must be the present, existential, concrete situation" (Freire 1970, 85). The web is a central component of students' present, existential, concrete situation; it situates them in an ersatz yet affective place that helps define who they are. Teaching through place, as I argue elsewhere, is a particularly effective pedagogical technique (Cravey and Petit 2012), and given students' affective relationship with the web, teachers in media and communication studies as well as the humanities and social sciences more broadly have an ethical responsibility to develop curricula that use the web to study the web so that students develop a richer, more self-reflexive understanding of their situation. The discussion of digital disaffect that follows is partly an outcome of such a pedagogical project, for turning away from the interface no longer seems possible or perhaps even desirable. Meg, in the cartoon strip *Dustin* (figure 11.2), may be satirically portrayed as obsessive and borderline pathological, yet her quip pointedly demonstrates more than just the web's centrality to the social, educational, and economic functioning of contemporary life; it demonstrates that the human-machine connection through the internet to information, other people, and machines has become definitional of a new Cartesian subject: "iPad, therefore I am." This is an ontological way of being that is far deeper than self-identification as an internet "user," or pretending to oneself that the internet is just a communications "tool."

In what follows, I divide my discussion of digital disaffect and pedagogy into two parts. The first, "As We May Think," considers pioneer American computer scientist Vannevar Bush's speculative and utopic proposal for "memex," a searchable information storage device. As one of the earliest manifestations of the idea that would come to be known as hypertext (Hillis, Petit, and Jarrett 2013), memex offers a historically grounded starting point to theorize affect, digital disaffect, and pedagogy in the context

Figure 11.2
Dustin © 2013 Steve Kelley & Jeff Parker, Distributed by King Features Syndicate, Inc.

of web browsing. Bush's memex, like the web, operates through the seeking and find-ing of associative interests and affective responses. His proposal operates within the belief that the rational and the objective lead to enlightenment. Through the memex, he writes, "Presumably man's spirit should be elevated if he can better review his shady past and analyze more completely and objectively his present problems" (Bush 1945).

Bush's memex as conceived appears to be a vision of pure rationality. The web, as memex actualized, however, is not, and in the second part of the chapter, "As We Do Think," I draw inspiration from memex to offer readers a series of associations in the form of print-based "hyperlinks." They include observations, an extract from a fac-ulty interview, snippets of a class assignment, and portions of interviews students con-ducted with their peers. All quotations are presented anonymously with no identifying attributes. Together these various moments provide a web of trails weaving around and through the chapter's title, and they convey an argument through affective resonance rather than linear structure. To the extent that affect escapes the structure of language, forms of affective writing attempt to mediate between the textual and the sensory (Paasonen 2011, 200–205). In engaging with affective writing in the second part of the chapter, my desire is to re-present to you something of the disaffected resonance that circulates through young adults and the classrooms they only ever partially inhabit. This is the world in which we now teach and in which we *must* think. My intent in organizing the course from which the excerpts are drawn was to let students produce a mirror onto their own ontological reality, a reality increasingly borne of technical affect. I can say that the project at least got their undivided attention, if only for the moment. As do we think.

As We May Think

Bush wrote his proposal for memex in his capacity as director of the US Office of Scientific Research and Development. It was published in the *Atlantic Monthly* in 1945 under the title "As We May Think" and condensed two months later in *Life* magazine, with illustrations by Alfred Crimi. Bush conceived the memex as an automated workstation containing libraries of books, pictures, periodicals, newspapers, and records of personal communications that "may be consulted with exceeding speed and flexibility" (Bush 1945) (figure 11.3). In explaining the concept, Bush notes that the human mind operates by association: "With one item in its grasp, it snaps instantly to the next that is suggested by association of thoughts in accordance with some intricate web of trails carried by the cells of the brain" (ibid.). Memex mechanizes this selection process: "any item may be caused *at will* to select *immediately* and *automatically* another. This is the essential feature of the memex" (ibid.; emphasis added).

MEMEX in the form of a desk would instantly bring files and material on any subject to the operator's fingertips. Slanting translucent viewing screens magnify supermicrofilm filed by code numbers. At left is a mechanism which automatically photographs longhand notes, pictures and letters, then files them in the desk for future reference.

Figure 11.3
Memex illustration by Alfred Crimi. *Life*, September 10, 1945. By permission of Joan Adria D'Amico.

In terms of theorizing a history of technological affect, Bush's careful eliding of agency is of considerable interest. The human mind "snaps instantly" in accordance to "the cells of the brain"; the memex responds "immediately" and "automatically"—"at will." But at whose will? That of the memex? Its operator? Or some combination of the two located at their interface? *Life* sensationalized the issue by giving its condensed reprint of "As We May Think" the subtitle "A Top US Scientist Foresees a Possible Future World in which Man-Made Machines Will Start to Think." Bush's proposal was for an analog device based on microfilm, viewing screens on which to magnify and project their contents, dry photography technology of the day, and the development of future technologies such as a walnut-sized camera worn on the forehead. Life termed it a "Cyclops camera" and Crimi illustrated the article accordingly (figure 11.4). The image today looks like a steampunk version of Google Glass (see Sundén, this volume).

Bush uses the term "trails" to describe the associative links provided through the memex, and he argues for their utility in allowing lawyers, among other professionals, to consider the "experience of friends and authorities" in making decisions by

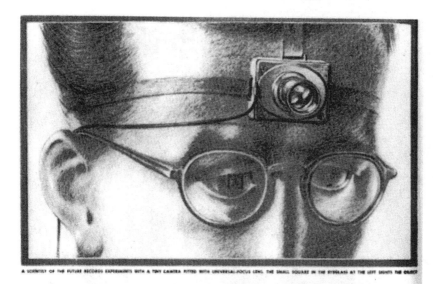

Figure 11.4
Cyclops camera illustration by Alfred Crimi. By permission of Joan Adria D'Amico.

consulting "new forms of encyclopaedias" that are "ready made with a mesh of associative trails running through them, ready to be dropped into the memex and there amplified." Bush predicts, "There will be a new profession of trail blazers, those who find delight in the task of establishing useful trails through the enormous mass of the common record." Bush would seem to refer to individuals focused on retrieval of specific forms of information in a logical, rational order. This differs considerably from an individual browsing the web, moving from link to link, randomly finding LOLcats and doing Facebook updates. Associative interest and affective response today also extend not only to those browsing for useful information but also to those randomly searching, even if their seemingly aimless quests result in "useless" information that nonetheless "grabs" their attention (see Dean, this volume). Information that is useless today may tomorrow be put to good use.

Memex was never built, but the fundamental idea of mechanized associative links has been realized through digitization and made more powerful still when networked. Now algorithms, human-machine intelligence, and crowd sourcing (today's rough equivalents of Bush's "profession of trail blazers") provide lists of linked associations—both useless and useful—as easily as doing a Google search, checking in on Reddit, or clicking forward to the next StumbleUpon site. Yet in leaving open the possibility that associative interest and affective response need not be produced solely through human agency, Bush implicitly suggests the rise of new forms of human-machine-based interactive thinking: human operators use a device that has some degree of unspecified agency to call up various materials for the purpose of discovering new links in "the enormous mass of the common record" and thereby contribute to the sum of human knowledge. After sixty years of development along these lines, Bruno Latour asks, "Why are we all held by forces that are not of our own making?" (Latour 2005, 43). This agency is an algorithmic sort of agency (see Karppi, this volume), able immediately and automatically to suggest additional associative links that may also contribute to human discovery and the development of new knowledge and understanding.

The establishment of new associations of which an operator (read student) was heretofore unaware is also the definitional apparatus of teaching. Memex, in effect, is a teaching machine. Teaching imparts information that students must absorb, coordinate, and accommodate within their existing intellectual framework, in order to thereby "learn." Their positive affective response to what is being learned (and to the teacher) greatly facilitates this process. As a technological form of pedagogical theory, memex assumes a distributed and networked model of learning that is the opposite of the inherently Lockean "banking" or "inoculation" model, in which teachers fill the supposedly tabula rasa of students' empty heads. Memex, rather, is more aligned with a problem-driven model of pedagogy, in which students necessarily already possess situated knowledge and experience, and build on it through guided encounters with associated material to learn more and, hopefully, arrive at knowledge formation. In this model of distributed learning, teachers act as facilitators; knowledge building flows back and forth, with teachers learning from students as students learn from teachers.

Consider Google, for example, as something of a contemporary memex and teaching machine that provides associative links immediately, automatically, and in the click-click-click rhythm of human-machine will. Any search draws on the existing situated knowledge of the operator-student and adds to it by providing linked (and Google-algorithm-approved) associations from known and expected sources—Wikipedia, for example, often among the top returns—and from unknown and unexpected sources that the machine has produced as if of its own volition. A degree of serendipity seems built in, a product of human-machine agency with the potential to add to the operator-student's knowledge in unpredictable, possibly even random, yet still memex-like ways. The speed and automation with which this can occur is new, and many changes in degree can result in a change in kind. In another sense, however, there is little that is new in all of this. Serendipity and chance associative encounters are part of life. This is why they, along with the seemingly random forms of association they induce, play a role in traditional classrooms and other learning environments. A teacher may provide unexpected information or new analytic-critical thinking tools that must be incorporated into a student's existing knowledge base, for example, and since students are not subject to knowing in advance the meaning of such encounters, their agency as to what is presented is circumscribed. While they may know the subject material, they cannot know in advance what their affective response to it may be and where this may lead. An unexpected or random encounter can be as illuminating as a lightning bolt and can orient a student on a new and unexpected trajectory, for good or ill, or both.

Mary Shelley's *Frankenstein* (1818), a novel focused in many ways on pedagogy and the process of learning, uses the metaphor of a lightning bolt to present the dark side of an unexpected encounter, even as it serves as a teaching text today that instructs readers that the desire for life-changing affective encounters has a lengthy history. When the adolescent Victor witnesses lightning strike a tree, the sight has profound affect and sets him on his quest for the knowledge that will allow him to create life from dead matter. His ill-advised adventure results in Aristotelian tragedy. While a Google search is unlikely to amount to such a profound life-changing pedagogical moment or hubristic fall, the associative links that search provides nevertheless have the potential to elicit surprising and unpredictably affective responses from operator-students. This potentiality extends across the web. It explains some of the allure of web browsing, and its centrality in classrooms where the web is always on suggests that it is better to engage with it through curricula than to ignore it (Davidson 2011).

Google as the "don't be evil" memex/teaching machine relies on a not-so-implicit pedagogical model in which information (and thus the potential for knowledge production) flows back and forth between teacher (here, Google) and student (here, the searcher). In exchange for receiving a list of associative links keyed to search terms (along with the possibility of unpredictable affective responses this might entail), operator-students agree to be surveilled, consumerized, and targeted by advertisements across the web as they click on and follow associative links. We learn from Google-the-teacher, even as we teach Google—a student with a most prodigious memory—our likes and dislikes, just as we teach Amazon, Netflix, and other intelligent agents to recommend books and other media we may want to purchase or watch. Any perceived asymmetry in this relationship may depend on the point of view of the observer, though Google gains most financially, since it is able to monetize its services by aggregating the associative trails taken by everyone, whereas we each can only know our own. Bush writes that memex cannot hope "to equal the speed and flexibility with which the mind follows an associative trail, but it should be possible to beat the mind decisively in regard to the permanence and clarity of the items resurrected from storage." Google capitalizes on its ability to remember with permanence and clarity to better identify and quantify our perceived needs and offer new associative links based in part on our past searches. Doing so successfully makes it more likely that Google will produce positive affective responses in its operator-students and, in a virtuous circle, improve its bottom line by being able to intuit our desires and target us with advertisements.

Bush's proposal, made at the end of World War II, is one of cautious optimism. Recognizing the destructive capacity of weapons made possible through the application of science, he thought it a more productive project to turn scientists to the task of finding ways to organize and mechanize the retrieval of human knowledge so as to preserve and advance it. His examples of individuals using memex are drawn from the professional class—lawyers, patent attorneys, physicians, chemists, and historians. These are highly educated information seekers, and their projected uses of memex directly relate to research necessitated by their individual professions. For Bush, then, memex was an elite device with the lofty goal of allowing humans "truly to encompass the great record and to grow in the wisdom of race experience." He might find it surprising that the memex-like device we call the web would be democratically available; that it would become accessible through a multipurpose computer on desks, or increasingly through mobile phones used openly everywhere; that it would be as much, if not more, for entertainment and social communication as it would be for research to advance human knowledge; that its joys would derive from its usefulness *and* its uselessness.

One can appreciate Bush's embrace of his own idea. The automatic and immediate production of associated links to any relevant book or document would seem magical indeed. Yet what seemed extraordinary science fiction in 1945 has become ordinary and at the current technological juncture no longer remarkable. For those born digital, the automated linking of associative interests on the web, and concomitant affective responses, have become so naturalized that they could be called "As We *Do* Think." One aspect of this way of thinking, being, and expectation of digital affectivity is beginning to manifest itself as a kind of hypnotic, engaged disengagement with the miasmic qualities of boredom, detachment, ennui, and malaise that collectively can be thought of as digital disaffect. If intensity is "more than," the sensation of digital disaffect is "less than." Figure 11.5 captures something of this sensation. Seen it before; been there, done that; nothing new to see; coupled simultaneously to a haunted and hypnotic longing for the affective promise of the internet. And so one click, followed by the next, followed by the next. Exemplifying the Tantalus myth, digital disaffect is the sensation of always being about to attain the one thing that will bring satisfaction, yet finding that it always, always, always lies just beyond reach (see also Dean, this volume).

As We Do Think

In the future, we shall have microscopic libraries of record, in which a photograph of every important book and document in the world will be stowed away and made easily available for the inspection of the student.

—H. G. Wells, *World Brain* (1938, 76)

From a student survey:

Do you feel bored when online or when surfing the web?

• Yes I do, very often. It is boring because it is the same thing over and over again, but I do it because I have nothing better to do.

Figure 11.5
FOXTROT © 2011 Bill Amend. Reprinted with permission of UNIVERSAL UCLICK. All rights reserved.

• I'm bored because I feel I shouldn't be when online. I feel I should be checking something, and when I can't think of anything, I become bored.

• I do feel bored sometimes when I'm surfing the web. Then I will start gaming.

Affectivity is not simply the human experience of mind and body, but also the realm of worldly experience beyond the bounds of the person. Just as weather produces affect, so too does the networked interface (Hillis 2009). In the case of web browsing, the affective promise of immediacy made available through interactivity is based on an implicitly McLuhanite understanding (McLuhan 1964) that the medium is the message and technology extends our human sensorium, including our affective capacities and dimensions. The promise of immediacy is built into the ability to click here and there and there again—to *move*, if only virtually (see Hillis, this volume). Its logic is reminiscent of Music Television's 1980s advertising campaign, "I Want My MTV … NOW!"—except that the demand for immediacy has become not only the default expectation but also the background structure of feeling (Williams 1960). Like weather, it produces affect that is at once pervasive and ethereal and not necessarily linked to any one single individual's psychology. Rather, as Sara Ahmed (2004) suggests, the affective, here as a demand for immediacy, is an integral part of social life itself.

Do you ever feel disconnected to the real world due to your internet use?

Yeah, definitely. I can spend hours watching shows online and I'm completely disconnected from the world. You come out of it and a whole day has passed that you haven't been a part of and you've just been in your room, on your laptop.

Do you consider yourself a productive person?

No.

Why is that?

Because I spend my life on my laptop and do nothing useful.

So seeing as you spend a lot of time at home, do you ever find yourself feeling lonely?

Well, I guess that I do sometimes. I think everyone does. I mean in a way I hang out with people on the internet, my Twitter friends, my Facebook friends. But it's not real-life interaction, it's more of this kind of distant disconnected superficial connection.

Digital disaffect infects the network like a virus. It hijacks the machinery for its own reproduction and is produced and reproduced through the server farms and cables that constitute the cloud and the routers, systems that operate to connect people to people, screens to screens, and machines to machines. Digital disaffect operates through interactive functionalities. Intertwined with affectivity, it hides in plain sight in the internet's affective promise of the immediacy of *now*. Click now for this, the web offers. Affectivity and interactivity are virtual and actual. The promise is valid, but its delivery sometimes seems on permanent hold.

From a classroom assignment:

Complete a full record of your daily online activities for the entire week. You should collect and report this data in table form (typed or handwritten). Include the following categories: A) date and time; B) what you were doing, including total time spent doing it; C) your emotional state(s) while doing it; D) your motivation for the activity; E) was the time well spent?

A	B	C	D	E
Jan. 11, 9:45–10:30	Tweet on phone from bed	Bored	Didn't have anything else to do so I tweeted away my problems	Killed like 45 minutes of my life until I passed out from being tired
Jan. 12, 7:30 am	Checked phone for updates and unanswered messages	Unemotional	Wanted to see who messaged me	Same routine every day when I wake up
Jan. 12, 7:20 pm	Browsing the internet	Bored	Had nothing better to do	No, wasted my time doing nothing

So you feel bored on the internet, or whatever you are doing on the internet. So what do you do when you are bored of the internet? Do you still go on it?

Yes, when I'm bored on the internet I still go on it hoping that there are some other things that would grab my attention and quench my boredomness. Since the internet is actually a site, like everything is there, might as well. There is always something that will pop out. … So if I'm bored, I go on the internet and surf. And if I find something fun, then I won't be bored anymore.

But it doesn't really last long?

It doesn't last long because I always find something good. I have to find something good in the internet. Like, let's say 9gag. It's never ending, but when you see the same pictures from the one you just visited earlier, then you get bored again, since you already saw that. Then the fun ends. Now you go on to a different website, let's say Reddit. You see a new picture, sure fun, then you see the same pictures again, and like the ones you visited earlier, boredom again. Now you go to YouTube. You see the cycle, right. So it's bored, not bored, bored, not bored, bored.

Brian Massumi notes that surfing the web "sets up a rhythm of attention and distraction" (Massumi 2002, 139). Every visual activity, he writes, has a pronounced tendency toward one pole or the other. Television, for example, fosters inattention and distraction by inviting us to zap between channels and engage in other activities while watching; movies and books are toward the other pole, demanding greater attention. Web browsing, Massumi suggests, combines both: "Link after link we click ourselves into a lull. But suddenly something else clicks in, and our attention awakens, perhaps even with a raised eyebrow. Surfing sets up a rhythm of attention and distraction" (139–140). This rhythm, both hot and cool, and which operates on a continuum from lull to intense affective attention, resonates with the pattern of an errant electrocardiogram: the flatline of disaffective lull punctuated by pulses of affectivity. Such pulses may occur, for example, in the midst of a flame war (Paasonen, this volume), when viewing online porn (Maddison, this volume), or when refreshing constantly to see if you've won a coveted item during the final seconds of an eBay auction. While the time between different kinds of pulses varies, the in-between time is the flatline of digital disaffect. Susanna Paasonen (2013, n.p.) comments on this phenomenon in terms of pleasure: "The promise and aim of pleasure [on the internet] is by no means always delivered—quite the contrary. Affective jolts of surprise or interest are often hard to come by whereas boredom and frustration lurk never far away."

Do you browse the internet even when you have nothing to look for?

Yes, I'm so used to turning to my social networks throughout the day, and sometimes I don't even know what I'm looking for.

What are some emotions you have after going on the internet?

I'm usually in a neutral state without drastic emotional changes, because going on the internet is something I do on a daily basis. It's almost like a routine for me.

I was just saying the other day about the fact that I'd get, like, a 4.0 GPA if there was no such thing as Facebook, Twitter, and any of these other distractions. Do you feel like the internet has impacted you academically?

I think it's technology as a whole. But realistically, we all have smartphones and most of us have some sort of data plan or social networking. So I think the way we have the internet at our finger tips causes us to depend on it and also live with it.

Do you check your phone frequently?

Yeah. I love how the profs don't mind the way everyone takes out their phones during lectures and tutorials. (Laughs)

How do you feel after you have been on Facebook for a while?

Pretty weird about myself. Like, I'll just say that "Wow, I've spent a lot of time on Facebook," and I'll try to shut it off, only to go back on my phone about five minutes later and just reaccess Facebook again.

From an interview I conducted through email with another media studies professor:

I asked my media theory class last fall to give me a five-minute media work describing their life in cyberspace.

• One student made a five-minute record of her online poker game: cartoon avatars betting real money through PayPal.

• Another provided a webcam record of his face as he surfed the net: an expressionless gaze … eyes darting, never making contact. In the background, a hallway full of meandering people seeming equally disinterested.

• Another student gave me a deeply layered sound collage of electronic media chatter. The piece stayed at the same sound level but was practically incoherent, due to all the discordant textures. I asked the student where she saw herself in this. She asked us to listen again for her very quiet voice in the distant background. We could barely hear small fragments of a conversation she was having with herself, but not enough of it to make any sense. With all the information surrounding her, she told us, she could never have a voice significant enough to matter much to anyone.

From what you say, I gather that you are dependent on the internet, so don't you suffer from anxiety at the thought of being cut off?

I think that if I was cut off from it, I would have grief, because I would think, "My internet, my email," but more than anything I would be relieved. And because the thing that I lack the most with the internet is self-control—I can't control it—and I realize that it's a problem. So if I was cut off I'd be upset, but in my head I'd think it is a blessing.

Memex has become oh-so-sticky. Associative interests. Disaffective, circular responses. As we now think. A virtual letdown. What else is going on?

Notes

1. "Inquiry and Reasoning in the Humanities" was taught at University of Toronto Scarborough, winter 2013. I would like to thank students for their thoughtful engagement in the work of the course and for their openness to sharing their research with a wider audience.

2. Marc Prensky's (2001) terms "digital natives" and "digital immigrants" have been widely influential, as has his contentious argument that as a result of new technologies students today think and process information differently from their predecessors.

References

Ahmed, Sara. 2004. *The Cultural Politics of Emotion*. London: Routledge.

Armstrong, Isobel. 2000. *The Radical Aesthetic*. Oxford: Blackwell.

Berlant, Lauren. 2004. Critical Enquiry, Affirmative Culture. *Critical Enquiry* 30 (2):445–451.

Bush, Vannevar. 1945. As We May Think. *Atlantic Monthly* 176 (1) (July):101–108. Available at http://www.theatlantic.com/magazine/archive/1945/07/as-we-may-think/303881/.

Cravey, Altha J., and Michael Petit. 2012. A Critical Pedagogy of Place: Learning through the Body. *Feminist Formations* 24 (2) (August):100–119.

Davidson, Cathy N. 2011. *Now You See It: How Technology and Brain Science Will Transform Schools and Business for the 21st Century*. New York: Penguin Books.

Freire, Paulo. 1970. *Pedagogy of the Oppressed*. Trans. Myra Bergman Ramos. New York: Continuum.

Hillis, Ken. 2009. *Online a Lot of the Time: Ritual, Fetish, Sign*. Durham: Duke University Press.

Hillis, Ken, Michael Petit, and Kylie Jarrett. 2013. *Google and the Culture of Search*. New York: Routledge.

Latour, Bruno. 2005. *Reassembling the Social: An Introduction to Actor-Network-Theory*. Oxford: Oxford University Press.

Massumi, Brian. 2002. *Parables for the Virtual: Movement, Affect, Sensation*. Durham: Duke University Press.

McLuhan, Marshall. 1964. *Understanding Media: The Extensions of Man*. New York: McGraw-Hill.

Paasonen, Susanna. 2011. *Carnal Resonance: Affect and Online Pornography*. Cambridge, MA: MIT Press.

Paasonen, Susanna. 2013. Irrational Users. Conference presentation, Association of Internet Researchers (AoIR) 13, Manchester, England.

Prensky, Marc. 2001. Digital Natives, Digital Immigrants, Part 1. *Horizon* 9 (5):1–6.

Sobchack, Vivian. 2004. *Carnal Thoughts: Embodiment and Moving Image Culture*. Berkeley: University of California Press.

Tomkins, Silvan. 1995. *Exploring Affect: The Selected Writings of Silvan S. Tomkins*. Ed. E. Virginia Demos. Cambridge: Cambridge University Press.

Wells, H. G. 1938. *World Brain*. Garden City, NY: Doubleday, Doran.

Williams, Raymond. 1960. *The Long Revolution*. London: Chatto and Wyndus.

Value

12 Getting Things Done: Productivity, Self-Management, and the Order of Things

Melissa Gregg

This chapter connects productivity applications—also known as Getting Things Done (GTD) apps—with the tradition of time management pedagogy that has developed in modern business culture over the past several decades. Both spheres have religious dimensions: I show how old ideas of confession, abstinence, and salvation appear as rehabilitative marketing spin in services touted by GTD prophets today. This context illustrates GTD's appeal as a secular ethics, and as what I will suggest is a kind of religious practice. In the shift from the printed page to the network, time management techniques accumulate some of the resonances of Silicon Valley mythology, and become a set of tenets that propel contemporary ideas of creativity and industry through association with vocation and religious calling.

The extent to which this appeal fails as religious comes down to the fact that GTD is a practice that is self-oriented, not other-focused—indeed, its main principles require investment in a default assholery (James 2012) that elevates an elite class of worker beyond the concerns of ordinary colleagues and social bonds. GTD produces an idea of human efficiency that is only imaginable through the mutually constitutive discourses of computation and management. Applying these principles of efficiency to the individual, productivity regimes enacted through new media hardware and software retrain seemingly natural aspects of social being toward more substantial and rewarding ends.

As we will see, time management renders a wide expanse of convivial activities as traps or annoyances best avoided. In this sense, GTD espouses asociality as superiority. It draws together troubling philosophical legacies of exceptionalism in the guise of successful entrepreneurialism. In the networked context, productivity's mandate is to obliterate what remains of voluntary sociability in the otherwise coercive networking context of the modern workplace (Gregg 2011). It takes seriously the possibility of focusing attention purely on the consequential, at least for predetermined periods. That individuals have the power to control life's unpredictability in such a way through the deployment of technological infrastructure is just the first fantasy GTD cannot fulfill.

Feeling Productive

To *feel productive* is to exude as a personal accomplishment the qualities sought and endorsed by modern computing technologies and management mantras alike. GTD apps allow users to achieve their goals and reclaim appropriate space-time perception in the face of network culture's immersive potential. This is done in a number of ways, from shutting down email and nonpriority communication to quantifying individuals' peak performance periods for maximum efficiency. The GTD industry thus epitomizes the trend toward *algorithmic living*, in which data bits and code become the impetus for enlightened behavior. GTD categorizes, with the aim of eventually finessing, different elements of a user's world. Services and pointers provided by productivity apps turn everyday activities into objects of measurement—and hence adjustment and improvement—by a "quantified self."[1]

GTD's "affect of efficiency" emerges from adopting specific techniques "of thinking about doing and not-doing" (Adrian Mackenzie 2008, 149). It transforms the volatility of contemporary living into actionable steps that provide a better pace and orientation for our encounters with time and things. Productivity apps are the harbinger of and contributors to this specific affective bearing: their promise is to deliver productivity regularly and reliably, cognizant of the pleasures to be found in uninterrupted work. GTD strives to deliver an enhanced relationship to time by maximizing opportunities for optimal work "flow" (Csíkszentmihályi 1990; Banks 2014). With names like Self Control, Omnifocus, Rescue Time, even Freedom, these services offer liberation as much as consolation from everyday demands. The objective is to provide mastery over extraneous matters—what time management manuals have long referred to as "trivia"—and to overcome the fallibility of human constraints, like memory. GTD responds to a condition in which the plenitude of data accessible online can lead to an inability to complete routine tasks, as one of the most popular reminder services, Remember the Milk indicates (www.rememberthemilk.com).

Advancing the technological optimism that has characterized key moments in the history of the internet (Turner 2006), GTD's spin on the original hacker ethic is to see personal and professional tasks alike as challenges to be overcome through efficient programming. As is the case in the shift to "cognitive capitalism" (Moulier 2011), life and labor are interchangeable versions of administrivia; GTD's gift is to deliver results in the private and public zones that are equally performative in the online spheres now crucial to displaying competent—which is to say profitable—subjectivity. The very need for so many reminder and scheduling services as digital devices proliferate illustrates certain shortcomings in our ability to "action" what is routinely demanded of us in networked life. GTD allows us to see that there may be a growing section of the population for whom the ability to prioritize without the prompting of computer platforms is either undesirable or unthinkable. In practice, GTD applications exacerbate as much as they respond to the fallibility of memory and motivation in the face of data overload. Productivity apps can be seen as one of the "genres of affect management" (Berlant 2011) critical to developing the forms of attention necessary for survival and flourishing in the present. GTD is an index that the seductiveness of online culture is a new opportunity and burden for those whose routine comforts and friendship communities increasingly take place in virtual environments. Time management techniques offer a technological solution to an ontological and empirical problem: that the network delivers more requests for attention than it is possible to act upon, and that these requests often come from colleagues, friends, and family simultaneously.

For workers, GTD encapsulates at least two priorities necessary to succeed within the "new spirit of capitalism" (Boltanski and Chiapello 2005):

1. *To create control*: over temptation, but also demands. One of the key aspects of contemporary online life is the inability to determine whether some notification or ping or contact will be an opportunity or a threat, a source of pleasure or trauma. This reconfigures notions of affect stemming from systems theory, elaborated in the work of Silvan Tomkins and circulated by scholars such as Eve Sedgwick, Adam Frank, and Teresa Brennan (Seigworth and Gregg 2010). A simple example of how networked affect operates is the habit of checking email. In spite of our knowledge that browsing an inbox is usually uninspiring and damaging to concentration, we still do so. The optimistic expectation of a magic message with happy news almost always ends in disappointment, but the cycle of checking nonetheless continues (see also Dean, this volume; Karppi, this volume). Our persistent return to the volatile affective sphere of the digital, in spite of diminishing returns, demands a theory of attachment that accounts for such ordinary practices of "cruel optimism" (Berlant 2011).

2. *To "thrive on chaos"*: a phrase from management monolith Tom Peters (1988) that appears in minor variations in the subtitle of many work-related advice manuals (e.g., Carroll 2004). The Peters dictum captures GTD's basic rationale: to maintain a functioning individual with an enhanced likelihood of greatness. Yet the ahistorical technocentrism of GTD's online subcultures has served to obscure the direct link between this new manifestation of time management techniques and previous examples of popular business pedagogy.

The remainder of this chapter suggests that these are alarming priorities for the majority of workers to accept. Their combination in the GTD lifeworld, in particular, signals a renewed appeal of the ideals popularized by figures like Ayn Rand who held sway over some of the earliest web pioneers (Streeter 2011; Curtis 2011). The heroic individualism characteristic of Silicon Valley myth, from Bill Gates to Mark Zuckerberg, Stewart Brand to Steve Jobs, is one that legitimizes notions of individual supremacy in the name of advancing civilization and success. It is a belief system that normalizes and accepts hierarchical power and collegial disharmony. In its efforts to streamline out of existence not just distractions but the purportedly unimportant neediness of other people, GTD continues a legacy of thought that is content with the mission of elevating the status of a few especially brilliant people above the struggles of others.

(Still) Getting Things Done

To focus solely on the technological dimensions of GTD is to miss some significant precursors that assist in understanding its function. *Getting Things Done* (Allen 2001) is one of the most successful recent titles among the countless time management publications that have been a feature of office life over the course of many decades. GTD owes a debt to this tradition of management self-help and the discourses of professionalism that typified the mid-century high modernity of Fordist production. As the ranks of middle management swelled in the organization era of the 1950s and 1960s, the genre of popular business pedagogy served as a training ground for a generally male business class seeking to secure reputational capital and the benefits of lifelong employment. By the 1980s, however, such literature was aimed at assisting managers charged with the task of mass layoffs and corporate restructuring. It is in this period, and moving into the early 1990s, that new efforts in professional strategizing took hold. Stephen Covey, author of the phenomenally successful *Seven Habits of Highly Effective People*, describes this move as an "inside-out approach to personal and interpersonal effectiveness" (Covey, in Mackenzie 2008, 141). Self-help publications expanded in scope from addressing an aspirational management elite to become fodder for the creative class of information workers. These employees not only exercised new varieties of power in team-based workplaces, they also enjoyed the luxury of company-funded air travel, with enough down time to peruse the departure lounge bookshops that are a pivotal site for productivity pedagogy.

A curious aspect of this lucrative publishing business throughout its transformations is the timelessness of its advice. From the subtle art of "wastebasketry" (Bliss 1993) to the finer skill of delegation, business self-help serves up a host of tried and true methods to escape "the time trap" (Mackenzie 1972, 1990). Indeed management manuals are notably ahistorical, with repetition not only of particular tips (ranked and refined to-do lists; daily affirmations; time logs; the Pareto principle, or 20 percent rule)[2] but also of highly repetitive and reciprocal suggested reading lists. Successful writers adopt a fearless approach to self-citation and appear to have no qualms in republishing predecessors' recommendations, even their anecdotes. Throughout, the authority of the writing is punctuated and enhanced with recourse to pithy quotations, which may derive from religious, spiritual, or conventional wisdom, alongside "quasi-scientific appeals to neurology and psychology" (Mackenzie 2008, 143).

An impoverished attention to precedent is one of time management pedagogy's key ironies. That its relationship to time and history is distinctly unreflexive mirrors the presentism of business culture broadly. If the formula for success is largely invariable over time, this only confirms the status of business self-help as a genre, for which there is an apparently insatiable market appetite. As a *popular* genre, however, productivity maintains an ambivalent proximity to any explicit training within the workplace. In-house time management training for corporate professionals is often optional rather than mandatory, marking productivity pedagogy as the stuff of cattle-class airline cabins and weekend sofas rather than office settings per se.

Personal productivity literature's recreational tenor exemplifies what Mark Banks (2009) calls "instrumental leisure." This incorporates the broader suite of lifestyle preferences necessary to ensure middle-class hegemony in social and cultural space. As we will see, GTD apps extend this practice, teaching "methods of working that fill gaps between the worlds of enterprise, government, education and everyday life" (Mackenzie 2008, 137). This is part of a wider process that is implicated in the transference of work-based priorities throughout all enclaves of the social (Berardi 2009).

As institutional cutbacks began to throttle the benefits of white collar work, for those lacking the formal guidance or explicit instruction once reserved for a vocation, and for the many increasingly coming to terms with the unlikely prospect of a secure career in an organization, productivity literature has filled a psychological void. In the context of Western secular business culture, it addresses a salariat in need of recognition and the reassurance that its members are not only gifted and capable but, with the right motivation, destined for a prosperous future. In its combination of solace and pragmatism, time management technologies are constituted through a recreational sermonizing in which the basic structures of religion come to fruition. The next section outlines at least three components central to this spiritual dimension as productivity pedagogy has moved online. Through its myths of origin,[3] its performativity,[4] and its constant appeal to disciplined repetition, GTD's networked subcultures address users as potential followers requiring indoctrination. As I will suggest, however, this is a religion of its neoliberal time, in that an inward focus avoids any theory of society that can serve to harness care for others.

The Individual as Failure—GTD and Confession

In his address to Google employees in 2007, Merlin Mann, creator of the 43 Folders website and icon of the online GTD movement, begins with an anecdote.[5] Appealing to workers on a personal level, Mann relates the history of his experience with email. The tale begins with infatuation and love, sharing the wonder and excitement of email as an "astonishing" new horizon for contact. As the volume of online communication increases, however, Mann admits to growing feelings of inadequacy. His relationship to email deteriorates over time to that of being overwhelmed and paralyzed by messages. Couched in Mann's endearing style, the GTD techniques he discusses are offered as a solution to a familiar kind of inertia. The anecdotal mode is purposeful here, as it is in so many pedagogical contexts. Mann draws on self-help's formulaic structure, which charts a recognizable course: "You think I'm not like you, but listen. I had your problem. I overcame it. Here's how. Copy me." Mann's Inbox Zero technique follows the same tenets of paperwork efficiency touted in time management manuals for decades. The only novelty is the technological development that makes email the primary platform now delivering information to workers.

Mann's career as a motivational speaker and creative talent trades on the popularity of his 43 Folders website and builds from the example of self-help pioneers such as Dale Carnegie (1988), whose lectures to Depression-era Manhattanites punctuated shrewd business advice with multiple anecdotes.[6] In Mann's case, the cathartic function of his introduction also draws on the Augustinian tradition of confession, dating back to the fourth century.[7] To confess is to speak the truth of oneself, to access and retrieve the essence of interiority and offer it to others for judgment (Foucault 1978). A generic trait of other self-help programs (twelve-step, AA), confession's retro-intro-spection calls for an honest and attentive self-criticism to generate a new manner of living. The conversion process initiated by the confessional has mobilizing power. The pattern or refrain—"I too had your problem, but look at me now. If you only adopt my methods, you can be cured"—encourages followers to identify with a leader, see the light, and find a path of better thinking that animates righteousness. In GTD, reinvention is reinforced by repetitive and habitual practices that include positive affirmations and carefully selected catchphrases. The latter are further endorsed by a populist neuroscience that encompasses an evangelical optimism, evident in the oft-cited maxim to "visualize" change.[8]

In combination, the GTD confession-conversion process succeeds on a religious level to the extent that it avoids inherently political structural questions and instead demands a leap of faith. The link between inward focus and individualism is ensured through the aura of the celebrity GTDer, whose visionary status facilitates the recruitment of others. Mann's stardom (he is introduced as a "superhero" by the Google host) rides the wave of enthusiasm for other dot-com prophets whose unique qualities and innate genius inspire others. But his personal charisma rests on a disavowal of this status. His website is *not* just another instance of the GTD trend, but "about finding the time and attention to do your best creative work."[9] For the regular GTD believer, the discourse of confession articulates a conjuncture between personal improvement and personal productivity. It is an articulation that makes two things appear natural in their alliance, even if they do not necessarily go together (Hall in Grossberg 1996).

Taking Control—GTD and Self-Discipline

Religious traditions are also evident in productivity techniques that encourage periods of abstinence and withdrawal from the network. Self Control and Cold Turkey are downloadable applications that block a computer's access to desirable online sites (those that occasion regretful indulgence) and the established peril of email. The tagline for Cold Turkey—"I'm watching you"—winks knowingly at dystopian visions of surveillance embodied in Big Brother in its promise to "temporarily block you off of social media sites, addicting websites, games and even programs!" (http://getcoldturkey.com). Also noteworthy in this genre, Self Control (http://selfcontrolapp.com) offers a "spirit of escape" for users faced with the challenge of too many online obligations. Creator Steve Lambert cites the influence of Merlin Mann's Inbox Zero speech at Google as formative in dreaming up his application's design (http://visitsteve.com/made/selfcontrol/). Self Control is his effort "to deliberately create time for me to create that even I couldn't sabotage." It offers assistance for individuals looking to focus "on the work that, hopefully, they care the most about, for their livelihood and for their well-being. It's about making the best of a bad situation" (Lambert 2012).[10]

Like the confessional process outline above, any success possible through using these programs requires users to acknowledge a problem. In this case it is the ceaseless temptation of stimuli available in a smorgasbord of online forums. Users of these platforms may remain skeptical of the deification attached to GTD gurus and have little to do with online subcultures in general. Their utilitarian outlook makes them unlikely candidates for conversion. Instead, the pleasures of online life are acknowledged to be the problem in maintaining a healthy balance of activities. Within the framework of productivity, these users respond positively to forced deprivation. Their more militant approach reckons with the sociability and coerciveness of the network, perhaps better figured as a challenge of will in an age of neuromarketing and attention-seeking design.

The block-and-avoid tactics underpinning these instances of GTD are a redeployment of pointers from productivity literature of decades past (e.g., the suggestion to schedule a "golden hour" of uninterrupted time each day, or the imperative to identify a "prime time" for performance).[11] But in the online context, the prevention model invokes a health-oriented moralism reminiscent of Catholicism, with its prevailing metaphors of denial, restraint, asceticism, and sin. Too much socializing with friends is a temptation to be trained out of workers if they are to remain appropriately productive. GTD's techno-fix provides a solution to this as well as to common etiquette dilemmas—the Facebook friend who sends constant messages, the IM buddy who ignores a "busy" status. To cope with these situations, GTD extends the moralizing and individuating tendencies of particular religious traditions as much as self-help more broadly in prompting the ultimate question: could your biggest productivity problem be *you*?

Omniscience and Omnipotence—GTD and Freedom

A third religious strain of GTD is its desire to produce the elevated perspective necessary to deliver improved productivity. Quantification apps such as Rescue Time (www.rescuetime.com/) and Vitamin-R (www.publicspace.net/Vitamin-R/) join project management suites like Omnifocus (www.omnigroup.com/products/omnifocus/) in the aim to deliver fully integrated maps of the territory of waking life. These examples allow users to track work/life cycles by day, hour, or minute, so that energy levels and communication patterns can be identified for improvement or discipline. The ultimate goal is to siphon off periods of greater concentration from the mass of undifferentiated data and demands.

The pivotal religious experience delivered by these services is the sense that *you* can be God, in charge of your destiny, for at least twenty-five minutes a day.[12] Their objective is to provide uninterrupted time to be creative—to get on with the "real" work of producing the product, idea, or insight that others in the office will likely miss. This process manipulates the unwieldy "order of things" (Foucault 1970) presented by the network to make space for guilt-free concentration. The cumulative habit of indulging this superior use of time enlivens awareness of productive opportunities throughout the workday. Such mindful attention to time may allow room for extraneous matters, but only after more noteworthy targets have been met.

GTD's Order of Things

The notion of freedom that GTD services animate updates for the network era regimes of prioritization first naturalized in time management manuals of the 1970s and 1980s, in which readers were taught how to classify tasks and disruptions from the urgent to the not so urgent, the important to the trivial. Thus categorized, anything that can be delegated is delegated, according to ruthless regimes of calculation. The "how to" section of Mackenzie's 1972 edition of *The Time Trap* shows the politics of order involved in these earlier precedents. The things that come to count as trivia include updates on overdue reports alongside telephone calls from one's wife. In describing tactics to avoid "the avalanche of paperwork," the author argues that everything comes down to assessing "which materials ought to come into your desk and which ought to be screened out mercilessly by your secretary" (Mackenzie 1972, 69). GTD apps extend time management's longstanding effort to produce a hierarchy of attention for workers whose jobs reward elite performance. This is the freedom to act and make history through the consequential decisions confined to the privilege of high office, once all other administrative burdens have been delegated down the workplace hierarchy.

A historical reading allows us to note that the rise of techno-mediated efficiency infrastructure occurs in tandem with post-Fordism's reconfiguration of the sexual contract. Productivity apps are the digital assistants increasingly required when the gendered labor of the secretary and the wife are not so easily available.[13] In postfeminist work cultures mediated by personal mobile devices, business and home-based administration are less likely to be delegated to others, even if, as we are realizing, a key component of GTD philosophy is to absolve responsibility for certain kinds of labor. In the wake of the significant rupture brought about by feminism, the affective labor of the secretary is a luxury fewer numbers of workers will know. As such, GTD allows us to appreciate the extent of the administrative and logistical labor once provided largely by women.

The notion of freedom GTD celebrates is, perversely, the freedom to work (Gregg 2007). In practice it typically means liberation from a raft of unrewarding labor that others must still perform. This understanding of freedom as the power to delegate fits with broader attitudes that have shaped the development of the internet for several decades. It is a vision that naturalizes the power of men over women, to the degree that the freedom it promotes is understood "in terms of the power to command, to walk out the door, to deny the work of nurturing and the material fact of interdependence" (Streeter 2011, 13). It is also a vision that is specifically American, a "habit of understanding freedom negatively, blindly, as freedom from government, freedom from dependency, freedom from others" (Streeter 2011, 13). The idea of freedom through creative labor relates to the broader glamorization of work in successive dot-com booms and the origin stories attached to pivotal leaders (Jobs and Wozniak, Gates, etc.). The quasi-religious appeal of these narratives resonates strongly with the elements I have been describing as crucial to the GTD worldview.

GTD resembles a religion in providing a solution to the inadequacies of an individual who, following successful inculcation of its systemized set of practices, is ultimately destined for a higher calling. In the first category of techniques identified above, conversion to a productivity program is initiated through confession. Recruitment is premised on admitting a deep truth—being a fallible human and therefore in need of repair. This acknowledgment of personal failure becomes material to be rehabilitated through techniques of mastery, whether it is elevation above the day-to-day concerns of this life (Zen Habits, http://zenhabits.net) or the elimination of obligation (the "four-hour work week"—see Ferriss 2007). In the second category, the seeker similarly admits to character flaws, acknowledging the sin of relationships outside work, which in the logic of productivity amounts to quasi-incompetence close to a lack of will. The sinner calls upon a higher power to reward productivity and punish unproductive activities through the policing tactics of blocking and surveillance. This is, however, an ethics of resignation, one that effectively cedes control over access to seductive communication to a stronger force. Technology becomes a judging deity, a suprahuman fix for problems generated by technology itself. Finally, in the third category, GTD is the route toward the ultimate good: pure creativity. Quantification and metrics allow the user a divine perspective, that of a creator-God liberated from the fallibility of self *and* others. Elevated above the fate of peers through data insights and behavior tracking, the successful GTDer focuses attention on being brilliant and imagining a world of greater things.

Each of these versions of GTD orthodoxy involves a vision of mastery and control that entails freedom from obligation if not from work. There is no register for the materiality of other people, the infrastructure enabling freedom, or the mutual dependence that liberation requires. The accomplished individualism of the GTD subject enjoys what is claimed as a natural freedom. Yet this "natural" bearing is the result of technologies of self-management arising from a dedicated literature of popular pedagogy over many decades. This forgotten history has the cumulative effect of making GTD's myopia an acceptable good, even while its vision of personal emancipation requires segregation among workers. Productivity technologies thus provide protection from the pollution of incompetent others, a means to avoid "idiot compassion" (Carroll 2004). As a philosophy, GTD operates on the premise that "taking time for oneself is a form of liberation" (Lambert 2012).

The Territory of the Postprofessional

GTD's lack of novelty is only understandable given that it inherits a tradition of repetitive recommendations synonymous with the emergence of the modern business press. If motivational literature of the 1970s and 1980s helped managers to maintain their distance from those under their watch, GTD apps are a sign that, for many, the distance between manager and employee has collapsed. This collapse is a large part of the revolution that online connectivity has wrought upon organizations, "as knowledge workers began to discover the pleasures of online communication in substantial numbers, and elites groped for an organizational framework" capable of managing the "structure of desire" epitomized in web browsing's "endless 'what's next?'" (Streeter 2011, 25). In flexible, decentralized worksites today, time management has been one of the most prominent techniques cultivated by individuals to maintain employability in the face of growing occupational insecurity. Increasingly dissatisfied by (when they aren't also prevented from achieving) the predictability of a company career, employees have apparently gained fulfillment through proximity to "projects" and "networks," just as employers have offered the benefits of "flexibility" rather than stability in this "new spirit of capitalism" (Boltanski and Chiapello 2005). With their emphasis on streamlined workflow, the efficiency logics of GTD apps epitomize these broader cultural trends. They evolve in tandem with management protocols inviting employees to display autonomy and responsibility by "working smarter, not harder."

Unlike earlier individuals engaged in forms of professional strategizing, however, the self-sufficient worker downloading GTD apps today takes on the imperative of productivity in spite of a generalized lack of employment and institutional security. The difference between time management in the organizational era—defined by to-do lists, clock time, and a highly gendered division of labor—and GTD in the network era—where employees at all levels are equally responsible for their own productivity—is thus the difference between professional and *postprofessional* subjectivity. This is a work context in which prior versions of management surveillance are less obvious or necessary, since the innate value of productivity is no longer questioned. It is no coincidence, I have been suggesting, that it is also a moment in which the commonsense tenets of individualism and freedom have become so embedded in technology design that a cooperative politics seems elusive.

In contrast to the social ethic attributable to the organization era (Whyte 1956), in which workers gained status and privileges through association with a firm, GTD's asociality reflects a more widespread experience of mobile work. Flexible freelancers and remote workers of all kinds are liberated from the office because they are assumed to be willing to provide their own, ostensibly inexhaustible, resources. These resources begin with the logistical benchmark of constant connectivity and stretch to include the psychological resilience and composure entailed in day-to-day affect management. In this context, GTD's anti-institutionalism inaugurates a digital nihilism that obviates the need for, and reality of, mutual dependence and reciprocity in the workplace.

Productivity's self-inflating rhetoric positions the creative worker as a heroic individual who triumphs through the adoption of superior techniques. This is the pleasure individual workers feel in identifying with imperatives that are directly productive for capital. GTD produces meaning by providing an order in which to do things so that they appear superficially manageable. In doing so, GTD erases any need to question the overall structure determining *which* things are important.

GTD's individualized response to workplace inefficiency is a marker of the inchoate labor politics of the precarious white-collar worker. The careerist concerns of today's wannabe managers are matched only by the competitive mindset of the freelance entrepreneur battling for a break in the jackpot economy. GTD shows how the cutthroat requirements of even the most ordinary middle-class job are in the process of becoming detached from a horizon of ethical conduct once critical to participation in the bourgeois public sphere. Of course this horizon was always something of a fantasy. This chapter's brief history of time management is not intended to eulogize a golden age of good conduct that produced an ethics of business. The nine-to-five imaginary of Fordism may have allowed some to opt out of the careerist and managerial thinking now required of the majority, but it did so at the expense of what came to be known as "minorities," in relation to the particular gender, race, class, and sexuality assumed of the default worker (Mitropoulos 2006). Productivity apps extend GTD's "response-in-denial to the competitive pressures of the information economy" (Mackenzie 2008, 138) by consolidating what were already innate advantages for well-educated, because well-networked, men. That GTD emerges—as religion, as fad—within the growing demographic of information workers highlights the winning combination of poise, access, and literacy that defines participation in today's digital networks.

The further story GTD tells is that of the segregation between the information haves and "have-less" (Qiu 2009). Its cutting-edge user base jostles to stay at the top of the division of labor in an increasingly global economy. It provides "a delusional and probably short-lived self-satisfaction to individuals keen to keep abreast of the waves created by their own careers and their own enthusiasm for more communication and more speed" (Mackenzie 2008, 138). Mackenzie's analysis accentuates GTD's casual solipsism, which enables already privileged individuals "to differentiate themselves." GTDers are defined by productivity's circular reward structure, which holds that it is always better to "do more than their friends, partners, and colleagues." But such "enhanced efficiency only matters if some other people appear to be less mobile"—that is, if all agree to the same economy of activity (Mackenzie 2008, 143).

Alternatives to this regime of value are thankfully already available, for instance in the "refusal of work" legacy in the tradition of autonomist Marxism (Berardi 2009). The language of the "social factory" is useful for showing productivity's limitless ambition, and the pointlessness of "gaming" a system with predefined ends.[14] Recent feminist theory (e.g., Weeks 2011; McRobbie 2010) reads autonomist histories in combination with the ongoing devaluation of women's work—a move that is crucial to appreciate how the desire for time management underpinning productivity applications takes a particular notion of time for granted. It assumes that time, like the worker, can be managed according to the imperatives of capitalist production, and it does this in an unreflective way. Such a perspective cannot register the phenomenological or affective experience of multiple and conflicting stimuli: a reality that has long been the standard for working women, especially mothers, both within and outside the home. GTD's faith in technology as the salve for broader ontological insecurity in many ways exacerbates the hierarchies of labor inherited from previous configurations of work. A closer look at the "order of things" that it is GTD's mandate to reproduce reveals that the variety of labor valued within its system is highly selective.

As has always been the case, productivity logic offers a pedagogy of time that legitimates some workers' freedom over others. In its online manifestations, it provides a technical apparatus to deflect awareness of this fact, as it delegates work downward to those without the social or technical means to escape. GTD is in this sense an inkling of what has happened to the Protestant ethic in the new spirit of informational capitalism. Whereas capitalist values were once thought to align with the desire to move closer to God *in spirit*, productivity's mandate of outsourcing and delegating labor suggests that we now seek to become Godlike ourselves. The GTDer justifies his difference from the mass of workers, whose lack of self-discipline condemns them to administrivia. This is a particularly pernicious brand of nihilism, since it promotes *as* autonomy and freedom what is, in effect, a refusal to place any hope in improving conditions for others.

GTD's impossible promise is to transcend the competing affects of networked, which is to say contemporary, experience. Its religious valences seek a Pentecostal conversion of the Godlike power to control time and space. It is enough of an affront that this lifestyle actively endorses a form of living that substitutes action for thought (Mackenzie 2008). In joining the ranks of GTDers, we subscribe to a religion without an ethics, an ontology without an epistemology, along with a set of gestures meant to console us when faced with the knowledge that there are always too many things to do, but there may never be a sense of meaning behind the disorder.

Notes

1. Quantified Self, like GTD, is a trademarked movement focusing on the insights to be found in life tracking. See http://quantifiedself.com/. A useful overview is Nafus and Sherman (2013).

2. The Pareto principle, "the law of the vital few," is based on a formula first outlined by Italian economist Vilfredo Pareto (1848–1923) to explain the unequal distribution of wealth in his country. In time management pedagogy, this has been repurposed variously to explain that the least important work takes up eighty percent of our time—or, alternatively, that the top twenty percent of workers triumph because they focus on the most meaningful results/projects/clients. In either case, the principle is used to encourage better attention to prioritizing tasks and producing the right order of things.

3. An example of one such myth is a story told repeatedly in time management publications (e.g., *The Time Trap*, 1972 and 1990 versions) regarding Charles Schwab—an early president of Bethlehem Steel. Interested in how he could improve his productivity, Schwab engaged a consultant who urged him to write a daily to-do list with only one or two items on the list that, no matter what, had to be completed before anything else that day. This simple technique is said to have saved the company major ongoing costs, and the source of the advice was given a $25,000 check in gratitude. In a footnote, Mackenzie attributes the story to an anecdote reproduced in another productivity manual, further obscuring the source of the original tale.

4. Time management manuals typify Butler's (1990) notion of performativity, in that they produce a compelling and mobilizing ideal image that is itself based on a copy for which there is no original.

5. The address to Google employees is available on YouTube at http://www.youtube.com/watch?v=z9UjeTMb3Yk. Mann is unique in time management pedagogy circles for addressing his debt to predecessor Dave Allen in an FAQ on his popular 43 Folders website (http://www.43folders .com). Yet the origins of Mann's blog, as an attempt to implement the GTD philosophy, follow generic conventions on at least two other fronts: in documenting a project inspired by a book; and also, as we have seen since, in the retrospective renouncement of the very principles that contributed to his rising celebrity (see Babauta, 2011).

6. First published in 1929, *How to Win Friends and Influence People* set the standard for self-help, perhaps for all time, and has been reimagined in recent years to address the context of social media specifically in Carnegie and Associates (2011).

7. This passage arises from conversation with Jason Wilson.

8. The combination of pseudoscience, spirituality, and motivation in business self-help is especially great in the US. A striking example is Lewis (2008, 192–193): "Your mind holds all of the

power necessary to propel you toward your goals. You may have heard the expression 'If you can believe it, you can achieve it.' I know that statement is true. Nothing can take you farther or make more of a difference in your life than the incredible power of your own mind."

9. His FAQ section further states: "I am the guru of nothing," even while "my out-the-door price for a one-day visit inside the lower 48 starts around the price of a nice Honda Civic. Goes up from there": http://www.merlinmann.com/faqs/hiring-merlin/okay-so-whats-it-cost-to-hire-you.html.

10. Lambert offers a generous engagement with early sections of this paper in Lambert (2012).

11. Both appear in various forms in Mackenzie (1972, 1990) as well as Bliss (1993).

12. This marks their synergy with life-hacking philosophies such as "The Pomodoro Technique." See www.pomodorotechnique.com.

13. This chapter is partly inspired by reactions to Twitter's acquisition of the early GTD app I Want Sandy. Mourning the closure of the service online, a remarkable number of users invoked gendered language which fit with the retro-secretary aesthetics of the application itself. See Dornfest (2008).

14. The gamification of GTD is evident in productivity apps like Epic Win (www.epicwin.net). In its sample screenshot, pushups and garbage duties attest the interoperability of labor and life, with some schoolboy fantasy to boot (in the to-do item "to marry the Queen of England").

References

Allen, David. 2001. *Getting Things Done: The Art of Stress-Free Productivity*. New York: Viking.

Babauta, Leo. 2011. Toss Productivity Out. *Zen Habits*. Available at http://zenhabits.net/un.

Banks, Mark. 2009. Fit and Working Again? The Instrumental Leisure of the "Creative Class." *Environment and Planning A* 41 (3):668–681.

Banks, Mark. 2014. "Being in the Zone" of Cultural Work. *Culture Unbound*, special issue on "Capitalism and Culture," 6: 241–262

Berardi, Franco (Bifo). 2009. *The Soul at Work: From Alienation to Autonomy*. Trans. Francesca Cadel and Giuseppina Mecchia. Cambridge, MA: MIT Press.

Berlant, Lauren. 2011. *Cruel Optimism*. Durham: Duke University Press.

Bliss, Edwin C. [1976] 1993. *Getting Things Done: The ABC of Time Management*. Clayton, Australia: Warner Books.

Boltanski, Luc, and Ève Chiapello. 2005. *The New Spirit of Capitalism*. Trans. Gregory Elliott. New York: Verso.

Butler, Judith. 1990. *Gender Trouble: Feminism and the Subversion of Identity*. New York: Routledge.

Carnegie, Dale. [1936] 1988. *How to Win Friends and Influence People*. Rev. ed. North Ryde: Eden.

Carnegie and Associates, with Brent Cole. 2011. *How to Win Friends and Influence People in the Digital Age*. New York: Simon and Schuster.

Carroll, Michael. 2004. *Awake at Work: 35 Practical Buddhist Principles for Discovering Clarity and Balance in the Midst of Work's Chaos*. Boston: Shambhala.

Csíkszentmihályi, Mihaly. 1990. *Flow: The Psychology of Optimal Experience*. New York: Harper and Row.

Curtis, Adam. 2011. All Watched Over by Machines of Loving Grace. BBC2 (May):23.

Dornfest, Rael. 2008. A Fork in the Road (An Important Announcement about I Want Sandy). Available at https://getsatisfaction.com/iwantsandy/topics/.

Ferriss, Timothy. 2007. *The 4-Hour Workweek: Escape 9–5, Live Anywhere, and Join the New Rich*. New York: Crown.

Foucault, Michel. 1970. *The Order of Things: An Archaeology of the Human Sciences*. New York: Pantheon.

Foucault, Michel. 1978. *The History of Sexuality: Volume One*. New York: Pantheon.

Gregg, Melissa. 2007. Freedom to Work: The Impact of Wireless on Labor Politics. *Media International Australia* 125 (November):57–70.

Gregg, Melissa. 2011. *Work's Intimacy*. Cambridge: Polity Press.

Grossberg, Lawrence. 1996. On Postmodernism and Articulation: An Interview with Stuart Hall. In *Stuart Hall: Critical Dialogues in Cultural Studies*, ed. David Morley and Kuan-Hsing Chen, 131–150. New York: Routledge.

James, Aaron. 2012. *Assholes: A Theory*. New York: Doubleday.

Lambert, Steve. 2012. Comment on Home Cooked Theory. Available at http://homecookedtheory.com/archives/2012/11/05/the-territory-of-the-post-professional.

Lewis, Allyson. 2008. *The Seven Minute Difference: Small Steps to Big Changes*. New York: Kaplan Publishing.

Mackenzie, Adrian. 2008. The Affect of Efficiency: Personal Productivity Equipment Encounters the Multiple. *Ephemera: Theory and Politics in Organization* 8 (2):137–156.

Mackenzie, Alec. 1972. *The Time Trap: How to Get More Done in Less Time*. New York: AMACOM.

Mackenzie, Alec. 1990. *The Time Trap: The New Version of the Classic Book on Time Management*. Melbourne: The Business Library.

McRobbie, Angela. 2010. Reflections on Feminism and Immaterial Labour. *New Formations* 70:60–76.

Mitropoulos, Angela. 2006. Precari-us? *Mute Magazine*. January 9. Available at http://www.metamute.org/editorial/articles/precari-us.

Moulier, Yann. 2011. *Cognitive Capitalism*. Cambridge: Polity Press.

Nafus, Dawn, and Jamie Sherman. 2013. The Quantified Self Movement Is Not a Kleenex. CASTAC. Available at http://blog.castac.org/2013/03/the-quantified-self-movement-is-not-a-kleenex.

Peters, Tom. 1988. *Thriving on Chaos: Handbook for a Management Revolution*. New York: Perennial Library.

Qiu, Jack Linchuan. 2009. *Working-Class Network Society: Communication Technology and the Information Have-Less in Urban China*. Cambridge, MA: MIT Press.

Seigworth, Gregory J., and Melissa Gregg. 2010. An Inventory of Shimmers. In *The Affect Theory Reader*, ed. Melissa Gregg and Gregory J. Seigworth, 1–28. Durham: Duke University Press.

Streeter, Thomas. 2011. *The Net Effect: Romanticism, Capitalism, and the Internet*. New York: New York University Press.

Turner, Fred. 2006. *From Counterculture to Cyberculture: Stewart Brand, the Whole Earth Network, and the Rise of Digital Utopianism*. Chicago: University of Chicago Press.

Weeks, Kathi. 2011. *The Problem with Work: Feminism, Marxism, Antiwork Politics, and Postwork Imaginaries*. Durham: Duke University Press.

Whyte, William H. 1956. *The Organization Man*. Harmondsworth: Penguin.

13 "Let's Express Our Friendship by Sending Each Other Funny Links instead of Actually Talking": Gifts, Commodities, and Social Reproduction in Facebook

Kylie Jarrett

A few years ago, the following image appeared in my Facebook newsfeed (figure 13.1). Shared by a friend in my network, it speaks directly to the contours of affective relationships shaped by digital media technologies.

The humor of this ecard lies in the tension it presents. It claims that the ways we communicate in the context of social networking sites (SNS) such as Facebook are

Figure 13.1
Let's Express our Friendship … : http://www.someecards.com/usercards/viewcard/MjAxMS1iYW QzOGU3MGU0MWYwNTNm.

hopelessly diminished by their status as a commodified exchange, often of commodified objects such as this ecard. The humor, however, comes from the implicit ironic inversion that such exchanges are experienced as manifestations of meaningful friendship, generating various responses ranging from the ubiquitous hit of the "like" button, great hilarity (ROFL), amused acknowledgment ☺, or even ennui (meh). The energy behind these reactions is the profound affective component of social interactions generated through digital networks.

The tension between rich affective interaction and cheapened commodified exchange from which this ecard draws its humor is the same as that which underpins a great deal of research into the economics of digital media. Affect is increasingly recognized as central to the functioning of the capitalist system, and, crucially, to its digital networks (for instance Negri 1989; Marazzi 2011; Dyer-Witheford 1999; Terranova 2000; Fuchs 2008; Gorz 2010). Yet affect's role in market-based exchanges is typically constructed as untenably contradictory. The dynamics of affective interactions, associated with gift economies and the exchange of use values, is deemed at odds with the dynamics of commodified markets involving alienated exchange values. Many critical studies of digital media economics have subsequently sought models for how, as this ecard tells us, consumer labor can be simultaneously commodified and not. This analysis contributes to the discussion by challenging a purportedly fundamental binary between exchanges of gifts (reciprocated objects with socially meaningful use values) and exchanges of commodities (alienated objects with abstract exchange value), a binary that underpins assumptions about digital media economics. Allowing for gift and commodity hybridity brings attention to the reproductive role played by affect, indicating how both forms of exchange are valuable to the capitalist economic system *as use value*. This chapter uses the social networking site Facebook, and the exchanges between its platform and users, to highlight the way in which affective energies contribute to the reproduction of the capitalist circuits of digital media networks (see also Karppi, this volume; Pybus, this volume).

Affect in the Digital Economy

Shaped by Tiziana Terranova's (2000) identification of the importance of unpaid, immaterial labor to digital media industries, a growing body of work has focused on the interactions between users that provide content and monetizable audience data, and which subsequently have a role generating profit for digital media industries (e.g., Cohen 2008; Fuchs 2008; Comor 2010). User activity that adds value ranges from the tangible production of content—such as game play, a tweet, a YouTube video, or a comment on a health support forum—to the traces of user activity gathered by the vast data collection systems of commercial sites that are then sold to advertisers, to the maintenance of the sociality that provides each site's inexorable attraction. The pivotal role of these tangible and intangible audience inputs corresponds with the centrality of knowledge, social relations, and communication—the troika of affective immaterial products—within contemporary capital (Negri 1989; Hardt and Negri 2000; 2009; Lazzarato 1996; Berardi 2009).

The centrality of affect in capitalist economics is particularly pertinent for Facebook, since it draws its revenue from advertising targeted through collections of user data. Practices on the site that generate this data have a significant, if not dominant, phatic function, intended not to convey information but to express social affinity (Miller 2008; Tufekci 2008). Users share various forms of text (audio, visual, graphic) that affirm, contradict, or generate affective responses and relational intensities within interpersonal networks. Facebook user data are, therefore, integrally associated with affect rather than instrumental exchange. They are also aggregated and sold to advertisers in complex ways. Unlike some other commercial digital media platforms, which only target advertising based on an individual's inputs, Facebook's databases also map an individual's relational intensities, measuring hits of the "like" button, through which users express approval or social solidarity, as well as taste information provided by closely connected users within a network. Advertising on Facebook is subsequently targeted to a particular user based on the aggregation of extensive affective activity from across her or his personal network. This directly links value to "users' creation of social relations, or at least relations of affective proximity" (Arvidsson and Colleoni 2012,144). The intensities of affect between users on Facebook can thus be seen as productive, contributing directly to the economic value of the media platform. As the title of Yochai Benkler's (2006) analysis of internet economics claims, there is wealth in these networks.

In the context of commercial websites, such data exchanges can be seen as a form of exploitation, as they are unpaid contributions to the content of the site and the economic surplus generated by the company. These exchanges thus manifest the alienation of the laborer from his or her product and laboring capacity inherent to capitalism (Fuchs 2008; 2009; Andrejevic 2013). What is assumed in this argument is that consumer inputs can be interpreted in the same manner as the labor time of industrial workers. In capitalist systems, human energy is rendered calculable and is finally undercompensated relative to output, in order to generate surplus value. These processes transform an intangible energy and the lived experience of the worker—instantiated labor power—into an objectified commodity suitable for exchange and value generation—labor time. Fuchs (2008) and Andrejevic (2013) describe the same process of commodification when affective relations between users generate value for digital media providers, and as rich social exchanges are transformed into abstracted and alienable objects, such as demographic data, with calculable value (exchange value). This alienation from "natural" cooperative states of affective complexity through the processes of capitalist valorization animates many critical responses to digital media economics and the labor of consumers (see also Benkler 2006; Cohen 2008; Petersen 2008).

But as Adam Arvidsson (2009) notes, identifying how value is generated, and thus how capital works, becomes increasingly complicated in the context of affective networks. Affect (and indeed many consumer contributions to the digital media economy) is almost impossible to measure in terms of labor time. As a process, affective exchange is not capable of being abstracted to a general equivalent; neither is it attributable to one individual (Arvidsson and Colleoni 2012; Gorz 2010). As Christian Marazzi (2011) says, affective labor often involves an intensity and a concrete singularity that makes it incommensurable with standard criteria of valuation. For affective relations to serve their social purpose, they must retain their unique, individual qualities—their use value—and remain beyond the generalizable calculations used in capital. On one hand, then, digital media users' affective relations are increasingly associated with generating surplus value. On the other, however, this association is problematic, since the use value of interactions between digital media consumers cannot simply be front-loaded into existing paradigms of revenue generation. This raises the obvious question of how to understand affect's relationship to the generation of surplus.

Yet is this the right question? The exclusive focus on transformation from gifted use value into market-based exchange value in the literature on digital media economics has generated insight into only one aspect of how affective relations contribute to capital. This approach fails to explore the importance of such relations to the *reproduction of capital*, to the generation and maintenance of modes of being, thinking, and feeling that legitimate and support capital as a suite of social relations. Social activity such as "liking" the status of another on an SNS, organizing a guild run in a multiplayer online game, or commenting on a user-produced video on YouTube may not only generate value in the form of surplus or monetary gain. Such activities may also be *of value* to the perpetuation of contemporary capitalism and capitalist industries through maintenance of the social relations specific to that historical mode of production. To assert this supportive relationship between affect and capitalist systems, however, involves first challenging the naturalized binary relationship of gift economies to commodity markets that is often mobilized in discussions of digital media economics.

Gifts versus Commodities

Any reference to gift economies must acknowledge the important contribution of Marcel Mauss. First published in 1954, Mauss's *The Gift* synthesizes various anthropological studies of economies in premarket societies. In the legal and economic systems of such civilizations, individuals are not involved in the abstract, contractually defined exchanges typical of capitalist systems. Rather, the dominant exchange form is gifting, which involves cooperative social relationships emerging from a fabric of social interaction and reciprocal obligation. Mauss describes gift exchanges as "total" social phenomena, expressing all of the institutions of a society within them.

First, it is not individuals but collectivities that impose obligations of exchange and contract upon each other. The contracting parties are legal entities: clans, tribes, and families who confront and oppose one another either in groups who meet face to face in one spot, or through their chiefs, or in both these ways at once. Moreover, what they exchange is not solely property and wealth, movable and immovable goods, and things economically useful. In particular, such exchanges are acts of politeness: banquets, rituals, military service, women, children, dances, festivals, and fairs, in which economic transaction is only one element, and in which the passing on of wealth is only one feature of a much more general and enduring contract. Finally, these total services and counter-services are committed to in a somewhat voluntary form by presents and gifts, although in the final analysis they are strictly compulsory, on pain of private or public warfare. (Mauss 2002, 6–7)

Gift exchanges as described by Mauss have served as counterpoints to the commodified market exchanges associated with industrial capital. In his criticism of this binary, John Frow (1997, 124) summarizes the typical opposition established between the two forms of transaction:

Commodity Exchange	Gift Exchange
Alienable objects	Inalienable objects
Reciprocal independence	Reciprocal dependence
Quantitative relationship between objects	Qualitative relationship between subjects

What is important to emphasize is the inalienability—the persistence of unique use value—attributed to the gift, as well as its possibility only in a context of reciprocal interpersonal relationality. These characteristics form its distinction from the abstracted objects of market-based exchange. It is this necessarily affective quality that associates gift exchanges with "preceding divergent types of moral economies that were dominant before the rise of political economy" (Prodnik 2012, 285).

Digital Gift Economies

This concept of gift exchanges as distinct from commercial exchanges has been used to explain the economics of the internet since its popularization in the mid-1990s. In 1998 Richard Barbrook (see also Raymond 1998; Ghosh 1998) described the internet as a high-tech gift economy not only because the content available through its platforms was provided for free. Internet exchanges were also gifts in that each input contributed to the cultural commons from which all network participants could draw. In the norms of late 1990s internet culture, the "giving and receiving of information without payment is almost never questioned. Although the circulation of gifts doesn't necessarily create emotional obligations between individuals, people are still willing to donate their information to everyone else on the Net" (Barbrook 1998, n.p.).

For Barbrook, this economic form was a manifestation of the anarcho-communism proposed by New Left activists of the 1960s, and offered a radical alternative to capitalist modes of production. The specific forms of gift exchanges have also been studied in various online communities (e.g., Bergquist and Ljungberg 2001; Veale 2003; Lampel and Bhalla 2007; Hjorth 2007; Pearson 2007), where valorization is associated with the socially emergent "moral economies" of particular user networks. Dourish and Satchell (2011, 34) also emphasize the moral economy of social media such as SNS, arguing that they need to be considered as spaces for social interaction that "entail reciprocal responsibilities and forms of social sanction that manifest themselves as moral and emotional pressures." Interpersonal reciprocity is the locus of valorization in digital media as much as in the premarket gift economies described by Mauss.

In his critical analyses Christian Fuchs (2008; 2009) identifies gifting practices as the core of digital media economies. He argues that because the free flow of ideas between users has been associated with the medium since its inception, what he terms "native" internet production can readily be associated with gift economies. Fuchs suggests that the cooperative relationship between users that marked the development of the internet continues on the contemporary social web in the many sites and practices that encourage meaningful, self-determined, and collectively organized participation. These practices transcend "the instrumental logic of accumulation, profit, competition, and commodification" (Fuchs 2008, 133) associated with market exchanges. It is these gift-like relations, based on an ethos of cooperation and reciprocal sharing, that Fuchs suggest must be maintained, and indeed fostered, in order to assure the radical potential of the internet and, ultimately, the flourishing of human society.

Curiously, this argument brings Fuchs's critical perspective into close alignment with Benkler's (2006) much less critical position that social exchanges—"sharing"—of the type associated with gift economies have become central to digital media economics. For Benkler there is some tension between gift or moral economies and market dynamics, but they nevertheless interact in ways that produce economic, and social, value. Others, working from more critical perspectives, suggest a greater incompatibility between internet gift economies and not only the economics of digital media but capitalism itself. Barbrook, for instance, notes that although "money-commodity and gift relations are not just in conflict with each other, but also co-exist in symbiosis, ... each method of working does threaten to supplant each other. ... The potlatch and the commodity remain irreconcilable" (Barbrook 1998, n.p.). Fuchs (2008, 2009) also argues for a complex dialectic between capitalism and gift economics on the internet, yet suggests that the two modes of production function as negating binaries. He assumes the absolute subsumption of the gift and its use value into the debased exchange value of the commodity form.

Thus, even while *all* commodities have both use value and exchange value (Marx 1990; Comor 2010), in such critical interpretations of digital media economics use values are supplanted when encountered in the context of commodified exchanges. This position is exemplified by Lewis Hyde (1979, 21), who says, "When gifts are sold, they change their nature as much as water changes when it freezes, and no rationalist telling of the constant elemental structure can replace the feeling that is lost." Gifts, this strand of thought suggests, are exhaustively incompatible with *any form* of economic valorization; gifts (use values) and commodities (exchange values) exist in necessarily "hostile worlds" (Zelizer 2005).

Alienability and Gifts

It is not necessarily true, however, that in capitalist market contexts the reciprocal dependence of use values is eradicated. In contemporary consumer capitalism, as much as in precursor economic systems (Read 2003), there is no clear distinction between alienable and inalienable possessions. Frow notes:

Almost all things may move between these contexts, and are defined and valued accordingly. If it is possible for governments to impose a gift tax, for example, it is because almost all gifts can, in the appropriate cultural context, be measured as commodities; conversely, most commodities are capable of being gifted, and indeed the majority of gifts in modern societies with capitalist social relations *are* (purchased but not given as) commodities. (Frow 1997, 131)

Like the ecard from my Facebook newsfeed, Frow's argument draws attention to the simultaneous coexistence of inalienable affective and abstracted commodified qualities within the same object or process of exchange. Similar points are made in Arjun Appadurai's (1986) and Igor Kopytoff's (1986) related arguments about the movement through inalienable and alienable states in the progression of "the social life of things." This hybridity is also central to Viviana Zelizer's (2005) argument about the range of complex, multiple, and ongoing social negotiations that work to define the boundaries between acceptable and nonacceptable commodification of intimacy.

Sara Ahmed's (2004) model of affective economies also pertains. She describes the perpetual circulation of affect, punctuated by moments and/or spaces of "stickiness" (see Paasonen, this volume) in which it temporarily fixes as an intensity. The movement from gift to commodity can be viewed as such a moment of formal fixity, where the relation becomes identified as gift or commodity exchange through the registered affective intensity. Any exchange at any time may thus involve elements associated with gifts, commodities, or both, and this status may change as an object or practice circulates, accumulating and losing affective resonance.

This hybridity and fluidity can be traced in the types of relations enacted on Facebook. While it is certainly true that affective exchanges among users within a friend network are implicated within a capitalist circuit of alienated exchange due to their role in advertising-based revenue generation, it is also true that they retain their function *and basis* in the inalienable, cooperative relations typical of gift economies. Andrew L. Mendelson and Zizi Papacharissi's (2011) study of photographs by college students on Facebook is illustrative. Their analysis reveals that comments associated with many posts to SNS are often unintelligible outside the shared communicative and social context of those involved. Like the ideal gift, Facebook posts cannot be experienced solely as an exchange of abstracted commodities and still serve their phatic function within an affective network. The meaning for those involved cannot be alienated from the relational context of these exchanges, especially when, as is typical of Facebook, users are known to each other beyond the confines of the digital system (Lenhart and Madden 2007). That the data exchanged are later transformed into alienable commodities does not mean that these posts do not at some point circulate as use value.

User-Platform Relations

To assert that affective relations between users persist within commodified contexts such as SNS is, however, not the central focus of this chapter. The more innovative aspect of my argument here is that *user-platform* relations are also shaped by traces of giftlike reciprocity. This initially counterintuitive proposition is, I suggest, a necessary framework for understanding the economics of digital media platforms, access to which typically requires no monetary outlay, obscuring the status of using such sites as a commercial transaction. This is further complicated by designating an SNS site as a platform, which, as Tarleton Gillespie (2010) argues, allows a company to position itself as a neutral medium, eliding the organizing agency of its own systemic and economic affordances. The consequent expectation of a platform in the contemporary web is that it provides free access for the practice of individual self-expression—it is both an economic entity and a figuratively free place from which to speak, create, distribute, and position ourselves politically. Overt processes of commodification and monetization primarily take place in back-channel communication between the company and advertisers or the financial market (Arvidsson and Colleoni 2012), all at a remove from users' interactions. In this opacity, there is an easy conflation of the social interactions between users (and the affective intensities generated in such interactions) with the data exchanged between the user and the platform at the interface. My interaction with the Facebook interface when updating my status constitutes, for me, interaction with my meaningful others, rather than with the parent corporation. Even the increasingly invasive advertising on the site, like advertising on television, is experienced merely as background noise for these meaningful exchanges. This context ensures that using the cost-free service of Facebook remains experientially that of a freely given, and freely accepted, gift.

The reciprocal obligation of users given the gifts of affect via Facebook's platform is to actively contribute data, such as status updates, the "liking" of pages, and comments, that provide valuable taste-identifying information. It may also take the form of passive data associated with, for instance, user IP addresses, which can generate location information for targeted geographic advertising. While these exchanges are not formally gifts, due to their organization through abstract legal and technical arrangements (the end-user license agreement, the system's affordances), they nevertheless bear some qualities of the "balanced reciprocity" that Marshall Sahlins (2004, 220) identifies in primitive economies, where socially distant participants come to terms about the validity of exchange through "some renunciation of hostile intent or of indifference in favor of mutuality." In SNS, each data transaction adds more value to all participants in the exchange: the user, her or his friends, the platform, and the company. Mutual advantage is accrued as the user is given access to affectively rich engagements, while the platform generates valuable data to exchange with the company. This in turn enables Facebook to continue to provide users free access to content they value.

Furthermore, like the reciprocity described by Mauss, these data are "somewhat voluntarily" provided by users. Even if this voluntarism is due to the opacity of the interface that naturalizes extensive data collection (Arvidsson and Colleoni 2012) and the normative social pressures to "be on Facebook," the user is always at liberty to reject the gift, leave the site, and avoid reciprocating with data. The popularity of SNS would suggest, though, that the affective intensity of the interactions with other users accessed through the platform adequately compensates for the obligation to supply this data. To use Jodi Dean's words (this volume), we do "get off, just a little bit" in using SNS, and this inalienable compensation allows us to "come to terms" with the obligations of the platform, at least temporarily.[1]

Gifts and Reproduction

The continued salience of gifting signals the retention of use values in this commercial context, and in so doing brings into relief the capacity of such interactions to generate value in circuits adjacent to the dominant circuit of monetary exchange. To understand this argument it is important to look more closely at Mauss's depiction of gifts as "total social phenomena." Gift giving, in Mauss's estimation, does not occur naturally but is governed by systems of rules that are translations of the social order of society. Each gift demands reciprocity, the form of which is shaped by, and shapes, power relations associated with that object and the relational status of exchange participants. The rules of reciprocity governing a gift create social interdependencies and become "a web upon which social structure is organized" (Bergquist and Ljungberg 2001, 308).

To receive a gift is to be bound to the politics of reciprocity encoded into that gift. It is to be involved in all the institutions—juridical, economic, ritual, aesthetic, political, and domestic—of the social system through which the gift takes meaning. Whether it is appropriate to acknowledge your birthday gift from a maiden aunt with a thank-you note, with a return gift of similar, or perhaps greater, value, with a general level of affection for her, or by later becoming her primary caregiver is a complicated calculation, and the adopted form will relate to social and familial institutional norms. Not to reciprocate the gift at all, or to do so in an inappropriate form (for instance, in returning money), is to risk disapprobation or various kinds of exclusion from society—you may no longer be invited to share in family events and rituals, for instance. Reciprocal obligations such as these reflect and often perpetuate existing power dynamics, leading Karl Marx to suggest that gift economies are inherently conservative (Marx 1993; Read 2003). Because of this involvement in producing and reproducing social relations, gifts are inherently disciplining.[2]

Gift politics, partly based on social exclusion, discipline primarily at the level of affect and the socially encoded logics that are inalienable to the individual who experiences them. Users are rewarded with sensorily or affectively intense experiences—such as the reassurance provided when receiving a "like" of one's Facebook post—and punished with the psychological, emotional, and physical effects of social alienation—experienced as reduced responsiveness to posting or exclusion from the meaning-making of your affective network. A gift, then, can be associated with the reproduction of the social order *through use values*; it is the inalienability of the gift that provides it with the resonance to effect social ordering. When that order is fundamentally shaped by capitalism, it is possible for a gift to contribute to capitalism prior to, or even without, any transformation into exchange value. This is not because it directly generates fiscal value, but because it generates subjective orientations that are *of value* to the maintenance and perpetuation of capitalist social relations.

In user-platform interactions it is, therefore, not only user data (which can be directly tracked into the commodity circuit) that are returned in response to the gifts provided by the Facebook platform. What is reciprocated is also a disciplined subject engaged in practices that support the perpetuation of the site and its associated practices. The successful intensification of social relations engendered in the providing or receipt of, for instance, a "like" on an individual's Facebook page places a premium on engaging with others through a microblogging site. It makes the commitment of time and energy valuable, rewarding those who continue to "express their friendships through funny links" by adding more and more inalienable, but ephemeral, sensation to the experience. This affective investment and the need for its constant renewal is the source of brand value, a key reciprocal obligation associated with exchange value and central to the economics of digital media companies like Facebook, which typically generate substantial capital only as they enter financial markets (Arvidsson and Colleoni 2012). But the constant making and remaking of affective intensities also guarantees a perpetual set of practices that normalize the models of self-expression and social relations of the site within the structural frameworks of contemporary sociality.

The discipline associated with Facebook use is overtly expressed in the following ecard (figure 13.2), which was shared in my newsfeed during a period of widespread outrage at one of the many ethically dubious structural updates of the site that have irritated the company's user base.

The implication of this quip is that the voluntary, giftlike nature of user exchanges with the platform justifies the company's absolute authority. To accept the gifts of the platform is also to accept a social relationship in which the site retains all power. Any possibility that social communication in public contexts could be structured in ways that limit the unilateral authority currently enjoyed by commercial media companies is not available. Read superficially, this image disciplines us to accept that Facebook is what social networking looks like, and if we don't like it, we can get out.

But it is not only on a representational level that this image normalizes the dominance of Facebook and its associated practices. In the response generated upon encountering it within an affective network—not only that materialized in the flurry of social activities such as commenting, sharing, and liking that are collected as commodifiable

Figure 13.2
I'm Appalled … : http://www.someecards.com/usercards/viewcard/d5a23e57b2500174fde71079 9bb2aec7.

user data, but also that manifesting in individual affective reaction to the image, its humor, and its message—is the continued performance of a subject engaging affectively through mediated platforms. To feel something—anything—through a digital media platform is to become a source of fiscal value (user data), but, moreover, to become the endlessly phatic subject who continues to express his or herself through, and because of, these mediating platforms. As such, it is to become a resource of capital. As Patricia Clough et al. (2007) argue, in the contemporary market, shaped by uncertainty, shifting terrains of consumer desire, and the flux of abstract fiscal exchange, the generation of affect becomes a measure of market effectivity. To generate affective responses is to generate the churn that makes markets function.

Becoming disciplined to perpetually produce and/or seek affective intensities in relatively unquestioned commercial contexts is thus to become the subject of this mode of capitalism. This does not make these sensations any less real or meaningful, but nevertheless binds us to a communicative capital that desires and demands affective responses in order to perpetuate, to *reproduce*, its economic logic. On Facebook, even negative responses, such as the irritation I felt upon receiving the above ecard, serve to marshal one's engagement with others and with the site into a form that generates revenue *and* the affective intensities that encourage continued engagement with the platform. In this way the intensity of our affective responses becomes indexed to the legitimacy we attribute to the site, and SNS more generally, as valid mediators of our interpersonal relations.

Feeling of Value

Affect is thus implicated in the reproduction of market dominance by particular corporations. But there is more at stake than merely the consumer lock-in of one company's successful marketing. In reproducing the dominance of a particular model of digitally mediated interaction, the affective intensities experienced by the user also reproduce a subjective positioning that reflects an ideological social relation in which even the most intimate of experiences are open to, albeit never entirely captured by, the structures of exploitation associated with capital. When articulated within the broad range of similarly shaped interpellations across the social fabric, the cultural logics normalized through the affective intensities of commercial digital networks become powerful agents of social organization. Thus Facebook, and SNS more generally, come to exert agency—to have power to shape our engagement with the world—*because of* the value generated in the intensity of the affective exchanges within the networks they mediate. In the form of their use value to users, the gifts exchanged between users, through exchanges with the platform, contribute to the symbolic dominance of Facebook, but more importantly to the naturalization of the commercial mediation of our inalienable relationships.

The normalization of this fundamental social relation of capitalism ties affect to the contemporary "social factory," where problems of profitability have been resolved by exploiting the intellectual skills, creativity, and other subjective qualities of "human capital," including that produced by collective, traditionally nonmarket activities such as education, leisure, parenting, and communication (Lazzarato 1996; Berardi 2009; Ilouz 2007). This leads to a context in which the alienating logic of the capital relation permeates all aspects of existence (Dyer-Witheford 1999). Affect is implicated in sustaining this mode of production not only because it is made alienable and circulates as exchange value, but also because it serves as a crucial mechanism for the reproduction of that particular socioeconomic dynamic. The perhaps bitter irony here is that it is the very inalienability of our affective intensities that makes it possible, legitimate, and valid for those same responses to be rendered alien to us.

Affect thus intersects with capital in complex ways within digital media networks. It does not simply follow a unidirectional path involving the inevitable and irrevocable subsumption of inalienable affect into alienated capital—of gift exchange into capitalist market dynamics. Rather, there is a coexistence of both forms of exchange that underscores the persistence of use values within commercialized spaces. Use value can also be derived from interactions with technological systems, such as a media site's platform, that are typically only interpreted in terms of exchange value. This persistence of use value does not, however, mean that these exchanges are oppositional to the political economy of those spaces. The affective intensities of the gifts we exchange with each other, and with the technological platforms with which we interact, provoke investments in the normative practices of these sites and their structuring ideological agenda. They create and recreate us as Facebook users, tweeters, YouTube viewers, and Instagram photographers, inclined toward sharing more and more of our lives within these proprietary spaces. Affect is not wholly subsumed, but it is nevertheless marshaled into servicing the broad needs of capitalism as lived culture.

I am not suggesting that there is "nothing but" (Zelizer 2005) ideological calculation in these sites. The persistence of use value also means the persistence of meaningful and socially generative affective resonances, which always have the potential to undermine the dominant order by supporting alternative subjectivities. My point, rather, is that the importance to capital of affective networks may be traced not only to that which can be abstracted and transformed, ultimately, into fiscal value. Their importance is also that which is *of value* in reproducing the subjects of a capitalism that has an enhanced capacity to extract value directly from our sociality. It is, therefore, more than our friendship that is expressed by sending each other funny links on Facebook. It is the capitalist system itself.

Notes

1. The analysis here does not present what happens when the burden of reciprocity, either with other users or with the platform (particularly when articulated around privacy and the intrusion of advertising), becomes untenable and the balance between cost and gain is lost. In such instances, users often leave the site, sometimes only temporarily (see Tufekci 2008), or engage in protest against the company (see boyd and Hargittai 2010; Meredith 2006). It is also important to recognize that this "coming to terms," or its imbalance, is not necessarily registered as an instrumental weighing up of benefits and losses, but may also be a nonrational response to a social obligation.

2. The concept of disciplining, as it is used here, is not to be confused with negative, violent coercion or repressive outcomes. Drawing on Foucauldian and Althusserian interpretations, the assumption is that all social practices, including the pleasurable, encode and perform a particular mode of being associated with an ideological formation, rewarding and punishing, in more or less subtle ways, an individual's alignment with normative forms of behavior. In this context, even to be socialized into a subjectivity expressing positively valued behaviors, such as care for others, is an effect of disciplining techniques and technologies embedded throughout the wide social fabric.

References

Ahmed, Sara. 2004. Affective Economies. *Social Text* 22 (2):117–139.

Andrejevic, Mark. 2013. Estranged Free Labor. In *Digital Labor: The Internet as Playground and Factory*, ed. Trebor Scholz, 149–164. London: Routledge.

Appadurai, Arjun. 1986. Introduction: Commodities and the Politics of Value. In *The Social Life of Things: Commodities in Cultural Perspective*, ed. Arjun Appadurai, 3–63. Cambridge: Cambridge University Press.

Arvidsson, Adam. 2009. The Ethical Economy: Towards a Post-Capitalist Theory of Value. *Capital and Class* 33 (1):13–29.

Arvidsson, Adam, and Elanor Colleoni. 2012. Value in Informational Capitalism and on the Internet. *Information Society* 28 (3):135–150.

Barbrook, Richard. 1998. The Hi-Tech Gift Economy. *First Monday* 3 (12). Available at http://firstmonday.org/ojs/index.php/fm/article/view/1517/1432.

Benkler, Yochai. 2006. *The Wealth of Networks: How Social Production Transforms Markets and Freedom*. New Haven: Yale University Press.

Berardi, Franco "Bifo." 2009. *The Soul at Work: From Alienation to Autonomy*. Trans. Francesca Cadel and Giuseppina Mecchia. Los Angeles: Semiotext(e).

Bergquist, Magnus, and Jan Ljungberg. 2001. The Power of Gifts: Organizing Social Relationships in Open-Source Communities. *Information Systems Journal* 11:305–320.

boyd, danah, and Eszter Hargittai. 2010. Facebook Privacy Settings: Who Cares? *First Monday* 15 (8). Available at http://firstmonday.org/ojs/index.php/fm/article/view/3086/2589.

Clough, Patricia Ticento, Greg Goldberg, Rachel Schiff, and Aaron Weeks. 2007. Notes towards a Theory of Affect-Itself. *Ephemera: Theory and Politics in Organization* 7 (1):60–77.

Cohen, Nicole S. 2008. The Valorization of Surveillance: Towards a Political Economy of Facebook. *Democratic Communiqué* 22 (1):5–22.

Comor, Edward. 2010. Digital Prosumption and Alienation. *Ephemera: Theory and Politics in Organization* 10 (3/4):439–454.

Dourish, Paul, and Christine Satchell. 2011. The Moral Economy of Social Media. In *From Social Butterfly to Engaged Citizen: Urban Informatics, Social Media, Ubiquitous Computing, and Mobile Technology to Support Citizen Engagement*, ed. Marcus Foth, Laura Forlano, Christine Satchell, and Martin Gibbs, 21–37. Cambridge, MA: MIT Press.

Dyer-Witheford, Nick. 1999. *Cyber-Marx: Cycles and Circuits of Struggle in High-Technology Capitalism*. Urbana: University of Illinois Press.

Frow, John. 1997. *Time and Commodity Culture: Essays in Cultural Theory and Postmodernity*. Oxford: Clarendon Press.

Fuchs, Christian. 2008. *Internet and Society: Social Theory in the Information Age*. London: Routledge.

Fuchs, Christian. 2009. Information and Communication Technologies and Society: A Contribution to the Critique of the Political Economy of the Internet. *European Journal of Communication* 24 (1):69–87.

Ghosh, Rishab Aiyer. 1998. Cooking Pot Markets: An Economic Model for the Trade in Free Goods and Services on the Internet. *First Monday* 3 (3). Available at http://www.firstmonday.org/ojs/index.php/fm/article/view/580/501.

Gillespie, Tarleton. 2010. The Politics of "Platforms." *New Media and Society* 12 (3):347–364.

Gorz, André. 2010. *The Immaterial: Knowledge, Value, and Capital*. Trans. Chris Turner. Calcutta: Seagull Books.

Hardt, Michael, and Antonio Negri. 2000. *Empire*. Cambridge, MA: Harvard University Press.

Hardt, Michael, and Antonio Negri. 2009. *Commonwealth*. Cambridge, MA: Harvard University Press.

Hjorth, Larissa. 2007. *Home and Away*: A Case Study of the Use of Cyworld Mini-Hompy by Korean Students Studying in Australia. *Asian Studies* (Quezon City, Philippines) 31 (4):397–407.

Hyde, Lewis. 1979. *The Gift: Imagination and the Erotic Life of Property*. New York: Vintage Books.

Ilouz, Eva. 2007. *Cold Intimacies: The Making of Emotional Capitalism*. Cambridge: Polity Press.

Kopytoff, Igor. 1986. The Cultural Biography of Things: Commoditization as Process. In *The Social Life of Things: Commodities in Cultural Perspective*, ed. Arjun Appadurai, 64–91. Cambridge: Cambridge University Press.

Lampel, Joseph, and Ajay Bhalla. 2007. The Role of Status Seeking in Online Communities: Giving the Gift of Experience. *Journal of Computer-Mediated Communication* 12:434–455.

Lazzarato, Maurizio. 1996. Immaterial Labor. In *Radical Thought in Italy: A Potential Politics*, ed. Paolo Virno and Michael Hardt, 132–146. Minneapolis: University of Minnesota Press.

Lenhart, Amanda, and Mary Madden. 2007. Social Networking Websites and Teens. Pew Research Internet Project. Available at http://www.pewinternet.org/Reports/2007/Social-Networking-Websites-and-Teens.aspx.

Marazzi, Christian. [1994] 2011. *Capital and Affects: The Politics of the Language Economy*. Los Angeles: Semiotext(e).

Marx, Karl. [1976] 1990. *Capital: A Critique of Political Economy*. Vol. 1. London: Penguin.

Marx, Karl. [1973] 1993. *Grundrisse*. Ed. David McLellan. London: Macmillan.

Mauss, Marcel. [1954] 2002. *The Gift: The Form and Reason for Exchange in Archaic Societies*. London: Routledge.

Mendelson, Andrew L., and Zizi Papacharissi. 2011. Look at Us: Collective Narcissism in College Student Facebook Photo Galleries. In *A Networked Self: Identity, Community, and Culture on Social Network Sites*, ed. Zizi Papacharissi, 251–273. Oxon: Routledge.

Meredith, Peter. 2006. Facebook and the Politics of Privacy. *Mother Jones* 14 (September). Available at http://motherjones.com/politics/2006/09/facebook-and-politics-privacy.

Miller, Vincent. 2008. New Media, Networking, and Phatic Culture. *Convergence* 14 (4):387–400.

Negri, Antonio. 1989. *The Politics of Subversion: A Manifesto for the Twenty-First Century*. Trans. James Newell. Cambridge: Polity Press.

Pearson, Erika. 2007. Digital Gifts: Participation and Gift Exchange in LiveJournal Communities. *First Monday* 12 (5). Available at http://firstmonday.org/article/view/1835/1719.

Petersen, Soren Mark. 2008. Loser-Generated Content: From Participation to Exploitation. *First Monday* 13 (3). Available at http://firstmonday.org/article/view/2141/1948.

Prodnik, Jernej. 2012. A Note on the Ongoing Processes of Commodification: From the Audience Commodity to the Social Factory. *Triple C* 10 (2):274–301.

Raymond, Eric S. 1998. The Cathedral and the Bazaar. *First Monday* 3 (3). Available at http://www.firstmonday.org/ojs/index.php/fm/article/view/578/499.

Read, Jason. 2003. *The Micro-politics of Capital: Marx and the Prehistory of the Present*. Albany: State University of New York Press.

Sahlins, Marshall. [1974] 2004. *Stone Age Economics*. Oxon: Routledge.

Terranova, Tiziana. 2000. Free Labor: Producing Culture for the Digital Economy. *Social Text* 18 (2):33–58.

Tufekci, Zeynep. 2008. Grooming, Gossip, Facebook, and MySpace. *Information Communication and Society* 11 (4):544–564.

Veale, Kylie J. 2003. Internet Gift Economies: Voluntary Payment Schemes as Tangible Reciprocity. *First Monday* 8 (12). Available at http://www.firstmonday.org/ojs/index.php/fm/article/view/1101/1021.

Zelizer, Viviana A. 2005. *The Purchase of Intimacy*. Princeton: Princeton University Press.

14   Happy Accidents: Facebook and the Value of Affect

Tero Karppi

Brian Massumi argues that "the ability of affect to produce an economic effect more swiftly and surely than economics itself means that affect is a real condition, an intrinsic variable of the late capitalist system, as infrastructural as a factory" (Massumi 2002, 45). This chapter puts Massumi's argument to use in order to understand how affect is turned into economic value in contemporary social media. I offer a case-based analysis of Facebook's Timeline as a diagram of contemporary political economy, in order to outline an infrastructure of the material and expressive conditions of affect. Following Tiziana Terranova's (2000, 38) take on digital economy, I consider the birth of Timeline as part of a larger capitalization of culture, the culture industry, and labor defined by capitalism. What follows is an elaboration of how business practices and the channeling of collective and cultural labor into monetary flows are immanently built into media technology (Terranova 2000, 39). To put this in more concrete terms, I assess how Facebook as media technology affords and enables certain activities instead of others (Paasonen 2011, 258; see also Dean, this volume; Pybus, this volume).

Value

Massumi's allusion to factory infrastructure relates to a material production of affects as a condition of a political economy. For Gilles Deleuze (1995) the factory is a diagram of political economy. It operates as a hierarchical system of centralized power, within which individuals are distributed according to their relations to one another. Everyone is given his or her own place and task, and the model itself is based on the enclosure of space and capitalist ownership of the means of production. Each individual in a factory constitutes a single body working for the benefit of the capitalist, the owner of the factory. On Facebook, this single laboring body is generally known as "the user."

Timeline's infrastructure is highly dependent on users and their actions. An individual's participation is managed through protocols that regulate her or his actions by, for example, translating websites into Facebook-compatible objects. One can, for example, read the *Guardian* website through Facebook's interface. Users are equally rendered Facebook-compatible. Their subjectivities are produced through their use of social media (Chun 2006, 249; Coté and Pybus 2007); their data is gathered and sorted by Facebook algorithms and sold to anyone who is interested.

Value on Facebook is produced, distributed, extracted, claimed, and performed in three intertwined ways. First, value is extracted from people and turned into financial capital. Second, Facebook is valuable to its users in ways that exceed value's economic definitions (see Jarrett, this volume). Cultural, symbolic, and social values accrue to people and are further performed by them. Third, value is tied to social relations that can be extrapolated into relationships of innovation, production, and consumption (Lazzarato 1996; Skeggs and Wood 2012, 6–8). In fact, Facebook's own definition of its value indicates that building a social relationship holds a key position as a value maker for users, developers, advertisers, and marketers (Facebook, Inc. 2012, 2–3). As Maurizio Lazzarato (2001) puts it, a thing can only have economic value if it produces a social relationship.

The idea that Facebook produces value through social relationships helps us to understand why CEO Mark Zuckerberg (Facebook, Inc. 2012, 68) argued, in a prospectus given before the firm's 2012 IPO, that "we [Facebook] don't build services to make money; we make money to build better services." Instead of maximizing profit, Facebook aims to build a more comprehensive infrastructure of value that is not reducible to instant income for the stakeholders. A practical reason for this is that Facebook can only partially prove to skeptical investors how direct income is produced. For example, Facebook can show how economic value can be extracted from its users even though the site remains free to use; instead of paying with money, users "pay" for the use of Facebook by providing it with their data, which are turned into financial capital when purchased by advertisers and other third parties.

Yet there is more to the infrastructure of "using while being used" (Chun 2006, 250) than the dimension of data mining related to tracking and monitoring the user around the web through cookies and IP addresses (Roosendaal 2011). Users do not browse the web in order to voluntarily give out their data. These individuals' ambitions lie elsewhere. The data as such have no direct use value for them. Instead, they are extracted like a shadow, without their direct involvement. The aim of this chapter is to further elaborate this dynamic, in order to understand how value is produced through affects and affective experiences. From an infrastructural point of view the affectivity of likes, recommendations, and activities, the capitalization of the potentiality of social activities to be turned into value, has a central position in this process (Gerlitz and Helmond 2011).

Timeline

Facebook's market value is connected to its mechanism of establishing social relations and enhancing user engagement. To sustain itself, Facebook needs to continuously create new functions, interfaces, and protocols that reciprocally revolutionize its means of value production (cf. Deleuze and Guattari 1983, 233). Infrastructural change to update the user interface brings a new point of view to the world, causing events and creating effects (cf. Buck-Morss 1995, 440). Such changes are how new forms of data mining and database structure are introduced to the public. Such changes arguably aim at better user participation and better means of extracting implicit and explicit data. This context helps in understanding the changes that Facebook went through when, in September 22, 2011, its new user interface, Facebook Timeline, was published.

The Facebook Help Center explains that Timeline "is your collection of the photos, stories, and experiences that tell your story" (Facebook Help Center 2012a). It is a visual archive that collects and displays an individual's previous posts, updates, and events in chronological order. It sorts these actions, puts them in the right place, and stores them for the future. This is emphasized on Facebook's official blog: "With Timeline, now you have a home for all the great stories you've already shared. They don't just vanish as you add new stuff" (Lessin 2011). Finding events, updates, and posts from the past is made easier in comparison to the previous interface, which provided no options other than browsing profile updates by continuously clicking backward through a number of posts. The user can browse her Timeline through years and dates, filling in blanks by going back in time and adding events, including those that took place prior to her having joined Facebook. Timeline marks a user's birthday by default, and Facebook's official blog tells us, "Now, you and your friends will finally be able to tell all the different parts of your story—from the small things you do each day to your biggest moments."

According to Facebook, the list of things one can do with Timeline is extensive. It is divided into three parts: *cover*, *stories*, and *apps*. *Cover* is a concise visual representation of the user that combines pictures, basic information, and details such as the number of one's Facebook friends. *Stories* include actions familiar to the user: she or he can edit personal information ranging from occupation to residence, view and add photos, and post status updates. *Apps* show users' app activity—for example, what music they listen to on Spotify or what they read on the *Guardian* and other news sites.

Historically, timelines have been connected to processes of archiving and mining data, as well as to governing the conditions of expression (Parikka 2011). Timelines divide time and organize it into sequences (Rosenberg and Grafton 2010, 13). Timelines control what can be seen and heard. Facebook's Timeline is an apparatus of power in a similar manner; it maps relations among forces (Deleuze 1988a, 37).

Mirko Tobias Schäfer (2011, 51) argues that the force relations of user participation in social media can be divided into categories of the explicit and the implicit. Motivation drives explicit participation and includes different content-providing activities, such as sharing photos, participating in discussions, and liking things. Implicit participation benefits from explicit participation but "does not necessarily require a conscious activity of cultural production" (Schäfer 2011, 51). Instead, implicit participation means tracking information from user activities performed on social media platforms and using this information—e.g., for targeted advertising, software design, or improving a platform's information infrastructure. In other words, the data that users provide while communicating and interacting in social media are also shared implicitly (Schäfer 2011, 44, 78). The line between consumers and producers is blurred, and forms of labor are transformed (Terranova 2004, 91–94). Implicit participation in particular involves "unacknowledged" labor or "unconsciously performed" labor (Schäfer 2011, 78). On one hand, digital labor increases creativity, produces new cultural inventions, and helps people solve problems in large groups. On the other hand, the content created and the digital labor used to create it become means of exploitation. "Besides uploading content, users also willingly and unknowingly provide important information about their profile and behaviour to site owners and metadata aggregators" (Van Dijck 2009, 47).

Timeline is situated somewhere along a continuum running between the categories of explicit and implicit user participation. Its visual design is based on user-generated content such as photos and posts, but simultaneously it becomes the organizer of implicit participation. Facebook's massive trove of data includes information generated by explicit sharing, such as wall posts, photos uploaded and tagged, lists of friends, and information about login times and internet protocols used (McCown and Nelson 2009, 252; Carioli 2012). While implicit participation is mainly invisible, its operations are indicated, for example, in the targeted ads appearing next to users' News Feed streams.

While implicit and explicit participation are suitable terms to describe what is or can be shared, as forms of categorization they do not exhaustively explain value production in social networks. Arguably, these terms serve to commodify processes of sharing and the content shared as if these could be acquired and marketed like any other commodities. They too easily neglect the activation of future participation that is crucial to Facebook's business operations. In other words, while user data have both use value (for example, data in the form of pictures serves as a constitutive element for the site) and exchange value (data sold to third parties), on their own, data do not produce a surplus of power for Facebook. In the context of Timeline, the surplus of power (see Lazzarato 2001) flows from mechanisms that generate more clicks, actions, and interactions. The surplus of power, then, is constituted in an economy of forces operating on the levels of the actual and the virtual. It is embodied in the functions of Facebook's interface, such as the "like" and "share" buttons through which web pages are translated into Facebook-compatible objects (Gerlitz and Helmond 2011). Simultaneously the surplus of power withholds a virtual dimension of potentiality. Almost anything that is incorporable into Facebook can generate a new click.

Affect

The discussion of Timeline presented above suggests two interrelated questions concerning value production. The first is the well-discussed question of how to track information provided by users and then translate it into value (Van Dijck 2009; Cheney-Lippold 2011). Equally important but less discussed is the question I am addressing here: how to produce more clicks, more actions, and more interactions on social media platforms? What makes us tick parallels the equally compelling question: what makes us click?

At the Facebook's F8 Conference 2011, held for IT developers, entrepreneurs, and innovators, Zuckerberg (2011) announced that Facebook had been developing its Open Graph protocol, which would help users connect anything, such as communications, games and media, and lifestyle applications, to their Facebook experience. Open Graph would help users track and express their lives on Facebook more thoroughly. It also would provide content for an individual's Timeline but, more importantly, would help him or her discover new things through his or her friends. According to Zuckerberg, the protocol would draw on the principles of "frictionless experience," "realtime serendipity," and "finding patterns" in friends' activities. In short, "frictionless experience" refers to applications that publish things automatically to Timeline, and "realtime serendipity" refers to finding these things and interacting with them without leaving Facebook's interface. These changes imply a relatively passive user, a follower who accidentally stumbles upon things. Hence a typical Facebook user does not actively search for information but instead is affected by things shared on the Facebook platform. Such serendipity clearly differs from, for example, the way in which Google's platform constructs a user's profile. Google positions the user as an actor who actively searches for information. What Google's platform fails to offer, however, is the affective feeling of the randomness of discovery, the happy accident upon which Facebook relies.

Things shared on Timeline are directed to "feeds" and "streams." The News Feed, in particular, is a stream familiar to most Facebook users. According to Facebook (Facebook Help Center 2012b), News Feed is a "constantly updating list of stories from people and pages that you follow on Facebook." In addition to these postings, the feed includes photos, tags, and events. News Feed is controlled by algorithms that use "several factors, including: how many friends are commenting on a certain piece of content, who posted the content, and what type of content it is (e.g., photo, video, or status update)" to determine what objects will be shown for an individual user (see also Bucher 2012).

These flows of objects constitute Facebook's intangible assets (Pybus 2009) and are essential to producing value for users. They manifest the promise of a happy accident: that there is always something interesting to find on Facebook, that every time one logs in one might stumble upon something unique and original, unseen and interesting—something affective. Indeed, as Jennifer Pybus (2009) maintains, the production of affect is at the very core of social media operations that rely on the double axis of social participation and data mining. Accordingly, affect and affectivity are crucial concepts for understanding how Facebook produces value for both users and shareholders. As

Skeggs and Wood (2012, 5) maintain, affect is that which makes us do or not do certain things. It is that which grounds our experiences of the surrounding world (Pybus 2009). Affect, then, operates in the present moment. It extends toward possible actions, ideas, and emotions. It is present in every situation as potentiality, as the virtual possibility of encountering and experiencing something that only later can be manifested in words and emotions, or, in the language of Facebook, in clicks and recommendations.

The potentiality of affect has a central position in Deleuze's (1988b) reading of Spinoza. According to Deleuze, the body is an assemblage of force relations, and the power of being affected determines how such assemblages may take place. Bodies are formed in the processes of affecting and being affected. For Massumi, the transaction that alters bodies' capabilities takes place during moments of affection:

> When you affect something, you are at the same time opening yourself up to being affected in turn, and in a slightly different way than you might have been the moment before. You have made a transition, however slight. You have stepped over a threshold. Affect is this passing of a threshold, seen from the point of view of the change in capacity. (Massumi, n.d.)

This passing of a threshold is Timeline's central mode of operation. It controls the stream of affect to create points where a double orientation of data production and affect generation takes place. In a most concrete sense, these points are Facebook-compatible objects managed by protocols, which, following Alexander Galloway (2004, 7–8), regulate "how specific technologies are agreed to, adopted, implemented, and ultimately used by people around the world."

Facebook's Open Graph protocol in particular is designed to include third-party websites and pages that people have liked on the Facebook interface. Redesigned along with Timeline, Open Graph now includes "arbitrary actions and objects created by third party apps and enabling these apps to integrate deeply into the Facebook experience" (Facebook Developers 2012a). Practically any website can be made Facebook-compatible, and such actions as reading, listening, and watching can be given Facebook-compatible objects:

> The Open Graph allows apps to model user activities based on actions and objects. A running app may define the ability to "run" (action) a "route" (object). A reading app may define the ability to "read" (action) a "book" (object). A recipe app may define the ability to "cook" (action) a "recipe" (object). Actions are verbs that users perform in your app. Objects define nouns that the actions apply to. We created sets of actions and objects for common use cases and a tool for you to create your own custom actions and objects. As users engage with your app, social activities are published to Facebook which connects the user with your objects, via the action.

Open Graph recognizes three actors: "user," "action," and "object." Its purpose is to create Facebook-compatible objects that an individual then can deploy. As usage gets posted to an individual's Facebook page, the object becomes visible and potentially affective, thereby attracting new interactions.

A Facebook-compatible object is filled with potentiality created by the coupling of affect and effect. Stumbling upon a Facebook-compatible object creates a virtual relation of contagion and communication (Massumi 2008, 23). For example, when a user likes something, this like is posted on her News Feed and shown to a group of users selected by Facebook's algorithms (Bucher 2012, 1167–1168). Sometimes the like is translated to an advertisement. This relation is of potentiality. The affect produced is a carryover of the qualitative nature of what happens (Bucher 2012, 24). A post can become an advertisement, but that does not mean it necessarily does so. Neither does it necessarily induce affect, since there are other possible relations that might or might not happen. While Facebook tries to premediate (cf. Grusin 2010) affect and predetermine user actions and reactions, such outcomes can only be partially achieved, since the relation between the object and the affect is always immanent and virtual, and hence impossible to predetermine (Massumi 2008, 22–24). This problem is well known to Facebook, and the company endeavors to bypass it by creating an abundance of affect flowing through different streams: the more affect there is, the more chances for affection and affectivity.

Users, then, are turned into affecting bodies in a very concrete manner. The event of getting a job is transformed into a post that can be liked, for example, and the act of listening to music is transformed into a Spotify track that can be clicked on. Timeline mediates the incipience of emergence. It entices us to become interested in things. It invites us to click, share, and recommend. For the user, these approaches become thresholds through which new experiences are potentially gained, things found, and relationships formed. For Facebook, they accrue the data of user interests and actions and hopefully improve the firm's bottom line by so doing.

Applications

The affective dynamics of social media give rise to a human subject who is both an agent of digital labor and an object of processes of data extraction, or, as José van Dijck (2009, 46) maintains, "User agency ... encompasses a range of different uses and agents, and it is extremely relevant to develop a more nuanced model of understanding its cultural complexity." Focusing on the human subject seems to undermine the role of other actors involved in the generation and circulation of affect. Indeed, Jane Bennett argues that we need to consider more thoroughly the participation of nonhuman material in everyday events. For Bennett (2010, 21–22) all actors, even nonhuman ones, are social in the sense that they are bodies with a capability to affect and be affected. A similar understanding of affect and affectivity can be traced from Spinoza to Deleuze to Massumi. Deleuze and Guattari, for example, address bodies in a nonhuman sense when they maintain that

[w]e know nothing about a body until we know what it can do, in other words, what its affects are, how they can or cannot enter into composition with other affects, with the affects of another body, either to destroy that body or to be destroyed by it, either to exchange actions and passions with it or to join with it in composing a more powerful body. (Deleuze and Guattari 2005, 257)

Expanding the focus to include nonhuman operators is necessary in order to understand what Bennett (2010, xii) calls impersonal affect: that is, affect that is not "transpersonal" or "intersubjective" but "intrinsic to forms that cannot be imagined … as persons." Impersonal affect, then, points to a body as a composition that does not have essentialist features but is formed as an assemblage of different force relations. Interestingly, however, while Bennett argues that impersonal affect is intrinsic to a form that cannot be imagined as a person, we see a reverse operation in the case of Timeline. In fact, Timeline does its best to transform impersonal affect into something imagined as persons (hence also Facebook's one-user-account and real-name policies). It is always the named user who does something, who likes something, who listens to something. This does not mean that the named user, however, is a person or even will become a person. On the contrary, named users are nonhuman and human compositions that appear personlike but cluster around impersonal affects. To elaborate further, a look into Facebook applications and their specific role in Timeline is in order.

According to Facebook Social Design, Open Graph uses third-party apps to include "arbitrary actions and objects" in the Facebook experience. As the Facebook Developer page puts it,

After a user adds your app to their Timeline, app specific actions are shared on Facebook via the Open Graph. As your app becomes an important part of how users express themselves, these actions are more prominently displayed throughout the Facebook Timeline, News Feed, and Ticker. This enables your app to become a key part of the user's and their friend's experience on Facebook. (Facebook Developers 2012a)

In essence, News Feed, Ticker, and applications form the core infrastructure of Facebook's impersonal form of affect. While News Feed is a stream of content provided by named Facebook users, sometimes applications themselves can be authorized to post on News Feed. To post autonomously on behalf of the user, applications need only to request publishing permissions for "publish_stream" and "publish_actions" (Facebook Developers 2012b). The latter permission is used, for example, by games to automatically post high scores on an individual's Timeline. While they relate to a person, these affects are impersonal, replicated by nonhuman operators.

The Ticker is a second factor along the continuum noted above. Through the Ticker, user actions become visible to other users. A variation of News Feed, Ticker displays a real-time stream of friends' activities. While News Feed shows the actual things shared, Ticker shares what becomes actualized as clicks, likes, and comments. When clicking on a post on Ticker, one can see conversations on friends' walls, as well as photos posted by total strangers that one's friends have commented on. Ticker is automatic. It extracts affect from user actions. With Ticker, the personal becomes impersonal and the impersonal becomes affects.

Even private user activities, such as reading an article or listening to music, can be translated into social and clickable experience through applications. For example, Spotify, the music streaming service, can be integrated with Facebook so that the music to which a user listens appears in the News Feed, Ticker, and on its own section in Timeline. Other users can click on the track and start playing the same music. This information is also then posted to their News Feed, Ticker, and Timeline. The Spotify integration generates an affective experience of music even when not audible. According to Facebook's blog (Lessin 2011), Spotify represents a new kind of social app "that lets you show the things you like to do on your Timeline—the music you listen to, the recipes you try, the runs you take and more." Arguably, however, the user is not showing anything, for it is the app itself that exposes the user and translates her music preferences into impersonal affects. This visible data then generates an affective flow that potentially attracts new users.

Harnessing the power of impersonal affect that emerges automatically, unintentionally, and uncontrolledly may be regarded as the biggest change in the Facebook interface. Its autonomous model of affection indicates that we have shifted from identities constructed in social media to impersonal entities constructed by social media. The autonomous dimension of a happy accident complicates evaluations, especially in the field of psychology, that assess Facebook on the basis of self-presentation or digital narcissism (see Mehdizadeh 2010). This autonomous dimension may remove the possibility of users portraying themselves as "hoped-for-possible-selves" (Zhao, Grasmuck, and Martin 2008), since carefully constructed self-presentations are replaced with an abundance of uncontrollable information, save for users' privacy settings. Indeed, questions of identity and subjectivity may be superseded by bodies' capabilities to affect and be affected impersonally.

It should be clarified, however, that the generation of impersonal affect neither implies a diminished role for users nor diminishes the importance of self-presentation on Facebook. On the contrary, they remain important motivations for participation. Objects, actions, and users disconnected from the human actor, however, have increasingly begun to generate impersonal affect. As a consequence, the human user is no more than a critical point where multiplicities of selections are activated and selections can be made (Massumi 2002, 32).

The novelty of happy accidents on Facebook lies less in data-gathering mechanisms than in algorithms and protocols that translate things into affects and feed them back to users' streams. Affects interfere with our sensing, thinking, and acting; they offer us different connections and new modes of connectivity (Massumi 2002, 24–26), but they also disconnect us from ourselves. In Deleuze's (1995) terms we become *dividual*:

being split by digital technology into a series of codes that circulate in data banks and information networks. The dividual is a composition, a new body with new powers to affect. It alters the ways in which we become users in and of network culture.

Affect's Value

To evaluate the value of affect we need to consider how things become affective in the first place. Thus the value of Facebook can be understood not only in terms of Marxian economics but also with reference to Gabriel Tarde's (2007) economic psychology: in other words, how value emerges from beliefs and desires that move from individual to individual, following the logic of contamination and contagion controlled by the social media platform (see Latour and Lépinay 2009, 8–10). Correspondingly, the concept of the user does not indicate an affected individual, but an individual that is in the state of becoming affected. It points to the subjectivity that is just becoming an individual (or dividual) through social media. The production of such subjectivity is connected to the production of affective flows and translating them into value.

What I want to emphasize is that Facebook's value is less related to market value per se than to its capability to affect its users. Arguably the former is based on the latter. Happy accidents describe the ways through which users are effectively and affectively engaged with the platform. Affirming the accidental, the random, the surprise, the affect is Facebook's way to build better services and make money along the way. Happy accidents retain a promise that the user will find something interesting every time she logs in. The experience, however, can be frictionless only if one participates explicitly. One has to be connected to the platform in order for the happy accident to take place. Stronger still is the peril of happy accidents: the user will miss something interesting if she is not engaged with the activities undertaken in the platform. The happy accident demands that the user is constantly signed in and never leaves the platform. This is how a monthly user becomes a daily user. This is user engagement *ad extremum*.

While my analysis of happy accidents suggests that affects and affectivity can to some extent be captured, produced, and monetized through the social media platform, I do not suggest that affect is entirely deprived of autonomy. The creation of new subjectivities and different forms of collectivities emerges when everything from objects to arbitrary actions to human subjects can be rendered Facebook-compatible through protocols and interfaces. This includes the potential to find new things. Affects, as Massumi (2002, 25) puts it, enable "a different connectivity, a different difference, in parallel." Affect always escapes the confinement of a particular body and extends toward new potential futures (Massumi 2002, 35). These futures include wanted modes of user engagement but also modes that challenge it, such as glitches, trolls, and malware, which exploit both the contagious nature of affects and Facebook's infrastructure, tweaked for spreading them. Thus the economic effects of affects are unpredictable and the modes of user engagement unsteady. For Facebook, building its business on affect is a huge opportunity and a huge risk.

References

Bennett, Jane. 2010. *Vibrant Matter: A Political Ecology of Things*. Durham: Duke University Press.

Bucher, Taina. 2012. Want to Be on the Top? Algorithmic Power and the Threat of Invisibility on Facebook. *New Media and Society* 14 (7):1164–1180.

Buck-Morss, Susan. 1995. Envisioning Capital: Political Economy on Display. *Critical Inquiry* 21 (2):434–467.

Carioli, Carly. 2012. When the Cops Subpoena Your Facebook Information, Here's What Facebook Sends the Cops. *Boston Phoenix* (April 6). Available at http://blog.thephoenix.com/blogs/phlog/archive/2012/04/06/when-police-subpoena-your-facebook-information-heres-what-facebook-sends-cops.aspx.

Cheney-Lippold, John. 2011. A New Algorithmic Identity: Soft Biopolitics and the Modulation of Control. *Theory, Culture and Society* 28 (6):164–181.

Chun, Wendy Hui Kyong. 2006. *Control and Freedom: Power and Paranoia in the Age of Fiber Optics*. Cambridge, MA: MIT Press.

Coté, Mark, and Jennifer Pybus. 2007. Learning to Immaterial Labour 2.0: MySpace and Social Networks. *Ephemera: Theory and Politics in Organization* 7 (1):88–106.

Deleuze, Gilles. 1988a. *Foucault*. Trans. and ed. Séan Hand. Minneapolis: University of Minnesota Press.

Deleuze, Gilles. 1988b. *Spinoza: Practical Philosophy*. Trans. Robert Hurley. San Francisco: City Lights Books.

Deleuze, Gilles. 1995. Postscript on Control Societies. In *Negotiations, 1972–1990*, trans. Martin Joughin, 177–182. New York: Columbia University Press.

Deleuze, Gilles, and Félix Guattari. 1983. *Anti-Oedipus: Capitalism and Schizophrenia*. Trans. Robert Hurley, Mark Seem, and Helen R. Lane. Minneapolis: University of Minnesota Press.

Deleuze, Gilles, and Félix Guattari. 2005. *A Thousand Plateaus*. Trans. Brian Massumi. Minneapolis: University of Minnesota Press.

Facebook. 2012. Introducing Timeline. Tell Your Life Story with a New Kind of Profile. Accessed September 6, 2012. No longer available.

Facebook Developers. 2012a. Open Graph. https://developers.facebook.com/docs/opengraph. Accessed June 11, 2012. No longer available.

Facebook Developers. 2012b. Publishing Permissions. May. Available at https://developers.facebook.com/docs/publishing.

Facebook Help Center. 2012a. Introducing Timeline. Available at https://www.facebook.com/help/467610326601639.

Facebook Help Center. 2012b. News Feed Basics. Available at https://www.facebook.com/help/?page=132070650202524.

Facebook, Inc. 2012. Form S-1. Registration Statement. Washington, DC.

Galloway, Alexander R. 2004. *Protocol: How Control Exists after Decentralization*. Cambridge, MA: MIT Press.

Gerlitz, Carolin, and Anne Helmond. 2011. Hit, Link, Like, Share: Organizing the Social and the Fabric of the Web in a Like Economy. DMI Mini Conference. Amsterdam.

Grusin, Richard. 2010. *Premediation: Affect and Mediality after 9/11*. New York: Pargrave Macmillan.

Latour, Bruno, and Vincent Antonin Lépinay. 2009. *The Science of Passionate Interests: An Introduction to Gabriel Tarde's Economic Anthropology*. Chicago: Prickly Paradigm Press.

Lazzarato, Maurizio. 1996. Immaterial Labor. *Generation-online.org*. Available at http://www.generation-online.org/c/fcimmateriallabour3.htm.

Lazzarato, Maurizio. 2001. Towards an Inquiry into Immaterial Labour. *Makeworlds* 1. Available at http://makeworlds.org/node/141.

Lessin, Samuel W. 2011. Tell Your Story with Timeline. September 22. Available at https://www.facebook.com/blog/blog.php?post=10150289612087131.

Massumi, Brian. 2002. *Parables for the Virtual: Movement, Affect, Sensation*. Durham: Duke University Press.

Massumi, Brian. 2008. The Thinking-Feeling of What Happens: A Semblance of Conversation. *Inflexions* 1 (1):1–40.

Massumi, Brian. n.d. Interview by Mary Zournazi. *Assembly International*. Available at http://www.assembly-international.net/Interviews/html/brian%20massumi.html.

McCown, Frank, and Michael L. Nelson. 2009. What Happens When Facebook Is Gone? Proceedings of the 9th ACM/IEEE-CS Joint Conference on Digital Libraries, Austin, Texas, 251–254.

Mehdizadeh, Soraya. 2010. Self-Presentation 2.0: Narcissism and Self-Esteem on Facebook. *Cyberpsychology, Behavior, and Social Networking* 13 (4):357–364.

Paasonen, Susanna. 2011. *Carnal Resonance: Affect and Online Pornography*. Cambrdige, MA: MIT Press.

Parikka, Jussi. 2011. Operative Media Archaeology: Wolfgang Ernst's Materialist Media Diagrammatics. *Theory, Culture and Society* 28 (5):52–74.

Pybus, Jennifer. 2009. Affect and Subjectivity: A Case Study of Neopets.com. *Politics and Culture* 2007 (2). Available at http://www.politicsandculture.org/2009/10/02/jennifer-pybus-affect-and -subjectivity-a-case-study-of-neopets-com/.

Roosendaal, Arnold. 2011. Facebook Tracks and Traces Everyone: Like This! *Tilburg Law School Legal Studies Research Paper Series* 3:1–9.

Rosenberg, Daniel, and Anthony Grafton. 2010. *Cartographies of Time*. New York: Princeton Architectural Press.

Schäfer, Mirko Tobias. 2011. *Bastard Culture! How User Participation Transforms Cultural Production*. Amsterdam: Amsterdam University Press.

Skeggs, Beverley, and Helen Wood. 2012. *Reacting to Reality Television*. New York: Routledge.

Tarde, Gabriel. 2007. Economic Psychology. *Economy and Society* 36 (4):614–643.

Terranova, Tiziana. 2000. Free Labor: Producing Culture for the Digital Economy. *Social Text* 18 (2):33–58.

Terranova, Tiziana. 2004. *Network Culture: Politics for the Information Age*. London: Pluto Books.

Van Dijck, José. 2009. Users Like You? Theorizing Agency in User-Generated Content. *Media, Culture and Society* 31 (1):41–58.

Zhao, Shanyang, Sherri Grasmuck, and Jason Martin. 2008. Identity Construction on Facebook: Digital Empowerment in Anchored Relationships. *Computers in Human Behavior* 24 (5):1816–1836.

Zuckerberg, Mark. 2011. F8 Keynote. September 22. Available at https://f8.facebook.com.

15   Accumulating Affect: Social Networks and Their Archives of Feelings

Jennifer Pybus

Data is just like crude. It's valuable, but if unrefined it cannot really be used. It has to be changed into gas, plastic, chemicals, etc., to create a valuable entity that drives profitable activity; so must data be broken down, analyzed for it to have value. (Palmer 2006)

Welcome to the data society. Please log in and begin sharing information. Whether you are uploading a video on YouTube, posting an article on Reddit, pinning an interest on Pinterest, posting an opinion or link on Twitter, uploading a cool photograph on Tumblr, or sharing a favorite moment with your Facebook friends, you are actively engaging with social media. The massive migration to the web, which has brought hundreds of millions of people into the networked circuits of Web 2.0 platforms, has had a transformative effect on how we expect to receive and share information. For younger users, or "digital natives," those who see "new digital technologies ... as the primary mediators of human-to-human connections" (Palfrey and Gasser 2008, 4), posting content has become a necessary means by which to maintain intimacy with peers (Davis and James 2013, 6). Indeed, as Davis and James argue, given that over eighty-two percent of young people in the United States use social networking sites, those who do not actively participate are considered at risk of social isolation (Davis and James 2013, 6; Lenhart et al. 2011). Unlike many of their parents, or "digital immigrants" (Davis and James 2013, 5), this younger demographic is not as concerned about the visibility of their personal information (boyd 2006). Instead, they are more apprehensive about their ability to control what they have chosen to circulate online (Livingstone 2008). As such, young people find themselves confronted with the desire to connect with and remain current and visible within their networks of friends, while being acutely aware of and concerned about the consequences and risks associated with personal privacy (Davis and James 2013; Devitt and Roker 2009). While a more sustained discussion of privacy is beyond the scope of this chapter, I would like to focus on those social and affective perceived benefits that accrue through the ongoing sharing and circulation of user-generated content.

Social media create what Carrie James et al. (2009, 26) call a new "culture of disclosure," particularly for younger users, predicated on a distinct set of beliefs, norms, and affective practices that legitimate the constant uploading of personal materials. While there is a growing awareness that our digital footprint is increasing, a Pew Research Foundation report indicated that "surprisingly few people are using strategies to limit access to their information" (Madden et al. 2007). However, just a few years after this report was published, we see evidence to the contrary. In fact, Davis and James show "evidence that young people's privacy-protecting behaviors on social network sites have increased over time to the point where they are more likely to engage in these behaviors than older adults" (Davis and James 2013, 7). Clearly our relationship with the data that we produce is in the midst of a significant transformation, creating new opportunities for surplus value and exchange, different expressions of sociality, and new concerns over who sees and controls the user-generated content that circulates.

Given that the amount of data we are producing will only increase, I would like to introduce the concept of the digital archive, or what I call the "user profile archive." This concept can help us understand how our data affects us, and by so doing, provide insight into why our digital footprint will likely continue to expand exponentially. The starting point for this chapter, then, is how affect circulates in social networks, how it produces value, and what role these archives play within our information society. My interest is in the economic value accumulated in social networks, which rely explicitly on the immaterial and affective labor of users who continuously upload and update their online profiles, and subsequently generate vast amounts of usable data (Coté and Pybus 2007; 2011). Equally, I want to examine the "stickiness" of social networks (Ahmed 2010), the levels of intensity that reside within a user's virtual archive. Here I draw on Ann Cvetkovich's conceptualization of the archive as an affective and sentient "archive of feeling" to examine how affect accumulates within user profiles and moves people, producing another kind of value: social value.

Sites such as Facebook would not exist if they did not reproduce sociability. Users want to be where their friends are (boyd 2006), which is why they keep logging in. Within this context, we can perhaps understand why on Facebook alone, an average of 684,478 pieces of content are posted each minute (Tepper 2012). Moreover, as I will argue, it is precisely this social value that propels the production of our digital archives. Our data profiles are, in this sense, not just sites of surplus value but important spaces for sociality, and hence subjectivization. Yet such digital archives only exist when social and economic relations elide. Hillis, Petit, and Jarrett (2013) make a similar argument in the part of their work that explores the architectonic principles of Google Books, a project that seeks to scan and index every book into a digital library. Such an enormous (and impossible) undertaking requires the "general intellect" of users to circulate and produce economic value for Google. This is not, however, a straightforward process, given that, at least on the surface, the creation of such an expansive library could be viewed as both a service and benefit to the user. What should be emphasized is that in order to gain access to the Google Books archive, an individual must search, creating a unique result—a unique archival event. The act of searching thus becomes a part of the user-generated content that Google relies on—instantly subsumed—rendering the searcher into a "body of information" (Hillis, Petit, and Jarrett 2013, 169) and hence part of the archive. While we cannot move away from these inherent contradictory communicative relations, we can turn to the production of the personal user profile archive as a means of understanding this double articulation of value. The digital archive can therefore illuminate how the conflation of economic and social relations is not simply an alienated process but always already engaged and active.

Social Networks: Toward the Production of Social Value

Social networks are virtual spaces driven by the active participation of users. More specifically, according to boyd (2011, 42), what define these computer-mediated environments are the ways in which they allow users to: (1) construct a public or semi-public profile within a bounded system, (2) articulate a list of other users with whom they share a connection, and (3) view and traverse their list of connections and those made by others within the system. What is central, then, for a social network to function is relationships—affective relationships. Users don't typically go to these sites to meet strangers, but to maintain preexisting offline friendships (Lampe, Ellison, and Steinfield 2007). Equally, research suggests that people turn to social networks to be comforted when they are feeling down (Sheldon, Neetu, and Hinsch 2011), to be built up when they are feeling insecure (Zhao, Grasmuck, and Martin 2008; Gonzales and Hancock 2011), or, more generally, for positive emotional experiences (Sas et al. 2009). Thus, as more and more people log in to these sites, affect accumulates.

In the United States alone, eighty percent of teens between the ages twelve and seventeen, and eighty-seven percent of young adults between the ages of eighteen and twenty-nine, use social networks (Pew Research Center 2012). Such a high percentage of people on these sites coincides with the enormous amount of time they spend logged in and producing content. In 2008 the average person spent 3.2 hours a month on social networks. Just three years later, in 2011, we see a three hundred percent increase, with users averaging over 9.6 hours a month (Lu et al. 2012). Not surprisingly, of that time logged, seven hours and forty-six minutes were spent on Facebook (Parr 2011).

Marketers refer to the amount of time spent on a website as the degree of stickiness, which, in this industry, is an important measure of value. To account for this, a site's success is based on the number of times per month a user comes to any given website and the average number of minutes spent there. Social networks are typically the most sticky, because they are predicated on user-generated content. Without people actively logging in and inputting data, such sites would quickly lose market value (see Karppi, this volume). When we look at the amount of time users devote to Facebook, we can see that this site is one of the most successful examples of stickiness. There are, however, a number of other social networks that specialize in creation of sticky content, particularly those aimed at younger children, such as Club Penguin, Moshi Monster, and Fantage. Each lets young users build and maintain avatars by playing games with their friends as they use the social networking features.

For Ahmed (2010, 31), stickiness is what "sustains or preserves the connection between ideas, values and objects." The architectural structure of social networks is therefore critical in facilitating the sociality that flourishes among users. For Zizi Papacharissi and Alan Rubin (2000), this design typically includes several elements that bring people together, as well as engaging pastimes (which vary depending on the demographic). The design of social networks makes it easy to access information, provide entertainment, or simply find convenient spaces to interact with a large number of a user's friends. In short, the social network structure provides an opportunity for its users to engage in myriad affective social relations.

Do those affective social relations produced by users, however, obfuscate larger economic relations inherent in the design of these digital spaces? Every keystroke, every link, every comment that people generate can be extrapolated for surplus value. Therefore, are users, as Mark Andrejevic (2011) and Christian Fuchs (2008) argue, simply exploited or manipulated by these larger political and economic forces to produce value for the information economy? Or do users have an inherent understanding of these forces but nonetheless enjoy the effects of networked sociality generated when they engage with their divergent groups of friends? The point here is not to resolve these inherent contradictions, but to emphasize that the affective value experienced within these circuits should not be underestimated (see Jarrett, this volume). Such value is arguably what keeps people logged in and drives the production of a user's profile archive—an archive that represents and produces subjectivities, an archive based on choices that determine those subjectivities, an archive that will grow exponentially over a lifetime (or rather, if one is on Facebook, will grow over the expanse of one's Timeline) and eventually outlive its user.

Social Networks and Their Archives of Feelings

In theorizing the virtual archive I want to begin with Michel Foucault, "who first tried to re-articulate [the archive] into a more general epistemological category and then, in his later work, re-defined it as a primarily sociological reality marked by power differences" (Laermans and Gielen 2007, 2). In other words, the archive that Foucault envisioned in *The Archaeology of Knowledge* was never only a material construct that contained and organized documents. Foucault argued that the archive should not be understood as simply "the sum of all the texts that a culture has kept upon its person as documents attesting to its own past, or as evidence of a continuing identity" (Foucault 2002, 129). Instead, it is immanently productive and operates as that which "differentiates discourses in their multiple existence and specifies them in their own duration" (ibid., 146).

Here the archive is anything but a static storage facility; instead, it is an important space of interpretation and contestation that has the power to make meaning through its ability to privilege certain discourses over others. Who and what gets remembered, and who gets to make these existential decisions, are issues with important social, political, and economic ramifications (Pybus 2013). The moment something is brought into the archive, or, rather, what Derrida (1998) calls the "event," has a profound significance. Typically, an event was once a carefully curated moment in which the archivist allowed one narrative to unfold as opposed to another. Archives are, in this sense, inherently about choices. The distributed networks, and hence those digital flows that make up the web, have opened up new possibilities for the production of a multiplicity of archives that can all be easily stored and accessed by a large number of people (Pybus 2013).

Social networks are radically user-oriented; thus the digital user profile archives present the opportunity for a plethora of "imagined communities" that are housed within. Unlike the static repositories of information stored in a traditional archive, digital archives are constantly being worked on, their contents always in the middle of being recombined, recontextualized, and re-searched. This constant updating is a direct consequence of the new paradigm of permanent transfer, and fits with how Foucault characterized the evolution of the archive: that is, not as a monument for future memory but, as Laermans and Gielen argue, as "a document for possible use" (2007, 2), one that allows for the constant (re)formation of histories and counter histories, alongside the production of those imagined social, political, and economic communities (Coté and Pybus 2011).

Ann Cvetkovich takes our understanding of this dynamic archive a step farther through her conceptualization of an "archive of feelings" predicated on "an exploration of cultural texts as repositories of feelings and emotions, which are encoded not only in the content of the texts themselves, but in the practices that surround their production and reception" (Cvetkovich 2003, 7). She moves beyond traditional means of archival documentation to include new genres of self-expression, by accounting for those ephemeral moments that can link the larger lived experiences of queer collectives. For Cvetkovich, objects extend and are hence steeped in cultural meaning, each with its own affective history. Her archive of feelings preserves not just knowledge but emotions, captured in those discrete moments when we are affected by intimacy, sexuality, love, and activism (Cvetkovich 2003, 240). The culmination of those sensory moments is, for her, what builds "emotional memory."

The feelings, or lived experiences, that Cvetkovich wants to privilege in her archive echo those which cohere Baruch Spinoza's "conative bodies"—what Jane Bennett calls "associative or social bodies" (Bennett 2010, x). In this sense, affect is put forward as something generated from the inside of bodies that moves outward, connecting the individual to other bodies (Ahmed 2004a). It is a relational process that can propel bodies to act, as described by Spinoza and later by Gilles Deleuze (1978). In addition, affect is produced outside the body in what Ahmed calls "a realm beyond representation" (Ahmed 2004a, 4). Here she raises questions about how "emotions shape the very surfaces of bodies" on which they operate, thereby orienting bodies ontologically, in relation to social, economic, and political discourses. Ahmed is interested in understanding why we experience immediate affinities toward particular objects and subjectivities, and therefore she finds that affect is something external, something that "aligns individuals with communities—or bodily space with social space—through the very intensity of [our] attachments" (Ahmed 2004b, 119). Affect has the ability to shape, constitute, and transform bodies, particularly as they circulate and reproduce over time (Ahmed 2004a; 2004b). Her argument resonates with how Deleuze speaks about bodies as propelled into motion by the potential that resides in any given moment. Such propulsion is, at least in part, what coheres user practices in social networks. In other words, each message, note, and photo that gets uploaded carries with it the ability to affect not only a friend in the network but equally the individual user, based on the way that this object is received by the members of his or her respective community. Such a relational, affective model is apposite for understanding social networks like Facebook.

To be able to capture an essence of what procures a memory, and hence what lies in between and propels bodies into action, is what "marks a body's belonging to a world of encounters" (Gregg and Seigworth 2010, 2). In this, the "archive of feeling" can only exist within a larger composition of bodies—assemblages "with distinctive histories of formation but finite life spans" (Bennett 2010, 4). Such unusual archives are highly specific, fragmented, and ultimately resist the coherence of a linear narrative. It is these uneven topologies of lived experiences that make digital archives in social networks so dynamic. When a user places something into the archive, he or she is uploading an object that has social, and hence affective, value. The object in question has the potential to affect as it moves between the user and the larger network of friends who come into contact with whatever has been uploaded. Thus affect accumulates, sediments, and provides additional cultural significance to that which gets circulated (see Paasonen, this volume).

To exemplify how affect accumulates in social networks, let us consider what goes into uploading a photograph on a site like Facebook. Mendelson and Papacharissi show in their study of college students' use of Facebook that photographs help to maintain relationships and memories while facilitating the production of highly performative subjectivities. As such, most photographs tend to foster community through the sharing of common experiences and values (Mendelson and Papacharissi 2011, 26). Most of the pictures taken by college students tend to be highly conventional and include photos of peer groups, parties, and other events such as holidays. Moreover, when these pictures are posted, they are often meant to generate large numbers of posts from friends. This would suggest that the point of uploading a photograph is not simply to preserve a moment in time but, as Papacharissi and Mendelson argue, to ensure that it becomes visible. Such a highly curated moment brings about an intentional archival event. Here nothing is random: while the photo may appear banal, it has been deliberately chosen—one of many curated moments that comprise a user's archive. The act of placing the photograph into one's profile allows it to become a part of one's archive of feeling, accumulating affective meaning as it begins to circulate.

Brian Massumi's (2003, 1) theorization of the archive argues that language is what allows us both to archive and to remember. His "archive of experience" complements Cvetkovich's archive of feelings. However, instead of looking specifically at how affect accumulates within objects and bodies, he is interested in how shared experiences between "forms of life" produce "vitality affect"—that which gives form to the parts of our lives that are fundamentally shared through the rhizomatic movement of affect. Massumi takes this concept from Daniel Stern, who argued that affective relations are not emotional responses to biological needs or drives and therefore should not be considered as either discrete or isolated moments (Massumi 2008, 5). Instead, the active notion of vitality encompasses the very complex dynamics that are experienced when subjects engage with other subjects and/or objects. For Stern, this in part explained how humans remain fundamentally attuned to one another: "Tracking and attuning with vitality affects permit one human to be with another in the sense of sharing likely inner experiences on an almost continuous basis. This is exactly our experience of feeling-connectedness, of being in attunement with another" (Stern 1985, 157). Objects within the archive equally weave a complex web of interconnectivity; hence for Massumi, there is a deep resonance imbricated within the relational traces that these always already embody. As such, the production of affect within a social network like Facebook should never be understood as a singular process. While users might be affected by the content they upload, ultimately the site's popularity comes from the highly relational and participatory means by which the individual archives circulate. What is posted always has the potential to be worked on by friends. In these instances affect slides, becoming "vital" as users make decisions to affiliate themselves with particular people and particular pieces of content, thereby momentarily linking archives. Thus, as more comments and likes are added, as more links and photographs get shared, an inherent desire for affiliation grows.

Massumi's theorization of vitality affect (2003, 149) thereby provides another way of understanding the deeply relational process inscribed in circulating content and, more importantly, the role affect plays in the production of digital subjectivities. The more we use sites such as Facebook, the more we post, the more we are motivated to generate and share additional content (Wang, Tchernev, and Solloway 2012). Thus, while Massumi does not specifically envision digital archives, the very architecture of social networks is predicated on networked sociality that requires users to share experiences. Vitality affects thus take objects that may have formally existed on their own and bring them into a larger composition and system of meaning. Here our archives produce sociality, as they bind and cohere relations based on the circulation of our data. More importantly, if these profiles did not exist in this composition with other archives, then their resonance within our everyday lives would be significantly diminished.

There is an inherent paradox here, given that what gets inscribed can only ever be a replication, or rather a representation. The impossibility of totality is in part what drives the continued exponential growth of user profiles on social networks and is exemplary of Derrida's "archive fever" (1998), or rather of the inherent drive to place everything in the archive. If the digital archive has a singular purpose of collecting information, however, it could become what Baetens and Van Looy (2007) have called an "absolute archive, that is to say, a perfect memory ... without any loss shown." Such an archive would not only be utopian and perhaps somewhat perverse, it would have the effect of erasing memory all together. Given that one of the key characteristics of an archive is to be selective, digital subjectivities are in part reproduced by the act of forgetting. What is then remembered is the result of an ongoing process of curating the self. As such, there can never be a totality of links, likes, photos, comments, quotes, or even geolocations with digital archives. Instead, users continuously make choices to build a digital subjectivity (Thayne 2012).

To return to the individual user profile archive, each time we upload something about ourselves, an intention or desire motivates us to do so. What we choose to upload is part of the construction of our virtual subjectivities, yet we are not fully actualized until whatever we have chosen to circulate is received by members of our networks. The user profile archive must circulate among our peers to be externally valorized. In the moment of recognition, through a like or a comment, the archive becomes that much more sedimented a part of who we are. Affect, therefore, bridges the gap between our intentions (based on the content we choose to circulate and hence bring into our archives) and what we perceive (how it gets received by others). Affect is also what allows our content to resonate beyond ourselves, so that we can actually experience the moment when data is uploaded as an important archival event, one that facilitates the procurement of our virtual subjectivities through our affective archives. Such acts are not just embodied in the letters or images that appear on the screen but also in the affect generated among users, who constantly valorize each other's content.

The conceptualization of identity within networked environments is somewhat contested. For Sherry Turkle, the self is multiple and partitioned. We present different versions of ourselves to our friends, our family, and the world at large. While there is a "moving fluidity" among these disparate selves, how we come to express who we are online is driven more by the medium than by the individual user. Thus Turkle argues that "technology is the architect of our intimacies," and it determines how we come to express ourselves (2011, 19). Each social network has a different modality of self-expression that affects how we come to construct who we are within the specific circuits it operationalizes. Conversely, for Papacharissi (2011) identity formation is somewhat more cohesive, with all of our multiple selves coming together to produce a more singular, albeit fractured, identity, driven not only by the architecture of the technology but also by an active need for sociality. Despite the fundamental differences between these positions, each points to a more complete elision between the online and offline subject. Where once we could easily point to a singular material body, today we coexist simultaneously within multiple networked publics across multiple technological platforms.

People do not log in to social networks to live anonymous lives, but instead to live what Zhao and colleagues refer to as "nonymous" or (semi)public lives. In other words, people do not go to these spaces to completely reinvent themselves but, typically, to upload more truth than fiction (Zhao, Grasmuck, and Martin 2008). As social networks become important sites of identity formation, the (re)production of vast amounts of usable data increases. Thinking about a user profile as an archive (not a simple database) offers a more nuanced way to conceptualize the sheer amount of the data that gets uploaded. A database does not distinguish what is amalgamated; rather, it stands as an undifferentiated vessel that continues to amass as much data as possible. Conceptualizing the digital profile as an archive allows us not only to think about how "we write ourselves into being" (Sundén 2009) but, more importantly, to think about those related power/knowledge questions that emerge when we begin to examine the choices that determine what information will come to represent us, affect others, and subsequently affect ourselves. Moreover, such choices crystalize why so many corporations are investing vast amounts of capital to produce the algorithms that will allow them to sort through these databases and produce something usable (Gallagher 2012).

Economic Value

Within the subjectivizing moments noted above, users are always creating important opportunities for marketers, who intuitively understand that new economic possibilities now reside in the generating of passionate interests, as people increasingly come to express their intimacies publicly (Thrift 2010, 293). Therefore, while I have largely focused on the social value that originates within the archives that users produce, it would be a mistake to negate the plethora of new marketing practices, and hence the economic value generated as a result of the active procurement of profile archives. As

Mark Andrejevic has argued in the context of social networks, such forms of sociability rely on privately owned and operated infrastructure (2011, 86). Thus, though Facebook has experienced economic uncertainty due to the drop in its share price that followed its initial public offering (Ryan 2012), it would be a mistake to discount this data-generating behemoth, given the enormous amount of personal information to which it has access.

The value produced on Facebook does not come from the full subsumption of all the immaterial objects that its users collectively upload. Instead, it is generated in the specific combinations of data that can be broken down, organized, and analyzed, as the epigraph at the opening of this chapter suggests. The ability to select and make meaning is thereby tantamount to extracting value from the vast production of user-generated data (see Karppi, this volume).

One technique for extracting such value that is attracting ever more attention is known by marketers as "sentiment analysis" (Liu 2010; Cvijikj and Michahelles 2011). In the United States alone there are between twenty and thirty companies trying to capitalize on the opinions and feelings that users have expressed, by recourse to either sentiment analysis or "opinion mining" (Liu 2010, 1). Instead of relying on expensive and imperfect research studies based on consumer opinions, marketers now go right to the source. As they would argue, why commission a study when you can have access to what people really think? The value of social networks therefore resides in the perceived authenticity and continued flow of data produced by their users. And while sentiment analysis techniques are still relatively crude, many marketers agree that their development is the key to the future. Currently, only five billion dollars are generated annually (Brooks 2012) from the data produced on social networks. By 2017, however, some technology organizations predict that this industry will be worth over fifty billion dollars (ibid.). What is missing are the sophisticated tools to extract precise value and meaning from the vast amounts of usable data now produced daily.

The choices, then, that facilitate the formation of archives, either by users or by corporations, function as a key attribute for the data society. Yet if we are to think of Facebook as one giant archive, we are again confronted with the problem of memory. What is required is more research on the role algorithms play, given that these proprietary formulas are precisely what allow meaning to be extracted from the vast amount of data that is stored about every user. The more adept these formulas are at producing meaning, the more confident advertisers are (in Facebook's case) that they will reach their target markets. Without selection, without Derrida's (1998) archons—those who decide what and how something will be housed in the archive—there can be no means of gathering content that will come together to produce meaning. To select, here, is to produce surplus value. However, without users to produce their own archives, the profitability of these sites quickly comes to a standstill, as already seen with the demise of MySpace.[1] Thus, without the constant immaterial labor of users who participate in social networks, there would be no data that could be rendered into surplus value (Coté and Pybus 2007; 2011).

The user profile archive allows us to speak of the enormous amounts of data that we both produce and circulate online. According to *Forbes* magazine, "data is the new oil" (Rotella 2012). However, data still needs to be broken down to be useful. As Jay Parikh, Facebook's vice president of engineering, stated in August 2012, "The world is getting hungrier and hungrier for data. Big data really is about having insights and making an impact on your business. If you aren't taking advantage of the data you're collecting, then you just have a pile of data, you don't have big data" (Red Orbit 2012). The archive that Facebook accumulates offers both practical and theoretical means to examine the body as it extends into the virtual circuits of social networks, and it also provides a framework for understanding the kinds of value being generated. To focus only on the material outcome of this value is to negate how and why we generate so much data. Capitalism does not simply create "worlds" (Thrift 2010), or spaces to procure surplus value, but (here I am following a more autonomist tradition) also seeks to exploit the very real social practices that are poured into these social networks. To focus only on how corporations extrapolate our data negates those very real affective relations that propel the increased production and circulation of data by users. As we move further into the data society, we must focus on both—on what propels the production and circulation of user-generated content *and* on the immense amount of capital tied up in extracting the usable data from the affective archives we collectively produce.

Note

1. From 2005 to early 2008 MySpace was the most visited website in the world, surpassing even Google as the most visited site in the United States. When Rupert Murdoch bought this social network, membership was nearing its peak of one hundred million active users. Once Facebook came online in 2008, MySpace began to steadily lose its user base. In June 2011, it was bought by Justin Timberlake for thirty-five million dollars.

References

Ahmed, Sara. 2004a. *The Cultural Politics of Emotion*. Edinburgh: Edinburgh University Press.

Ahmed, Sara. 2004b. Affective Economies. *Social Text* 22 (2):117–139.

Ahmed, Sara. 2010. Happy Objects. In *The Affect Theory Reader*, ed. Melissa Gregg and Gregory J. Seigworth, 29–51. Durham: Duke University Press.

Andrejevic, Mark. 2011. Social Network Exploitation. In *A Networked Self: Identity, Community, and Culture on Social Network Sites*, ed. Zizi Papacharissi, 82–103. New York: Routledge.

Baetens, Jan, and Jan Van Looy. 2007. Digitising Cultural Heritage: The Role of Interpretation in Cultural Preservation. *Image [&] Narrative* 17.

Bennett, Jane. 2010. *Vibrant Matter: A Political Ecology of Things*. Durham: Duke University Press.

boyd, danah. 2006. Identity Production in a Networked Culture: Why Youth Heart MySpace. Talk given at American Association for the Advancement of Science, St. Louis, February 19. Available at http://www.danah.org/papers/AAAS2006.html.

boyd, danah. 2011. Social Network Sites as Networked Publics: Affordances, Dynamics, and Implications. In *A Networked Self: Identity, Community, and Culture on Social Network Sites*, ed. Zizi Papacharissi, 39–58. New York: Routledge.

Brooks, Chad. 2012. Big Data Expected to Drive Big Revenue over Next Decade. *Business News*, March 6. Available at http://www.businessnewsdaily.com/2146-big-data-expected-drive-big-revenue-decade.html.

Coté, Mark, and Jennifer Pybus. 2007. Learning to Immaterial Labour 2.0: MySpace and Social Networks. *Ephemera: Theory and Politics in Organization* 7 (1):88–106.

Coté, Mark, and Jennifer Pybus. 2011. Learning to Immaterial Labour 2.0: Facebook and Social Networks. In *Cognitive Capitalism, Education and Digital Labour*, ed. Michael Peters and Ergin Bulut, 169–194. New York: Peter Lang.

Cvetkovich, Ann. 2003. *An Archive of Feelings: Trauma, Sexuality and Lesbian Public Cultures*. Durham: Duke University Press.

Cvijikj, Irena P., and Florian Michahelles. 2011. Understanding Social Media Marketing: A Case Study on Topics, Categories and Sentiment on a Facebook Brand Page. Presented at MindTrek '11, Tampere, Finland, September 28–30.

Davis, Katie, and Carrie James. 2013. Tweens' Conception of Privacy Online: Implications for Educators. *Learning, Media and Technology* 38 (1):4–25.

Deleuze, Gilles. 1978. Gilles Deleuze, Lecture Transcripts on Spinoza's Concept of Affect. Available at http://agentcode.wikispaces.com/file/view/deluze_spinoza_affect.pdf.

Derrida, Jacques. 1998. *Archive Fever*. Chicago: University of Chicago Press.

Devitt, Kerry, and Debi Roker. 2009. The Role of Mobile Phones in Family Communication. *Children and Society* 23 (3):189–202.

Foucault, Michel. 2002. *The Archaeology of Knowledge*. London: Routledge.

Fuchs, Christian. 2008. *Internet and Society: Social Theory in the Information Age*. New York: Routledge.

Gallagher, Ryan. 2012. GCHQ to Trawl Facebook and Twitter for Intelligence: Civil Liberties Fears as Eavesdropping Agency Recruits Maths, Physics and Computing Experts to Analyse Social Networks. *Guardian* (October 31). Available at http://www.theguardian.com/technology/2012/oct/31/gchq-facebook-twitter.

Gonzales, Amy L., and Jeffrey T. Hancock. 2011. Mirror, Mirror on my Facebook Wall: Effects of Exposure to Facebook on Self Esteem. *Cyberpsychology, Behavior, and Social Networking* 14 (1–2):79–83.

Gregg, Melissa, and Gregory J. Seigworth. 2010. An Inventory of Shimmers. In *The Affect Theory Reader*, ed. Melissa Gregg and Gregory J. Seigworth, 1–28. Durham: Duke University Press.

Hillis, Ken, Michael Petit, and Kylie Jarrett. 2013. *Google and the Culture of Search*. New York: Routledge.

James, Carrie, et al. 2009. *Young People, Ethics, and the New Digital Media: A Synthesis from the Goodplay Project*. Cambridge, MA: MIT Press.

Laermans, Rudi, and Pascal Gielen. 2007. The Archive of the Digital An-Archive. *Image [&] Narrative* 17. Available at http://www.imageandnarrative.be/inarchive/digital_archive/laermans_gielen.htm.

Lampe, Cliff, Nicole Ellison, and Charles Steinfield. 2007. A Familiar Face(book): Profile Elements as Signals in an Online Social Network. Paper presented at the CHI 2007, San Jose, California, April 28–May 3. Proceedings, 435–444.

Lenhart, Amanda, Mary Madden, Aaron Smith, Kristen Purcell, Kathryn Zichuhr, and Lee Rainie. 2011. Teens, Kindness and Cruelty on Social Network Sites: How American Teens Navigate the New World of Digital Citizenship. Pew Research Internet Project (November). Available at http://www.pewinternet.org/2011/11/09/teens-kindness-and-cruelty-on-social-network-sites/.

Liu, Bing. 2010. Sentiment Analysis and Subjectivity. Handbook of Natural Language Processing, 2nd ed. Available at http://www.cs.uic.edu/~liub/FBS/NLP-handbook-sentiment-analysis.pdf.

Livingstone, Sonia. 2008. Taking Risky Opportunities in Youthful Content Production: Teenagers' Use of Social Networking Sites for Intimacy, Privacy and Self-Expression. *New Media and Society* 10 (3):393–411.

Lu, His-peng, Kuan-yu Lin, Hsiao-lan Wei, and I-hsin Chuang. 2012. Exploring the Stickiness of Social Networking Sites from the Perspective of Uses and Gratification Theory. *Business and Information* (July 3–5):386–395.

Madden, Mary, Susannah Fox, Aaron Smith, and Jessica Vitak. 2007. Digital Footprints: Online Identity Management and the Search in the Age of Transparency. Pew Internet and American Life Project. Available at http://pewresearch.org/pubs/663/digital-footprints.

Massumi, Brian. 2003. The Archive of Experience. In *Information Is Alive: Art and Theory on Archiving and Retrieving Data*, ed. Joke Brouwer and Arjen Mulder, 142–151. Rotterdam: V2.

Massumi, Brian. 2008. The Thinking-Feeling of What Happens. *Inflexions* 1(May 1):1–40.

Mendelson, Andrew L., and Zizi Papacharissi. 2011. Look at Us: Collective Narcissism in College Student Facebook Photo Galleries. In *A Networked Self: Identity, Community, and Culture on Social Network Sites*, ed. Zizi Papacharissi, 251–273. New York: Routledge.

Palfrey, John, and Urs Gasser. 2008. *Born Digital: Understanding the First Generation of Digital Natives*. New York: Basic Books.

Palmer, Robert. 2006. Data Is the New Oil. *ANA Marketing Maestros: Thoughts, Ideas and Insights Directly from the ANA* (blog). November 3. Available at http://ana.blogs.com/maestros/2006/11/data_is_the_new.html.

Papacharissi, Zizi. 2011. A Networked Self. In *A Networked Self: Identity, Community, and Culture on Social Network Sites*, ed. Zizi Papacharissi, 304–318. New York: Routledge.

Papacharissi, Zizi, and Alan Rubin. 2000. Predictors of Internet Use. *Journal of Broadcasting and Electronic Media* 44 (2):175–187.

Parr, Ben. 2011. You Spend Eight Hours Per Month on Facebook. *Mashable*, September 30. Available at http://mashable.com/2011/09/30/wasting-time-on-facebook.

Pew Research Center. 2012. Teens 2012: Truth, Trends and Myth about Teen Online Behavior. Pew Internet and American Life Project. Available at http://www.slideshare.net/PewInternet/teens-2012-truth-trends-and-myths-about-teen-online-behavior.

Pybus, Jennifer. 2013. Social Networks and Cultural Workers: Towards an Archive for the Prosumer. *Journal of Cultural Economics* 6 (2):137–152.

Red Orbit. 2012. Facebook Data Growing at 500 Terabytes a Day. Red Orbit, August 24. Available at http://www.redorbit.com/news/technology/1112681207/facebook-data-by-the-terabyte-082412.

Rotella, Terry. 2012. Is Data the New Oil? *Forbes* (February 4). Available at http://www.forbes.com/sites/perryrotella/2012/04/02/is-data-the-new-oil.

Ryan, Peter. 2012. Facebook Market Value Halved. *World Today* (August 17). Available at http://www.abc.net.au/worldtoday/content/2012/s3569960.htm.

Sas, Corina, Alan Dix, Jennefer Hart, and Ronghui Su. 2009. Emotional Experience on Facebook Site. Presented at CHI 2009: Spotlight on Works in Progress, Boston, April 4–9, 4345–4350.

Sheldon, Kennon, Abad Neetu, and Christian Hinsch. 2011. A Two-Process View of Facebook Use and Relatedness Need-Satisfaction: Disconnection Drives Use, and Connection Rewards It. *Journal of Personality and Social Psychology* 100 (4):766–775.

Stern, Daniel. 1985. *The Interpersonal World of the Infant*. New York: Basic Books.

Sundén, Jenny. 2009. Transformations in Screen Culture. Screen Culture: JMK Seminar Series. Available at http://www.youtube.com/watch?v=UAMDJCmCUKk.

Tepper, Allegra. 2012. How Much Data Is Created Every Minute? *Mashable*, June 22. Available at http://mashable.com/2012/06/22/data-created-every-minute/.

Thayne, Martyn. 2012. Friends Like Mine: The Production of Socialised Subjectivity in the Attention Economy. *Culture Machine* 13. Available at http://www.culturemachine.net/index.php/cm/article/view/471.

Thrift, Nigel. 2010. Understanding the Material Practices of Glamour. In *The Affect Theory Reader*, ed. Melissa Gregg and Gregory J. Seigworth, 289–308. Durham: Duke University Press.

Turkle, Sherry. 2011. *Alone Together: Why We Expect More from Technology and Less from Each Other*. New York: Basic Books.

Wang, Zheng, John Tchernev, and Tyler Solloway. 2012. A Dynamic Longitudinal Examination of Social Media Use, Needs, and Gratifications among College Students. *Computers in Human Behavior* 28:1829–1839.

Zhao, Shanyang, Sherri Grasmuck, and Jason Martin. 2008. Identity Construction on Facebook: Digital Empowerment in Anchored Relationships. *Computers in Human Behavior* 24:1816–1836.

Contributors

James Ash is Lecturer in Media and Cultural Studies at Newcastle University, UK. His research interrogates the relationship between technology and embodiment through the lens of affective design. He has published on video games and video game design in journals such as *Theory, Culture and Society*, *Body and Society*, and *Society and Space*. For information on his research and publications please visit his website: http://www. jamesash.co.uk.

Alexander Cho is a PhD candidate in the Department of Radio-TV-Film at the University of Texas at Austin. His dissertation explores how LGBTQ young people use social media. He is also a research assistant with the John D. and Catherine T. MacArthur Foundation's Digital Media and Learning initiative, and a teaching affiliate with the Center for Asian American Studies at the University of Texas.

Jodi Dean is the Donald R. Garter '39 Professor of Humanities and Social Sciences at Hobart and William Smith Colleges in Geneva, New York. She is author or editor of eleven books, including *Democracy and Other Neoliberal Fantasies* (2009), *Blog Theory* (2010), and *The Communist Horizon* (2012).

Melissa Gregg is Principal Engineer in User Experience Research at Intel Labs, and codirector of the Intel Science and Technology Center for Social Computing. She is coeditor of *The Affect Theory Reader* (2010, with Greg Seigworth) and author of *Cultural Studies' Affective Voices* (2006) and *Work's Intimacy* (2011). Her current research looks at technology's role in the domestication of management principles and the development of professional subjectivity.

Ken Hillis is Professor of Media and Technology Studies at the University of North Carolina at Chapel Hill. He has published widely about the intersections among technology, practices, and desire. His books are *Digital Sensations: Space, Identity and Embodiment in Virtual Reality* (1999); *Everyday eBay: Culture, Collecting, and Desire* (2006); *Online a Lot of the Time: Ritual, Fetish, Sign* (2009); and *Google and the Culture of Search* (2013).

Kylie Jarrett is Lecturer in Digital Media at the National University of Ireland Maynooth. With Ken Hillis and Michael Petit, she is coauthor of *Google and the Culture of Search* (2013) and is currently investigating consumer labor in digital media using Marxist feminist frameworks.

Tero Karppi is Assistant Professor of Media Theory in the Department of Media Study at SUNY Buffalo. His research focuses on disconnections in network culture.

Stephen Maddison is Head of Humanities and Creative Industries in the School of Arts and Digital Industries at the University of East London. He is a member of the Centre for Cultural Studies Research at UEL, and of the editorial board of *Porn Studies*. His work on pornography, embodiment, and cultural politics has appeared in several major collections, including *Mainstreaming Sex* (2009), *Porn.com* (2010), *Hard to Swallow* (2011), and *Transgression 2.0* (2012). He is the author of *Fags, Hags, and Queer Sisters: Gender Dissent and Heterosocial Bonds in Gay Culture* (2001).

Susanna Paasonen is Professor of Media Studies at University of Turku, Finland. With an interest in studies of new media, affect, and sexuality, she is the author of *Carnal Resonance: Affect and Online Pornography* (2011) and coeditor of *Working with Affect in Feminist Readings: Disturbing Differences* (2009).

Jussi Parikka works at the University of Southampton, Winchester School of Art. He is author and editor of several books, including *Digital Contagions* (2007), *Insect Media* (2010), *What Is Media Archaeology?* (2012), and *The Spam Book* (2009, ed. with Tony Sampson). Parikka blogs at http://jussiparikka.net.

Michael Petit is Director of Media Studies and the Joint Program in New Media at the University of Toronto Scarborough. He is author of *Peacekeepers at War* (1986); coeditor of *Everyday eBay: Culture, Collecting, and Desire* (2006), and coauthor of *Google and the Culture of Search* (2013). His research focuses on technological affect and the intersection of digital media and pedagogy.

Jennifer Pybus is a Teaching Fellow at University of Southampton, at the Winchester School of Art, and a Research Associate at King's College London on the Our Data Ourselves project. Her research focuses on digital culture, affect, and youth, with a specific interest in social media, citizenship, and digital pedagogies.

Jenny Sundén is Associate Professor in Gender Studies at Södertörn University, Sweden. She is the author of *Material Virtualities: Approaching Online Textual Embodiment* (2003) and coauthor of *Gender and Sexuality in Online Game Cultures: Passionate Play* (2012, with Malin Sveningsson).

Veronika Tzankova is a PhD candidate in the School of Communication at Simon Fraser University, Vancouver, Canada. Her background education in civil law was obtained in Turkey, where she spent seven years exploring the cultural influence of Islam on social and moral values. Her current research focuses on online expressions of alternative secular identities in the gradually Islamizing political landscape of Turkey.

Index

Abortion, 64
Activism
  altporn and, 154
  archive of feelings and, 239
  craftivism, 147–148n1
  ecoactivism (*see* FuckforForest)
  gift economy and, 207–208
Actor-network theory, 8–10, 11, 81
AdSense, 108
Adultery, 64
Adventure Time!, 51
Advertising. *See also* User-generated content
  business model and, 7–8, 20, 176–177, 204–205, 209–211, 216n1, 222, 223–224, 244
  demand for, 179
  distraction and, 121
  as economic imperative, 19
  networked/distributed pedagogical model and, 176–177
  porn sites and, 153
  software art and, 108
  targeted, 177, 205, 211, 223–224, 227
  user data and, 244
Aesthetics. *See also* Art
  affect and, 7
  allegory and, 82
  altporn and, 157, 159, 161
  avatars and, 86
  gift economy and, 211
  oversaturation by media and, 121
  processual, of new media, 105–106

  semiotic theory and, 152
  steampunk and, 136, 137, 141
  Tumblr and, 44, 46
Affect. *See also* Affect theory; Body; Circulation; Drive; Excess/more than, as quality of affect; Immaterial and affective labor; Intensity; Movement; Networked affect; New materialism; Stickiness
  accumulation of, 237, 240–241
  ambivalence and ambiguity and, 11, 63
  communication as, 85–86
  as contagious, 115n1, 230
  context and, 6, 120, 121, 130, 131
  definitions of, 1, 6–7, 28, 44–45, 61–62, 75, 142–145, 170
  emotion and, 1, 4–5, 13, 32, 44–46, 75, 103, 115, 120, 130, 142, 152
  ever-greater, desire for, 78, 176
  as impersonal and autonomous, 6, 19–20, 227–230
  in-betweenness and, 84, 103, 104, 105, 112–113, 120, 145, 181
  interpretation and, 7, 130
  mixing of conceptual categories and, 61–62, 67, 72n1
  nonhuman, 6, 12–13, 76, 179, 227–230
  political, 62–71
  precognitive, 9, 11, 131
  predetermination of, 227, 230–231
  queer, 49, 50–53
  sensation and, 120, 122–125, 130, 131